An Account of Abuse

Written by

Beth Tester

MUG: An Account of Domestic Abuse

Copyright © [2024] by Beth Tester

All rights reserved.

No part of this publication may be reproduced, distributed, or transmitted in any form or by any means, including photocopying, recording, or other electronic or mechanical methods, without the prior written permission of the author, except as permitted by UK copyright law. For permission requests, contact @bethtestermug on instagram. Contact details can vary in different editions and likely to be correct the more recent the edition published.

For privacy reasons, all names, locations, and dates have been changed.

Beth Tester is a pseudonym for the author. The author's legal name is known to the publisher.

Book Cover by Beth Tester.

First edition. 2024.

This book is dedicated to those who have lost their lives due to domestic abuse, whether their death resulted directly from physical violence perpetrated towards them or because they chose to end their lives to escape the misery and trauma associated with it.

In Memory of Becky 'Blue' -

'Because I can'.

Trigger Warning:

This book is not a guide to domestic abuse, trauma, or self-care. It is a personal account of domestic abuse, with some information withheld for security reasons. This account discusses many forms of abuse, including stalking and harassment, sexual abuse, sexual assaults, and rape. There is frequent mention of physical violence. There are also mentions of suicide, infertility, and fear of child loss.

Contents

Introduction

Chapter One – *The Language We Use*

Chapter Two – *They Made Me Leave*

Chapter Three - *Katia*

Chapter Four – *Artificial Christmas Trees*

Chapter Five – *The Most Wonderful Time of the Year*

Chapter Six – *It was Christmas Eve, Babe*

Chapter Seven – *Hoovering and Harassment*

Chapter Eight – *Sex and The Perpetrator*

Chapter Nine - *Affaires*

Chapter Ten - *Violence*

Chapter Eleven – *Psychological Abuse*

Chapter Twelve – *Do You Remember the First Time?*

Chapter Thirteen – *Abuse and Misogyny*

Chapter Fourteen – *Sex & Love & Addiction*

Chapter Fifteen – *Non-Ethical Recovery and Narcissistic Abuse Experts*

Chapter Sixteen – *A Plague Upon Both Your Houses*

Chapter Seventeen – *Rape*

Chapter Eighteen – *As We Forgive Those Who Sin Against Us*

Chapter Nineteen – *Stalking and Harassment*

Chapter Twenty – *Freedom*

Chapter Twenty-One – *Freedom Fleeting*

Chapter Twenty-Two – *Dating With Trauma*

Chapter Twenty-Three – *Post Traumatic Stress*

Chapter Twenty-Four – *Speaking Out and Post-Separation Abuse*

Chapter Twenty-Five – *The Future*

Useful Resources

Thankyou:

Sources, Citations and References

Introduction

Finishing this book is a weird, unfamiliar feeling. I've been writing stories since I was five years old, with the dream of one day publishing a novel and being a successful author. I never expected that the first book I ever completed would be a type of memoir about living with violent abuse and how my body, mind, and soul have been subjected to horrendous violations because of dysfunctional, fucked up men. But here I am, writing the introduction at last, after four years of writing this account on and off, pondering about what I leave in, what I remove, what I reinsert, what I soften, what I don't soften.

Much of this time was thinking about how on earth I will be able to publish a book that details abuse yet doesn't put me in further danger with the perpetrator(s). I realised that, sadly, unless they are no longer earthside, that will never be an option for me, and I am silenced for my own safety, just like other people living with abuse, all over the world. But I refuse to be completely silenced. Not because I enjoy being a 'victim,' like some trolls have suggested on social media, during the days when I was more protected through the courts and could write cathartically about what I had lived through.

Social media is amazing when it comes to bringing awareness to topics close to our hearts, that we feel passionate about – but on the flip side, the more we open ourselves up, and the wider our platform becomes, the more at risk we are of a different kind of abuse; trolling. It all falls under misogyny and entitlement, but it's an abuse that I and many others have had to battle through when openly declaring we have lived with a male perpetrator who has caused us psychological, emotional, and physical harm, endangered the life of ourselves and our loved ones. Under this patriarchal society, we are simply not believed by those who are keen to keep living in one, despite their denial that a patriarchy even exists, regardless of it being evident in all our everyday lives.

Those of us who decide to speak out about abuse are not believed – particularly those of us who are not men. If we are fortunate to have loving family and friends, then we may have people close to us to hold us while we recover and heal; but generally, we aren't believed. There is very little to gain from speaking openly about being abused because we are met with criticism, judgment, disbelief, and accusations. It also puts our lives in danger because the perpetrator of the abuse we have lived with may try to harm us for doing so. We are trolled, ridiculed, made fun of. One of the worst times of my life during my recovery from abuse was the 2022 trial between Amber Heard and Johnny Depp. Whether you believe Amber Heard is irrelevant; if you laughed at videos mocking her descriptions of abuse or reenacted it yourself, you are complicit in minimising the lived experiences of survivors. That's hard for me to say because I saw for myself survivors of abuse share those mocking videos and respond with humour. It wasn't a celebrity, whether she was innocent or not, being mocked. It was all of us. Some would argue that it was Amber Heard herself who mocked survivors. I would argue that it was the man who opted to have a court case in Virginia, partly so that it would be televised, to the detriment of survivors everywhere. During and since the trial, I have spoken to countless women who have disclosed to me that they will never speak out about the abuse they have lived with after the trial, as they won't be believed.

I had already begun speaking out. During the trial, I was trolled by one man in particular who had convictions of abusing women and children, and he repeatedly kept calling me 'Amber Heard,' to say that I was lying. I understand why people don't want to speak out. The damage of that trial being televised was massive and life-threatening.

Then there is the fact that now we fear being sued for 'defamation' if we speak out. And after much thinking, despite knowing I could potentially sell hundreds of copies of this book if I promoted it on my Instagram page, I have had to publish it under a pseudonym and change every name of anyone mentioned in my story. If I sell 50 copies in my lifetime, then that will be a huge achievement to me. I am going to publish this book because I have been living with abuse since I was twenty years old. I am now in my mid-thirties. And while I have been able to take much of my power back, I won't let him control my story. Yes, I cannot write it under my actual name, but I can still share it and hope that it brings awareness to why leaving abuse is so difficult.

I think that's the aim of this book. It's not a guide; it's not an example of a correct way to do things. It's not advisable to copy how I've gone about things or give to someone else as a way of saying, 'why don't you do what she did?' But it might be an answer for those questions that we get: 'why did you go back?' 'Why did you let him do that?' 'Why are you letting your child see him?' 'Why don't you just go back to court?' etc., etc. So many questions. Why don't you...?

Why don't we?

Because we're scared. Because this is what happens when we try to leave. This is what happens when we do leave. Because it's painful, excruciatingly painful to break away.

I couldn't write this account of abuse and the beginning of my healing journey in a neat timeline because nothing about healing while living with abuse is neat. It's treacherously hard, incredibly painful, and full of setbacks and slip-ups. It can be easily assumed that abuse just stops once there's been a separation, but not only does abuse often increase, but our lives are more in danger. We live with post-separation abuse. Our entire existence can be exhausting and, as my dedication will suggest, some of us choose to end our misery because of the impact of the trauma we are living with.

This book is far from a comfortable read. In fact, it goes into heavy detail and descriptions of living with abuse and of sexual violence. I ask that you read this book if you feel you are in the headspace that will allow you to read it without it doing harm to your health.

I also ask that any aunts of mine – and my mum and dad – do not read it. Please.

At the end of this book, you'll find a list of recommended resources on violence against women and girls. Additionally, I've curated a playlist for readers. Add the listed songs to your preferred streaming platform and, if you wish, listen to the songs as we walk through the story together.

I want to take a moment to acknowledge that this book is written by a woman who has lived with violence perpetrated by men and worked with only women, most of whom were abused by a man. I am also a white, English woman living in the UK and understand that my circumstances, no matter how awful, were lived by myself, someone who is privileged to know that statistically, I'm more likely to be believed, taken seriously, and supported better by the police and British justice system. Domestic abuse, stalking, and harassment and rape are all serious crimes that happen all over the world, not just to a white girl living in an affluent village, like me.

I am feeling like an imposter right now. Who am I to be publishing a book? And I'm telling myself, 'It's not even that good!'... but it's my story. Mine. And I choose to tell it.

Chapter One -
The Language We Use

One of the things I had to get my head around when I realised that I was in an abusive relationship was the jargon used around domestic abuse and toxic partners. While this book is in no way a self-help guide to abuse, I would like to talk about the language used around abuse by 'experts', educators, influencers, and in support groups. I wish that someone had presented me with a dictionary of jargon with definitions to help me understand what everything meant. And while I've tried to write in a language that is simple for anyone to understand, being inclusive of people who do not know much about abuse or haven't lived with abuse themselves, I felt that before I start this account, perhaps some context may help navigate the story.

I think it's important to state that I do not use all of the common words and phrases associated with domestic abuse, but at one point, I did. At the beginning of my healing journey and recovery from abuse, I was using terminology that I wouldn't necessarily use now and have refrained from using in this book.

Narcissist

My relationship with the word 'narcissist' has been at two extremes; I went from working with a narcissistic abuse expert and referring to all the terminology used by narcissistic abuse experts to do my job effectively, listening daily to the same podcasts over and over again, and learning everything I could about narcissistic personality disorder, counting myself a mini-expert... to refusing to describe individuals as narcissists because of my belief that mental health should not be stigmatised in such a way.

I strongly advocate for mental health, and I believe that by labelling people with a personality disorder that they have more than likely not been diagnosed with because of how extremely difficult it is to diagnose anyone with narcissistic personality disorder, we are implying that we can label anyone with a mental health condition. Why stop at calling the man showing signs of extreme entitlement, predatory behaviours, and undeniable charm a 'narcissist'? Why not label the woman with instability, impulsive tendencies, and noticeable swings of mood as 'bipolar'? Why not label the kid who speaks to themselves, withdraws, and believes in conspiracy theories as 'schizophrenic'? Labelling people with personality disorders is not only judgmental and unsympathetic to the individual but also harmful to people who have mental health problems, where they present actual symptoms of a condition for which they have been diagnosed. Disorders such as 'ADHD' and 'OCD' get so much attention on social media, where people self-diagnose based on a TikTok video made by an unprofessional. And while it may be true that you resonate with symptoms of a disorder and you deserve to be seen, heard, and reach a point of diagnosis, some people are just throwing names of disorders about to describe their own or others' actions when it's simply not the case. How many times do we hear someone who likes to take control of the cleaning in their house described as having 'OCD'? OCD can be debilitating to live with, and for someone whose life is negatively impacted by their obsessive-compulsive behaviours, hearing others describe themselves as having 'OCD' because they like their home to be clean can be frustrating.

The same applies to the word 'triggered'. As someone living with a diagnosis of C-PTSD, I don't appreciate some random person on the internet describing themselves as being 'triggered' by a meme that may speak to them and their behaviours on a personal level, because that's simply not what being triggered is. Being triggered, in the true sense of the word, is living with a sudden trauma response that has a negative impact on a person's entire day or week. It can encourage hallucinations and flashbacks. It can cause a person to feel deep fear, depression, and self-hatred. It can make a person react in ways they feel they cannot control. Being triggered is an awful thing to happen – the word and its meaning should not be taken lightly.

By not labelling a perpetrator as a 'narcissist', we're not protecting them, but the vulnerability of other people who may be labelled with disorders for the way they act or behave – which in too many scenarios, isn't because they're 'disordered', but because they are traumatised. Which brings me to a point I feel passionately about, and why I decided to suggest reading 'Sexy but Psycho' by Dr. Jessica Taylor, despite personally disagreeing with some of her work. Psychiatry has a lot to answer for when it comes to diagnoses of personality disorders. I have worked with so many victims of abuse who have lived with severe violence, who have been diagnosed with personality disorders such as 'borderline personality disorder,' 'bipolar disorder,' 'ADHD' and more. I understand that it is believed that trauma can be a precursor to disorders, but I do believe that in many cases, it is trauma that someone is living with, not a mental disorder. I absolutely hate it that I have been diagnosed with a disorder. I prefer to refer to myself as living with 'Post Traumatic Stress' or 'Post Traumatic Stress Response'. It is very, very real.... but I'm not disordered. I'm traumatised. In the same way that I believe a person who has lived with severe childhood trauma may not grow up to be 'disordered', but profoundly traumatised. From working with women across the world, I agree with Dr. Jess Taylor that women are subjected to being misdiagnosed rather than supported with the intensity of their trauma; that symptoms of disorders are treated with medication, rather than explored as a trauma response.

To be clear, I believe in mental illness. I am still exploring this way of thinking. But this is currently where I'm at.

I've yet to hear about a person described as a narcissist who doesn't have some form of childhood trauma, whether that's from the theory that they were the golden child in the family, the scapegoat or didn't have a family at all. That doesn't mean that we should empathise with someone who has abused us because of the way they were treated or not nurtured sufficiently as a child, like I have done; a perpetrator of abuse has no excuse for their harmful actions. It also doesn't mean that implying they have an undiagnosed personality disorder means they cannot help the way they act. This is how I felt when I was told by a criminal psychologist working with me that my ex-partner was a sociopath with narcissistic personality disorder. I said to my friends, 'he can't help it, he's unwell... he's got a personality disorder...' and I excused his behaviour because I felt his 'illness' was not his fault, not considering that even if he does have a personality disorder, it didn't mean I had to accept his dangerous behaviours.

The term 'narcissist' famously comes from Greek mythology, which describes the hunter Narcissus, who fell in love with himself when he saw his reflection and died miserably because he could only love himself. With Greek mythology in mind, I don't personally mind the term 'narcissistic tendencies' when we're talking about someone who shows such self-absorbed, entitled behaviours where they think about only themselves. But I try to refrain from doing so, and instead use 'toxic / abusive tendencies and behaviours'. I simply don't believe in stigmatising mental health; in the way I disagree with calling someone with a physical or 'visible' disability a 'cripple' or a 'retard'. Society apparently disagrees with offensive terminology towards people with physical disabilities, so why do we allow words such as 'hysterical,' 'lunatic,' 'insane,' 'crazy,' 'mental' to define people who may or may not have mental health conditions?

Survivor

I have a love/hate relationship with the term 'survivor'. I've used it for myself plenty of times, but it's never sat right with me. I feel like 'survivor' implies the ordeal is over, but after domestic abuse comes post-separation abuse and living with intense trauma. Therefore, I feel like most of us who have left an abusive relationship are still 'surviving'. I have never minded being called a victim because I know that I have been one. I don't feel like the word 'victim' shows weakness, but I understand that people feel the word victim has negative connotations linked to feeling powerless. I know that people prefer 'survivor' because it shows the strength and courage, we all have, to have lived with someone or something so horrendous.

I have noticed that in the last couple of years, organisations are using the term 'victim-survivor'. I don't mind this, as I feel it shows the equal amount of vulnerability and strength that we carry with us.

I did a survey on my Instagram page of what people who have lived with abuse preferred to be known as, and someone said, 'thriver', and 'surthriver', which I really like. It shows us that we can thrive after being chained to a restrictive, unsafe and unhappy life. But overall, the survey showed me that we all prefer to be referred as differently. To reflect that, in this book, I have included different ways of describing a person who has lived or are living with abuse, so that it can be inclusive of how people feel.

Common Terminology

One of the things that initially amazed me when discovering support groups online for people living with abuse is that it felt like all the perpetrators were reading from the same handbook. How could so many people be living different lives, unique to them, yet be living with similar kinds of physical, emotional, and psychological attacks by the person supposed to respect them?

As the years have gone by, and I've studied domestic abuse, I feel that one of the answers to this is due in part to domestic abuse being a male-dominated crime, and the entitlement male abusers feel is connected to the entitlement men are allowed because of the patriarchal society we live in. I have lived with a male perpetrator of abuse, and I have worked with a psychologically abusive boss, who is a woman, so I understand not all perpetrators are men. I acknowledge the pain and suffering of people who have lived with abusive mothers, partners, friends, colleagues, or strangers, who do not fit the narrative of abuse happening to them because of men. Nevertheless, statistics of deaths caused by domestic abuse perpetrated by men show us that male violence is extremely high, affecting all people – not just women and girls. The precursor to this anger and violence involves behaviours and actions constituting psychological, emotional, coercive, verbal, sexual and financial abuse, including manipulation and controlling behaviours. Due to the striking similarities of perpetrators' behaviours and actions, Victim-Survivors and educators have developed language that describes the common occurrences that happen when living in the Cycle of Abuse. While I have tried to refrain from using jargon, there undoubtedly will be words or terminology used that a person who hasn't lived with abuse or encountered these words and phrases may not understand. Originally, I spent a long time writing a type of dictionary at the beginning of this book. I decided to change the format because the definitions didn't fit the flow of my story. I contemplated creating a glossary, including examples and instances of terminology and jargon within my story. However, this proved difficult because of the method I'm using to self-publish. I encourage you to ask whatever search engine you use for the definitions of any words or phrases you're not familiar with, e.g., 'Gaslighting,' 'Trauma Bond,' or 'Hoover.'"

My written story doesn't start from the beginning of living with abuse; quite the opposite. I am going to start my account by describing the day I was rescued. I hope this highlights how abuse doesn't stop, and healing doesn't begin when the abused person is in a position to no longer hide what is happening to them. I hope this account resembles how messy, tangled, and terrifying it is to leave a person they love and to realise that they were never really loved in return, but a victim of a persistent hate crime.

MUG: An Account of Domestic Abuse

Chapter Two - They Made Me Leave

'On average the police in England and Wales receive over 100 calls relating to domestic abuse every hour.'

Her Majesty's Inspectorate of Constabulary (HMIC). (2019) Increasingly everyone's business: A progress report on the police response to domestic abuse.

Listen to: It's All Over Now, Baby Blue by Bob Dylan

It was the fourth time the police were called to my home due to domestic abuse. It is often read on the many inadequately checked social media groups for survivors that the recipient of abuse finally 'snaps'; that overnight, they suddenly realise they have had enough of the abuser's behaviour. But I did not have one of those big 'snap' moments. I just bounced about the years, experiencing multiple low points in the relationship, never reaching my conclusive moment of 'THAT'S IT.' My former partner's behaviour that led to me fleeing him in one

MUG: An Account of Domestic Abuse

wet autumn was not the final straw for me. In comparison to other incidents that had occurred because of his behaviour, I did not think his actions had been 'that bad.' However, when the police came round to arrest my long-term partner for the fourth time, they made me leave too.

I was prepared to leave the place where we cohabited together, but I was not prepared to emotionally leave him. That was too much of a scary prospect, for what the fuck was life without him? However, on that wet autumn morning, after hours of his incoherent rambling, intoxicated aggression, and threats to end my life, I managed to find the courage to message my sister. I couldn't use my phone because he had thrown it in the kitchen sink with the intent of damaging it. I knew that my daughter and I were in physical danger. Her father had locked the doors and windows of our home, preventing us from leaving. As a result, my daughter and I were trapped. I had my laptop open, charging on the kitchen table, so I managed to sneakily send a quick Facebook message to my sister... A simple, one-word plea for help: 'Police.' I feared what was happening in that present moment, but I was more petrified of the prospect of putting the final nail in the coffin of my relationship.

My sister called 999 at once, yet it took the police almost an hour to arrive at our home. This was not quick enough. The police in the UK are underfunded and face many logistical challenges. I am aware that they are not wizards who can zap themselves instantaneously to wherever they are needed. But during that hour, I endured further threats and fear while secretly awaiting their arrival. What if those threats had been carried out? The police would have turned up at a murder scene, with a shaken-up toddler sitting by her mother's lifeless body. Or worse, a double murder scene. We nearly died waiting for the police to save us.

When the police finally arrived, they did so in two vehicles. I can still hear the sirens, see the blue flashes on the playroom walls, witness the flicker of the net curtains from the neighbours opposite, and hear the crunch and scrape of the gravel on the driveway. I already regretted involving my sister and calling the police. He had unlocked the doors and started to 'calm down.' I felt immense guilt about what was about to happen to him. I knew he would be arrested, and the thought of him being taken away in a police van made me feel sick. It felt like he could sense the gravity of the situation. He even laughed with composure when he peered out the window and saw what awaited him. He had been arrested a few months prior, so he knew what to expect. He said one sentence to me: 'I will never forgive you for this.' Then, he graciously opened the door to the officers, politely said 'hello,' and was promptly arrested. I sat in the lounge, holding our daughter, a trembling mess, unable to witness his arrest. Outside, the police van door slammed shut, and the man who had just assaulted me was driven away.

In that moment of hell, I felt that everything in my life was shattered. What was going to happen to us? To our home? Our possessions? What were my parents going to say? How could he and I ever come back from this? Panicked, I decided that we would have to move away. Could we move to the coast, perhaps? Escape the demons in the South and head to the West Country? Start fresh in Devon or Cornwall, maybe?

Yes, we needed to start over, somewhere pretty, somewhere quiet, somewhere where nobody knew us... somewhere where we could begin our familiar routine of highs and lows all over again. Maybe the lows would go away now that it had gone this far? Maybe he had learned his lesson this time? Could we glue all the shattered pieces of our lives back together?

The police officers who remained said they needed to interview me. At the same time, my daughter asked to watch a film on TV. I remember the surreal feeling of everything in my entire world escalating dramatically, yet my daughter wanted the simplest of comforts to meet her basic needs of nurturing and feeling safe. I turned on a Disney Pixar film. I had a friend who worked in law, whom I knew from a parenting group I had been involved with. I messaged her on our group chat. I felt an intense sense of shame for messaging them. I said something like, 'He's just been arrested for assaulting me.' I thought to myself, 'God, they must be so tired of my drama,' a feeling that I associated with most of my twenties. With my toddler settled on the sofa, it was time to focus my attention on the two officers in my kitchen.

Listen to: Criminal by Fiona Apple

The two police officers taking my statement were both men. One was an experienced officer who had mentioned that he was soon leaving that constabulary in a casual conversation about the weather, work, and the way I had renovated the old kitchen chairs. The second officer was on his first day of the job. It seemed like he had never taken the lead in interviewing a victim of domestic assault before. He proceeded slowly and diligently, receiving constant guidance from his colleague. The new officer had also forgotten to bring a laptop to electronically record my statement. He sheepishly admitted this, looking worriedly at his superior, who displayed a look of irritation. "You'll have to write it all up when we get back then," his mentor said dismissively. "It's just another day at the office for them," I thought.

I was encouraged to provide an accompanying Victim Personal Statement (VPS). I knew that I didn't have to make the VPS right then; this wasn't my first experience of being questioned by the police. My ex had been arrested the previous January, and I had adamantly refused to make any kind of statement, hoping he would be able to come home quickly. For clarification, a VPS is used if the case goes to court and the perpetrator is found guilty. It supports the guilty verdict and can later influence the judge's decision on sentencing. I didn't understand it's purpose at the time, and I don't think the information was explained to me very well. Then again, my brain had managed to dissociate from what was happening, so the overwhelming amount of information being thrown at me went unheard. I was desperately thinking about how to drop the charges. He had been released from police custody the previous January, just a few hours after being arrested – tired, dishevelled, and pissed off. But this time, it was more difficult to drop the charges since it was my sister who had contacted the police and reported the domestic abuse. My mind was racing, trying to figure out how I could get him out of this situation.

My friend, who worked in law, was helpful. She arrived at the house shortly after I provided a witness statement to the police. My friend was with me when the officers asked if I felt ready to make the VPS, which focuses on how the assault has affected the victim and can be modified or added to later. That's when I began to cry. The officer explained that a VPS would be beneficial in court. The mention of "court" felt dreadful - I didn't want to go to court, why were they discussing it? It felt like the police were speaking in slow motion, while the events of the day were spiralling out of control. My friend intervened and firmly told them that I was not ready to give a VPS just yet. The experienced officer was stern and abrupt, telling my friend to back off. I timidly expressed that I wanted her there. Truthfully, I had no idea what I wanted, except for everyone to leave and for none of it to have happened.

At some point during the interview process, my sister arrived. She occupied herself by keeping my daughter busy in the lounge. I cancelled my shift at work at the last minute. One of my colleagues briefly came over to return my handbag that I had left in her car. Having known me for years, she could instantly sense that something was terribly wrong as she stepped through the front door and interrupted a police interview. She knew better than to ask. Instead, she embraced me in a warm, engulfing, and motherly hug. In that precise moment, I realised that it was the first genuine, protective hug I had received in years—and it was everything I had ever longed for. This marked the beginning of my world reopening to friends and family whom I had been emotionally isolated from.

The police proceeded with mandatory risk assessments, categorising the case as "High Risk" and informing me that Child Services would be notified. This news didn't come as a surprise; Child Services had already visited us earlier in the year following the previous arrest. During their last visit, I had lied and downplayed the domestic abuse, claiming it was just a disagreement that had been resolved. However, I understood that having a second safeguarding incident within a year was not indicative of a stable home environment, and this time I had to honestly cooperate. My brain acknowledged the seriousness of the situation, but I couldn't fully comprehend or process the impact. Any sense of safety had long vanished, and to cope, my brain instinctively recommended shutting down.

After sitting through two long hours of police statements, risk assessments, safeguarding protocols, and posing for photographs of my injuries, I was strongly advised to leave the property. The police explained that even though the man who assaulted me had been arrested, he would likely be released later, making it unsafe for me to remain in the family home. It surprised me that he would be able to return home, but our daughter and I would have to leave. My sister assured the police that my daughter and I would be staying with her. My friend, being practical, started listing the items I would need to bring with me and asked about my daughter's preferred toys. However, I couldn't fully comprehend their words. The idea that I might not have access to my belongings for an extended period felt surreal. It was as if I was watching everything unfold from a distant, detached perspective. My state of mind didn't allow me to consider which toys, clothes, toiletries, books, or paperwork I should take with me. In a daze, I collected random objects from around the house and haphazardly packed them into a sack, not realising that most of the items would be of little use later. The thought of our two pet rabbits weighed heavily on my mind. Thankfully, I had cleaned their living area out earlier that morning. But they typically spent their nights indoors with my daughter and me, sheltered from the cold outside where rats could pose a threat to them. I couldn't bring myself to say "Goodbye" to our bunnies; the guilt and sadness were overwhelming.

My parents were on holiday. It was no coincidence that there had been an escalation while they were away; this was his pattern. He knew I couldn't turn to them for help when they weren't at home, so the abuse often intensified and became more physical during their absence. Every time my parents informed me about their upcoming holiday plans, a sense of dread would fill me privately, knowing what to anticipate when they were gone.

My sister drove my daughter and me to her place. She lived about forty-five minutes away, across The Downs. As she took us across the familiar, chalky hills, I noticed the flecks of rain on the window and the misty grey that blocked the view of the landscape I knew so well. I turned my face so that neither she nor my daughter could see, and silently, I started to cry. Big, heavy tears fell purposefully, and I couldn't stop. I felt like I could easily vomit. The so-called 'love of my life' was distraught in a prison cell, and our secret was finally out: We were not the happy couple I had tirelessly pretended us to be.

Later at my sister's house, as we tucked into a takeaway pizza and my brother-in-law vented his thoughts about my presumed 'ex', we were visited again by a woman police officer. She came to take a witness statement from my sister. As they secluded themselves in the kitchen, I could hear murmurs and the mention of certain words. At one point, my sister entered the living room to retrieve her phone. She looked at me with a helpless expression and said, 'they need to go through my phone.' I had sent her messages that week expressing my frustration with the behaviour I had been putting up with. I silently berated myself for doing so. When my sister's interview concluded, it was my turn to answer more questions. This officer was kinder, gentler, less matter of fact. She wanted to gather more information about the background of my relationship. I couldn't be bothered, so I kept it brief. The officer explained that my partner would likely be released from custody later that night and warned me against returning home. I found her easier to talk to compared to the officers who had previously attended.

In the spare room of my sister's house, lying in a single bed with my tearful two-year-old, I cried until my eyes stung, and my throat felt raw. If it weren't for my precious daughter, I knew I would consider ending my own life. I truly didn't want to go on living if I couldn't be with him.

Listen to: Crazy by Alanis Morrisette

Neither my daughter nor I slept well. I woke up early, filled with determination that I had to rescue my partner from trouble. I sent a group message to his family members, assuming they were all aware by now. I asked them to inform him, whenever possible, that I would be waiting for him. I assured them that I would do my best to make things as easy as possible, hoping to minimise the trouble he would face. I believed some of his family would find the whole situation amusing. "They never thought we would last," I later wrote in my journal. I wondered who among his family would stand by him and what they would say about me behind my back. They seemed unfazed. I remember one of his relatives commenting something like, "Both of you need to work out your issues for the sake of your daughter." I didn't know how to respond to that. I was too exhausted to think about anything except ending the pain and heartache and finding a way to fix what was happening, so that we could resume our lives as a family.

The next two weeks passed in a blur; it was the first time in years that I had no contact with the man I loved. I experienced an agonising withdrawal. Our daughter was devastated - she adored her father, and the sudden separation, with no way to see or speak to him, deeply affected her. I didn't know how to explain to her what had happened. How could I soften the blow that we wouldn't be returning to the home she loved so much? The attic bedroom with its quirky charm, where her pet bunnies roamed freely at night. The white-framed double bed adorned with pink, flowery fairy lights, making her feel like a princess. The newly built treehouse in the garden. The plants she had nurtured. Her own playroom with a ball pit, Wendy house, and drawing desk. The toy kitchen that mirrored the real kitchen, where she cooked alongside me.

The two full bookcases holding her cherished books, collected from charity shops each month. How could I now explain that it was all gone? And that instead, we were living in a cramped house with her grandparents, in a cluttered room with limited toys, sharing a bed out of necessity? Every day felt like a haze of heartbreak. The world seemed dull and colourless, but I couldn't leave because I had a daughter who needed my presence. As an emotional person, my tears flowed constantly and unconsciously, and my child witnessed them. But I could, at the very least, provide her with my enormous love. Regardless of what I felt for him, my love for our daughter overshadowed everything else. Focusing on my child kept me going - my role as a mother gave me a reason to live. I noticed that, as much as I fantasised about ending my own life, I also longed for my daughter to have stability. That longing kept me on this earth, but it didn't erase my feelings for her father. Despite the damage that had been done, I resumed our relationship.

Years previously, just months before our daughter was conceived, her father suddenly and unexpectedly left me. Those months were the darkest of my life, and I deeply desired death. His departure seemed to come out of nowhere, leaving me desperate for answers. I pleaded with him to explain, but he stubbornly refused to discuss it. The escalating violence from him had also left me confused. I repeatedly asked why he felt the need to hurt me, but he never provided a satisfactory answer, instead blaming me for provoking his impulsive anger. I knew I would never get the answers I sought from him. However, in that wet autumn, my life was about to change when I met a woman who would have a profound impact on me. She was my Independent Domestic and Sexual Violence Advisor, assigned to me after the police referred me to a local domestic abuse organisation. Her name was Katia, and she held the answers as to why I had been abandoned for those few months way back, and why our relationship had continued to be dangerously tumultuous. It was that wet autumn that I discovered I was caught in the Cycle of Abuse.

Chapter Three - Katia

'The number of clients accessing Independent Domestic Violence Advisor (IDVA) services that use the SafeLives Insights tool decreased by 21.8% to 2,246 in the year ending March 2023, compared with 2,873 in the year ending March 2022.'

Evidence of the increase of Domestic Abuse during the pandemic.

Office for National Statistics (ONS) 2023

Katia called me, and from her no-nonsense tone, I sensed she was a straightforward and pragmatic person. She informed me that we would meet in person and arranged a date and time at a local library. Initially, we had planned to meet at a coffee shop, but on the day, Katia messaged me at the last minute, suggesting that it would be more discreet to have our conversation in the privacy of a quiet public place. When I arrived at the library, Katia was waiting for me by a window. She had already set up a laptop, with paperwork neatly laid out, a pen in hand, and a cup of coffee beside her. Her thick northern European accent reminded me of some of my Polish colleagues, some of whom I admired for their directness. Right from the start, Katia commanded respect. Her no-nonsense attitude and strong work ethic were evident as soon as I sat down. It was clear that Katia was there to perform her job thoroughly and efficiently.

I had no inkling of what I had gotten myself into when I agreed to meet Katia. I went to our meeting with low expectations and a desire to keep it brief. I had no intention of genuinely cooperating with her because, by that time, I was back in contact with Ethan. Naturally, I hadn't informed anyone about our reconnection. I had poured out my emotions, expressing my undying love for the father of my child, and he had begrudgingly accepted my apologies for causing him stress. Our primary goal was to get the professionals off our backs and resume our familiar family setup. Our daughter was thrilled to speak to Daddy on the phone every other hour and eagerly anticipated seeing him as soon as possible. He wanted to see us right away, but I insisted on waiting until we were "safe" from any repercussions with Child Services. In my mind, if I could swiftly conclude this meeting with Katia, I could then return home and erase the inconvenience from my memory.

Listen to: Doll Parts by Hole

Katia didn't approach our meeting in the same manner as I did. She drove straight into the heart of the matter, asking me uncomfortable questions to which I awkwardly responded. It felt as though I couldn't deceive her. She offered me help, something that had never been extended to me in the context of my relationship. I was intrigued. What help could this person possibly provide me?

Katia proceeded to explain her profession and her experience working with criminals and individuals with personality disorders. She had worked in prison settings, with people who had lied, manipulated, and, in some cases, committed murder. She shared this information right away, but I failed to see its relevance. I thought to myself that Ethan wasn't on that level. After all, Ethan was too clever to land himself in prison. I quietly (and mistakenly) felt confident that Katia couldn't comprehend the complexity of Ethan, as I knew he was more than just a criminal. Ethan had a dark side, and that had always been part of the attraction. Nevertheless, Katia posed questions that no one had ever asked me before. She interested me, and I felt compelled to engage in conversation with her.

I had occasionally hinted to others about Ethan's "true character." For example, I had become more open with one of his relatives, whom I had grown attached to. However, apart from the countless pages in my notebooks, I had never truly revealed to anyone the reality of our relationship. Yet, despite feeling uncomfortable, I spent an hour providing Katia with a basic background of our relationship. She took notes in front of me, highlighting key dates and organising the information to form a scribbled timeline. As I spoke, she nodded and continued jotting down words and phrases I used.

Next, using the timeline, Katia created a line graph. She used the key events as markers along the bottom of the chart and assigned numbers from 0 to 10 along the side, with 0 representing the most unhappiness and 10 representing the greatest happiness. We went through the key dates, and I described how each event made me feel on a scale from 0 to 10. It was a simple yet effective exercise. It was at that moment that I realised I had been ridiculously unhappy... but what surprised me even more was the realisation that I had rarely experienced *true* happiness.

Then came the "Power and Control" wheel (search google images!). Using the key events and the line graph, Katia outlined each section of the wheel. We marked each part of the Power and Control wheel that I had experienced with Ethan. By the end of this activity, I was staring in shock at a wheel filled with ticks: I had experienced every single form of abuse. The Power and Control Wheel wasn't just a hint of my partner's controlling character; it was a startling revelation of my reality.

Through her work, Katia has had to deliver this impactful revelation to different women, time and time again. I don't believe she took any pleasure in initiating the recognition that I was a victim of domestic abuse. It may sound silly, but even though I knew the name of the organisation she worked for, I hadn't believed that I was a victim until that moment. The police had informed me that the relationship I was in was considered "High Risk," but I hadn't grasped the full significance of that term. I can't recall if they explained what "High Risk" meant for my daughter and me, and if they did, I didn't pay attention. It felt as though I had been living in a dense fog throughout my twenties, and that fog was finally lifting, revealing a different reality than the one I had assumed. I wondered what it must be like to have Katia's role, being the person who initiates the process of lifting someone's fog.

"This is every part of your life, Beth," she stated firmly. I gazed at the documents spread out before me on the desk, seeing unfamiliar terms that didn't immediately register, like 'Gaslighting' and 'Discarded'. Phrases forcefully imposed themselves upon my consciousness, forming a distressing collage: 'Love Bombing', 'Tension Building', and 'The Incident'.

"This is a severe case of Domestic Abuse, Beth," Katia asserted. "You have been groomed, manipulated, and subjected to abuse by someone who, in my experience, likely has narcissistic personality disorder. I'll be frank with you - I'm astonished that you're still alive." Every inflection in Katia's voice reverberated within me. I felt the weight of each word.

"Statistically, if you were to return now, you would likely be dead within five years. But based on what I've learned today, I wouldn't be surprised if you didn't make it past the next two," she continued.

I was left utterly speechless.

Listen to: Narcissist by Avery Anna

I left Katia at the library, but my body had other plans. My legs seemed to have a mind of their own, making it impossible for me to go straight home. I trembled uncontrollably, like a rabbit struck by a car, not yet dead but paralysed with fear. Nausea washed over me, and I desperately needed to find a place to sit down. However, I found myself aimlessly walking in circles around the shopping centre, as if I were a remote-controlled car running out of battery, stuck in a perpetual motion.

My phone incessantly buzzed inside my bag. It was him. I entered the bookshop, then quickly walked out. I wandered into the clothing shop, hoping to see my friend who worked there, but she was nowhere to be found. I left the shop. People around me meandered between the vast window displays and under the towering glass ceilings. I halted and resumed my steps, torn between what I wanted to do and what I needed to do – two fundamental tasks. I longed to find a place to sit and process the overwhelming information I had received, but I also needed to return home to my toddler. Suddenly, I found myself on a bus, repeating the word "narcissist" over and over in my mind. Wasn't a narcissist someone who admired themselves in the mirror? Didn't they consider themselves godlike? I retrieved my phone to discover missed calls, messages, and voicemails.

I typed 'Narcissist' into Google for the first time and clicked on the first result that appeared.

'Overview. Narcissistic Personality disorder – one of several types of personality

disorders – is a mental condition in which people have an inflated sense of their own importance, a deep need for excessive attention and admiration, troubled relationships, and a lack of empathy for others.' (18 Nov 2017, https://mayoclinic.org)

That struck a chord; 'Lack of Empathy,' something I had noticed Ethan lacked considerably. He had seemingly possessed it in abundance all those years ago when we first met. I had considered this as a 'changed' aspect of his personality, connected to the continuous turmoil he had endured throughout his life. I knew he was a resentful, bitter person, but I had felt sorry for him rather than being critical of his inability to empathise anymore. I decided that I had been overwhelmed enough for one day and would investigate Narcissism another time.

Shortly after my first meeting with Katia, I went out for a coffee date with the girls from church - more about exploring faith later. It was the first time I had properly seen all of them since I had left the family home and, to their knowledge, left Ethan. I didn't want to tell them exactly what had happened. I was concerned that this group of inspiring women, who were relatively new additions to my life, would grow tired of my "drama." Besides, I believed that once everything had blown over, Ethan and I would officially reunite somehow. I hadn't figured out the logistics yet, but I felt it was important to downplay the assault and abuse. Little did I know that sitting opposite me was a new friend in my life, whom I was still getting to know, and who had a wealth of knowledge about domestic abuse, particularly narcissism.

"He's not well," I reasoned, excusing him as usual. "They say he has a personality disorder."

I still remember Rebecca's expression. She looked at me with her large, knowing eyes and a hint of a sympathetic smile on her face. She was going through her own hell at that time, a lengthy divorce with assets to divide. She hadn't revealed to me at that point why she and her husband had separated, but there were hints here and there that he was abusive. On the evening of our group coffee date, Rebecca was as shocking and straightforward as Katia had been.

"If you go back to him, you will die," she said with calm seriousness.

Listen to: Narcissist by Lauren Spencer Smith

Rebecca later introduced me to domestic abuse support groups on Facebook and helped me discover Narcissistic Abuse online communities. She has been a crucial influence in my understanding of narcissistic abuse and has been instrumental in starting my journey of recovery. Unlike most of my friends, Rebecca knew what I was going through, something I hadn't expected. She invited me to 'Like' Facebook pages, 'Follow' narcissistic abuse experts and coaches, join private recovery groups, and regularly sent me resources to equip me with information. Rebecca had resumed studying to become a counsellor, and I was more than happy to be her 'guinea pig.' I found her wisdom to be unavoidable since she had been in my position of self-denial and disbelief. I had been wrapped up in the assumption that I was the only person who had experienced Ethan's style of behaviour. So, when I was suddenly immersed in this world of individuals who had been treated similarly, it felt bizarre. Each evening, once my daughter was in bed, I would delve into a succession of private social media posts from people I could relate to. From Facebook groups to online forums, I was virtually surrounded by survivors of narcissistic abuse. I wasn't alone. Not only was I not alone, but I was far from it. I had stumbled upon knowledge that I couldn't unlearn or hide from — that domestic abuse was not only globally common but also a ferocious and deadly crisis.

I didn't immediately engage with other survivors in groups and forums. Instead, I "lurked," reading posts and reluctantly finding resonance. Sometimes, I would come across a post that felt as if I had written it myself. I faced multiple challenging revelations about the nature of my long-term relationship. One revelation troubled me more than the others: if Ethan was a narcissistic abuser, then there was evidence that he had never genuinely loved me in the way I had believed. If he was a narcissistic abuser, he appeared to be incapable of love as I, a non-narcissist, understood it. A narcissistic abuse expert personally informed me that narcissists "love" to their own version of love. As I navigated through the terminology and jargon of narcissistic abuse, my feelings of inadequacy were highlighted. Here I was, just another victim, deceived into thinking I had been with my soul mate. I didn't want to be a survivor. I wanted to be the exception. Now that I knew about narcissism, perhaps I could be the one who tamed the abuser, preventing further abuse? Could I fight for a happily ever after with the narcissist by understanding how to handle him and soften the cycle of abuse? Surely, there were other ways to regain my power without having to part ways with the man I loved. I continued to communicate with Ethan.

Autumn progressed into winter, and Ethan and I continued our secret contact. Every few days, we would meet up, bringing our daughter along. He would park in inconspicuous places, and I would make sure no family, friends, or neighbours would catch me before getting into his car. On a couple of occasions, we even returned to our family home. This turned out to be a massive mistake as it had a powerful and negative impact on our daughter. It messed with my own head as well, reminding me that we could still maintain our version of a "family." Yet, with the knowledge I was steadily acquiring about domestic abuse, I could also see that we were never truly a "family" in the real sense, only in sentiment. Despite my love for Ethan and my longing for things to return to how they once were, I couldn't ignore what I was learning about abuse and narcissism. I knew I should follow Katia's advice, as well as the guidance from Child Services, who were now heavily involved. Yet, I had had a complicated relationship with Ethan in one way or another for nine years—the entirety of my twenties. It didn't feel plausible for me to do as they suggested, which was to cut off all contact with him. As Christmas approached, Ethan and I continued to meet up, right under the noses of everyone involved in our situation.

Even though Ethan and I had resumed our "romantic" relationship, he continued to be unkind to me. I decided to press charges, and Ethan had to go to court. I did this because I felt like I was disappointing my family and friends if I didn't. He pleaded guilty to "assault by beating" and was given a fine of £80 and a community order. He was extremely unhappy with this punishment. My family, friends, and Katia were also disappointed with the lack of significant legal consequences for his actions. Katia said £80 was like a sick joke. I didn't even know there would be a fine for endangering my life, let alone a judge deciding my life was worth so little. Ethan didn't show remorse or apologise, as he hadn't done so in years. Instead, he blamed me for calling the police, for not dropping the charges, for making him go to court, for him pleading guilty, and for his sentencing. He frequently reminded me that everything that had transpired was "my fault," and I would routinely apologise in response. Ethan was in an unbelievably bad mood with me, and our interactions, whether in person or over the phone, were just as contentious as before our separation. He continued to be rude and physically hurt me when I said something he didn't like, like wrapping his knuckles on my head. He never paid the fine, as he always saw himself as "above the law." His sentence was merely an inconvenience that I had caused. Not much changed in the dynamic of our relationship, except for the fact that we no longer lived together. However, there was one significant difference: I began to realise, as Ethan continued to be verbally aggressive, physically violent, and emotionally brutal towards me, that Katia was right all along—we were dealing with severe abuse.

Chapter Four - Artificial Christmas Trees

'In the majority of female domestic homicides, the suspect was a male partner or ex-partner (74.7%),'

Office for National Statistics, 2023

Listen to: Playing God by Paramore

After my initial meeting with Katia, we had regular phone conversations. Despite my attempts to keep my contact with Ethan a secret, I couldn't maintain the pretence. Katia, being a skilled IDSVA, understood that survivors rarely cut off contact immediately. I felt incapable of lying to her.

Katia, in her brutally blunt manner, repeatedly emphasised that I would die if I continued to see Ethan. She urged me to go "No Contact" and suggested obtaining a non-Molestation order, as I would likely have one granted due to his conviction for assaulting me. I would sigh and feel guilty for disappointing her because I knew she genuinely cared for me. I would explain to her that going "No Contact" wasn't feasible since Ethan and I shared a daughter. Honestly, I wasn't ready to do it yet, and I wasn't sure what else I needed to be ready. I saw myself as a lost cause, full of excuses and lacking strength. But Katia continued to insist that I WAS strong, considering how long I had survived with someone so 'sadistic'.

I adopted one of Katia's suggestions, which was to write notes on my phone whenever Ethan said something offensive or abusive. The only issue was that Ethan would offend and abuse me so frequently that my phone became a constant presence in my hands whenever I was around him. He despised seeing me on my phone, so this activity proved to be dangerous. Ethan would attempt to snatch my phone while I was typing to see "who I was texting" or "what I was recording". This was a behaviour he routinely exhibited when we lived together as well. Katia's warnings resonated each time he commented on my notetaking. As a result, I only continued this method of documentation for a few weeks. I became adept at taking screenshots and created folders on my phone specifically for pictures of my injuries or our exchanged messages.

The lead-up to Christmas that year served as confirmation of Ethan's blatant narcissism. The more I read about Narcissistic Abuse, the more I could discern it in Ethan's everyday actions.

On our daughter's third birthday, Ethan's behaviour became erratic. It was a difficult decision, but I chose to exclude him from her celebration that day. Despite her excitement to see him, I organised a small birthday tea party at my parents' house, where we were living at the time. I explicitly requested that he not attend, as my parents were not welcoming of him. His behaviour was frantic, possibly drug-induced, and I worried about the distress it might cause our daughter to witness him in such a state. However, despite my pleas, Ethan chose to show up at my parents' house regardless. He took a selfie outside the garden gate, which he had installed himself, and immediately uploaded it to social media. While I sat on the sofa inside, I watched the "likes" pour in, fully aware that people approving the post were unknowingly endorsing a threat directed at me. I saw the post for what it truly was—an act of rebellion. It was a message of defiance, indicating that he could see the boundaries

I was attempting to establish but had no intention of respecting them, just like the boundary of the garden gate. He demonstrated how precariously close he was to unlock that gate and intruding into our safe space. He knew how to dismantle it from the outside because he had constructed it himself. He understood how to dismantle the defences I was erecting between us because he had built a domain that no one else had managed to breach. He knew how to gain access. I was fully aware of his capability to do so. He was showing me that my boundaries were not obstacles—they were ineffective. Ethan was inescapable. It shouldn't have come as a surprise that he tainted the memories of our daughter's third birthday, as he had a talent for tarnishing all events and occasions.

That Christmas was no exception to Ethan's yearly tradition of ruining it, even though our circumstances had changed. One day, I made the disastrous decision to bring our daughter back to the family home to decorate it with artificial Christmas trees. Deep down, I knew it was a terrible idea, but I was blinded by the idealisation of creating a "happy family unit" and giving our child the Christmas of her dreams. Every time we returned to our family home, it felt like I was teasing our daughter with what she wanted most, only to snatch it away before she could grasp it. I played Christmas music, illuminated the fairy lights, and adorned every available shelf with tinsel. While our daughter and I joyfully decorated the Christmas trees with our collection of inexpensive ornaments, Ethan expressed his dissatisfaction through sighs and muttered complaints. He was frustrated that we hadn't had any sex since the escalation that occurred a few weeks prior.

Listen to: There You Go by P!nk

Ethan had become fixated on Swinging sites during the last year of our relationship. He wanted us to have sex with another woman together. During the peak of his abuse, I found it easier to comply with his wishes to appease him. However, we never actually participated in Swinging together. Even after I left him, Ethan remained insistent on pursuing Swinging. On the evening that our daughter and I decorated the house for Christmas, Ethan was glued to his phone, messaging potential candidates for casual encounters. To avoid any arguments that night, I chose to ignore his behaviour and focused on creating a festive and joyful atmosphere for our daughter. Earlier that week, he had been excited to discover a profile of someone we both knew on the Swinging site. This person seemed to be discreetly offering services, and Ethan took pleasure in showing me how she was listed in an online directory of sex workers. Initially, I was taken aback and concerned for her safety, as I had limited understanding of the industry. I reached out to her to express my worries, and she reassured me that she and her partner were taking all necessary precautions for their safety. In the spirit of honesty, I also disclosed to her that Ethan and I were registered as a couple on the same Swinging site. I can't recall if I mentioned that I had no control over the account or who Ethan contacted through it. Keeping all of this as a shameful secret for some time, revealing it to someone who potentially saw me involved in taboo sex felt embarrassing.

It was while we were decorating the Christmas trees and Ethan was engrossed in the swinging site, that the male partner of the woman we both knew began to contact us. He was pissed off to discover that Ethan had been attempting to pay for his partner's services. Although I was unaware of this specific incident, I wasn't surprised as Ethan had often expressed his attraction to her and had a history of paying for the companionship of sex workers. Ethan didn't seem worried about being caught out; instead, he found it amusing. I could see the excitement in his eyes and hear the adrenaline in his voice as he engaged in an argument with the other man, employing his well-spoken yet subtly condescending manner. Despite always claiming to dislike drama, Ethan revelled in the opportunity for it when it presented itself. I observed how he enjoyed provoking the other man on the phone, relishing in his increasing frustration while maintaining his own calm demeanour. As the conversation continued, Ethan grew more animated and excited. It was a peculiar and sleazy display, entirely inappropriate in the presence of our three-year-old daughter, who was busy untangling tinsel from a cardboard Christmas box, overhearing the exchange. I requested Ethan to stop.

Ethan refused to stop. Despite my warnings that our daughter and I would leave, he

MUG: An Account of Domestic Abuse

simply laughed. My anger grew, and I demanded that he put an end to it, but he disregarded my pleas. The two men continued their argument over the phone, treating the woman involved as an object, as if she couldn't hear, but she could, and I heard her say, "Let me speak to Beth." In a fit of fury, I hastily put my daughter's shoes on her, much to Ethan's amusement, and with her on my hip, I screamed, "FUCK YOU ALL!" as I stormed out of the family home. My daughter, silent and shocked, clung to me as we ran into the bitterly cold winter night, tears freezing on my cheeks.

Ethan followed me, laughing to himself and telling me to stop being "so melodramatic." I begged him to go away, refusing to return. I told him that our daughter was scared, visibly trembling like a cornered mouse, wide-eyed and unable to speak. He wanted to hold her, coaxing her with words like, "Come on, baby, mummy's being silly for no reason, let's go back." She would reach out her arms to him, but I would pull back, keeping her away. I had already called my Mum to get us. We stood on the main road, outside the petrol station, seeking refuge in the light and the presence of CCTV cameras. Finally, Ethan walked away, shaking his head and calling back, "I love you both, see you tomorrow." And even then, despite knowing that I had been foolish and had put both our daughter and me at risk by returning to the family home, I still wasn't sure if he would see us tomorrow or not. I knew that Ethan wouldn't stop; it was clear to me. But the question remained: when would I stop?

Chapter Five -

The Most Wonderful Time of the Year

'On average, 2 women a week are killed by a current or former partner in England and Wales.'

Refuge. (n.d.). The facts.

Listen to: Mean (Taylor's Version) by Taylor Swift

That evening, once my daughter had settled into our shared double bed at my parents' house, I was able to try and process what had happened earlier. Part of me wondered if I should be feeling unhappy that Ethan had wanted to pay for the services of a person whom we both knew – but I felt numb. It was nothing new. I'd found out during our relationship that Ethan often visited sex workers and hadn't hidden his history of doing so prior to being with me. It also hadn't surprised me that Ethan was trying to organise a swinging encounter with a stranger while our daughter was present (his idea was that it could be after her bedtime, when she was peacefully dreaming upstairs). Ethan had made it clear that day that sex was the main thing on his mind. Before I had taken out the Christmas decorations, Ethan had tried to entice me into his bedroom while our daughter watched TV. His proposition was that I could dutifully perform oral sex on him, to which I had declined. I said I did not fit around his sexual desires anymore, and that I made my own mind up about when and where I wanted it – and besides, 'You don't deserve a blowjob,' I declared.

"Fit?" he laughed. "I don't fit around you two."

"Okay," I replied, "I'll remember that, then."

"You will remember it – I don't fit around you, I don't fit around her, I fit around me."

These were the types of conversations that I immediately documented in my phone notes. I also recorded some of them as audio.

Another conversation I had recorded was during an earlier visit to the family home. While there, I told him conversationally that one of my close friends was pregnant. I added, forlornly, that I was one of the only women in my various circles of friends who had just one living child.

"So? Loads of people just have one child," he scorned.

"I'm talking about myself within my circle of friends," I replied.

"Loads of people have NO children," he added, with his specialist way of verbalising every syllable in an aggressive tone.

"Yes, I'm just saying -" I started.

"YOU weren't even meant to have one child," he butted in, referring to my history of infertility.

"I know," I tried, "But -"

"You don't even think you're lucky!"

"I do, but -"

"Why does it matter how many children other people have?"

I didn't have a chance to say that I WAS happy for my friend; that I had been pointing out that all my friends were having second or third children. I never said I was not lucky; I never showed that I was ungrateful for only being able to conceive and keep one pregnancy to birth.

A few minutes later, with the atmosphere tense and discouraging, I said to our daughter, "We'd better go now."

"Yeah," he sneered at her, "You'd better go now, come on. Your Mum needs anger management. She can't cope."

Random assaults on my character, such as this instance, were far from unusual. As our relationship had progressed, I was subjected to daily verbal abuse. This one-sided conversation was immediately logged in my phone notes, which is why I can use it as a general example.

Our daughter started to cry. I said to her, "Could you please put your wellies on?" But she couldn't find them and cried even more.

"Yes, [your wellies] are outside, aren't they? Your Mum's just being special."

When our daughter did put her wellies on, she put them on the wrong feet. I asked her to take them off and put them on the right way. Ethan snapped,

"Are you going to bend down?"

I didn't understand. "What?" I asked.

"Are - you - going - to - bend - down?" he repeated slowly and condescendingly.

"I don't know what you mean."

"Your daughter is trying to put her wellies on. Are you going to bend down and put them on for her?" he replied. But before I could answer, he resigned by concluding, "You can't cope. You need to go on a course because you can't cope," then, to our three-year-old, "Your Mum needs anger management." He proceeded to point at my discarded bag of clothes and life admin that I had asked for.

"Are you going to pick this up?" Ethan snapped.

"Yeah, I'm just not ready to pick it up yet..." I responded, busy putting on my own shoes after sorting out our child's wellies.

"Yeah, it's because you're taking paperwork you don't need," he spat. The paperwork was formal documentation and paper bills I needed to sift through.

"Come on," I said, taking our daughter's hand, "Let's go to the car."

"Yeah, your Mum can't help you because she's taking stuff she doesn't need," Ethan continued bitterly. "Any excuse to leave. I love you both being with me, and YOU spend all the time stuck to your phone, as usual, trying to buy tickets you don't need. You should be at home, looking after your daughter." He was referring to a gig he found out I was going to.

Listen to: Boys Will Be Boys by Emelyn

The rain began to pour down as we reached the car. I had my hands full of bags – but I also had to lift our daughter into the car seat – it was always my job to load the car while he told me to "hurry up." I dropped one bag with the paperwork in it and swore to myself as the rain began to soften the contents. I bent to pick it up after settling our daughter in her seat, while Ethan started up and revved the car engine. Our daughter burst into tears, thinking he was driving off without me.

"Come on, Mum!" she panicked.

"Your Mum's just taking her time to be special with all her shit," her father consoled her.

Finally, as I sat in the back of the car and slammed the door shut, Ethan sped off before I had time to fasten mine or our daughter's seat belts. I leaned over to hold her in position, silently praying that we would return to my parents' house in one piece. She tried to push my hand away, irritably.

"You don't need her to hold you, we're going 20mph," Ethan told our three-year-old, as if she understood the highway code. Then he said, "I love you."

"I love you too, Daddy."

"Are you going to bed now?" he asked our daughter in a sweet, soft tone as he drove, windscreen wipers squeaking.

"NO!" she whined. She hated bedtime.

"Daddy is. Daddy's tired."

We arrived at my parents' house within a few minutes. He pulled up outside with a sudden brake.

"Right, wait here a minute because Mummy's got to take all her rubbish out of the car. She's got lots of rubbish."

I got out, pulled out the bags of clothes, folders, and paperwork, and said to our eager daughter as she tried to jump from her car seat, "Hang on, let me get hold of you properly."

"Yeah, because Mummy's got to take all her rubbish out," Ethan sneered. I snapped.

"And this is exactly why Daddy always ends up in debt! – because he calls all this paperwork rubbish!"

"Bye," Ethan sighed, emphasising that he had directed it only at our daughter. She returned the goodbye. I closed the car door, and no sooner had it shut, Ethan sped away.

Within two minutes of walking down the front garden path and entering my parents' home, I had dozens of missed calls and messages. Apologies. "I'm just tired, I'm working hard, and I miss you."

I was tired too. Exhausted.

MUG: An Account of Domestic Abuse

The countdown to Christmas Day continued to be unpleasant, with Christmas shopping proving to be an especially stressful experience. Ethan, our daughter, and I went to a retail park in a nearby town. We parked, but before we had even gotten out of the car, Ethan was urging us to "hurry up." He was always terribly impatient.

As I stepped out of the vehicle, I heard him mumble about the boots I was wearing, which were my favourite black suede ones with laces and a thick heel. I politely asked him what he had said. He told me I needed to do my shoelaces up. I looked down. They were already tied.

Ethan was carrying our daughter. He went straight into a popular craft store. I called after him as he entered, saying that we did not need to go into that shop. He turned around, stormed out, gave our daughter to me, and said to her, "Come on, let's go." He walked off.

"Daddy! We're behind you!" she called after him, as she wriggled from my arms, her little toddler legs trying to keep up with his stride.

We entered a clothing store. I said something normal and mundane. So much so that I couldn't recall what it was when I logged the dialogue in my phone notes shortly afterward. Ethan snapped at me in response - "Be quiet." I wrote a note next to this, saying "I think he forgets himself."

I saw a corduroy pinafore dress in the clothes store that I thought about buying as a present for someone. Ethan kept pressing me to say who the dress was for.

Our daughter was tired, and she fell asleep in his arms while he carried her around the shop. We walked about the shop separately, him bored and me actively looking for Christmas gifts. And then suddenly, I lost sight of them. Where were they? I began to feel the familiar fast rhythm of my heartbeat with its fix of adrenaline. I looked for them all over the first floor and the ground floor, and scary scenarios started entering my head. Was our daughter hurt? What had happened to them?

Listen to: Red Flags by Mimi Webb

After a while of searching, I received a text from him – they had returned to his car. After queuing for ages with hastily grabbed items, I returned to the car. The windows were steamed up, but I could see through the condensation that he was on his phone, playing a game. I opened the door to the passenger side and placed my shopping bags on the front seat, startling him.

"Knock before you open the door," he scowled, then added, "You've written about me on Instagram again."

I said I hadn't written about him on Instagram, and that was the truth. He was referring to my public account. At the time, I consciously refrained from airing our "dirty laundry" about our breakup on that account.

"You have, Beth, but I'm not going to argue with you about it. I just find it rude."

I was genuinely confused. I even took out my phone and checked Instagram to see if I had written about him, despite knowing I hadn't.

Ethan had been to a probation meeting that day, something he regularly attended after being convicted of assaulting me a few weeks prior. The services involved with us still didn't know that Ethan and I were meeting regularly. Ethan was grumpy every day, but on this day, he seemed even more agitated. As we left the retail park and the early evening darkness descended, we found ourselves in a queue of traffic in the car park. Our daughter continued to sleep in the back seat, where I was also seated, and I rested my head against the window as he described his meeting with his "rude bitch" of a probation officer. He mimicked the questions she had asked him that day, particularly when she dared to inquire if he would be seeing his family over the Christmas period. Unbeknownst to the probation officer, politely inquiring about Ethan's family was a mistake on her part. Ethan despised being questioned about anything, as if he was on trial every time a regular response was expected from him. Asking Ethan about his family, however, was especially hazardous, as he didn't have a healthy relationship with them. It's likely that the probation officer quickly learned that Ethan was not inclined to freely share information.

"Fucking hell, how boring is she?" he complained after recounting their conversation about Christmas plans. "I'm not working with her. She's not intelligent. [Our daughter] is the only important person, not them [his family]."

On the drive back, I began to doze off in the back seat of the car, resting my head against the window.

"WAKE UP!" he yelled and abruptly swerved the car, causing my head to collide with the window as he shouted. I startled awake, feeling annoyed but accustomed to this routine; Ethan despised me sleeping, not just in the car, but at all. I didn't utter a word. I knew to keep quiet and conserve my energy.

Was this the worst Christmas with Ethan involved? Nope. In fact, it seemed like one of the better ones at the time. However, I was still living in survival mode, still operating on autopilot, still exhausted. So tired. Completely drained.

Chapter Six -
It was Christmas Eve, Babe

'Careful planning is important because abusers can become more violent and controlling and their actions can continue to pose a danger after you have left too – so it's a time to be especially cautious. Remember: ending the relationship will not necessarily end the abuse.'

The Survivor's Handbook, Women's Aid

Listen to: Fairytale of New York by The Pogues and Kirsty MacColl

On Christmas Eve, my daughter and I had homemade cards and gifts to deliver to our friends. It has become our tradition to wait until Christmas Eve so we can drive around, admire the beautiful fairy lights, and keep an eye out for the glow of Rudolph's nose. Ethan picked us up from a discreet location near my parents' house to avoid being seen by them. I opened the car door and began to put our daughter in her car seat, as usual. It was immediately clear that Ethan was unhappy.

"Come on, for fuck's sake," he grumbled. I strapped her in and sat down next to her in the back. I always sat in the back ever since our daughter was born because Ethan didn't allow me to sit in the front, insisting that our daughter "needed" me in the back.

"Ethan, we won't go out with you if you're going to be grumpy," I warned him.

"I'm not grumpy," he replied. "Three times you've gone to the wrong car door to put her in the car seat. It blows my mind." I thought about how he often removed her car seat from the car, so I wasn't always aware of which side it would be fixed to, but I didn't bother mentioning it. So far that day, our daughter and I had a lovely morning at the Church Christmas play, and we wanted to enjoy our afternoon as well.

"Where are you going?" Ethan asked.

"I thought we could deliver our cards," I replied.

"Where are we going then?" Ethan responded impatiently.

"We're going as far as Rambley, if that's okay." Rambley was one of our neighbouring villages.

We stopped at a petrol station. I told him he could use my bank card. "I'm not exactly sure how much is in there, but there should be enough."

"How much?" he demanded.

"I'm not 100% sure, but I said there should be enough."

"What's the PIN then?"

I gave him the PIN number, and he slammed the door. I quickly opened the door and called after him,

"Ethan!? You don't need the PIN number, it's contactless."

"I'm not using contactless," he shouted back without looking around, heading towards the cashpoint.

Panic started to set in. How naive of me. I had allowed him to have my bank card and shared the PIN... now he was withdrawing MY money. I hurriedly got out of the car and called after him repeatedly at the petrol station,

"Ethan! Ethan! Ethan!?"

He didn't listen and continued towards the cashpoint.

When he returned to the car, he was shaking his head. He accused me of being rude for shouting at him. I explained that I had been worried he was withdrawing cash from my card when I thought he was only using it for petrol. I asserted that he had no right to look at my bank account and balance. We drove away.

"Where are we going?" he asked again.

"I've already told you, to deliver the cards," I replied.

"Where?"

"I've already said. It would be nice if we could go to Rambley. I have a little something for [my friend's] children."

"You were so rude. You were shouting at me," he complained.

"I was calling after you," I defended myself.

"You were shouting at me across the petrol station." There was no point in arguing back.

On the short journey to Rambley, our daughter wanted to tell her father about the Christmas play we had attended that morning. She excitedly shared how the vicar had dressed up as a shepherd.

"Did he?" Ethan responded, "Yeah, some people are alright there [at the church]. Only some."

Soon, our daughter, exhausted from the busy day, started yawning and rolling her head back. However, every time she started to drift off, Ethan deliberately said something loudly to wake her up.

"I don't know where I'm going," he said once we arrived in Rambley.

"You know where they live," I replied.

"I don't."

"Well, you just keep-" I tried to continue, but he interrupted me again.

"I don't. I said I don't. I don't."

"You just keep going down this road," I managed to respond.

MUG: An Account of Domestic Abuse

As we pulled up at my friend's house, he began muttering to himself. They were not home, but I was sure I had already informed Ethan about it.

"They're not even here," he grumbled.

"I know they're not; I'm just delivering this through the letterbox," I replied. I did not catch what else he muttered.

Finally, our daughter fell asleep in the back seat as we drove home along country roads. Ethan pulled over into a passing space on a small lane and started unbuckling his belt.

"Come on then," he said, pointing to his exposed erection.

"No," I growled. "I'm not going to suck your cock after the way you've been today, as if I'm your slave."

Ethan pushed his erection back in and fastened his belt.

"I'm not interested then," was his response. "Stop bothering to see me. She's asleep. Take her home. I'm not playing games."

Listen to: Why Do You Hate Me? By Marmozets

Christmas Day that year was no different from previous years, despite our separation. I managed to persuade Ethan to take us to his elderly grandmother's house on Christmas morning, where many of his family members would be. He was angry about this and complained throughout the entire journey, never once wishing me a "happy Christmas." I wasn't upset by it because he hadn't wished me a happy Christmas for years. I was determined that our daughter was going to have an amazing day and remained cheerful throughout the car journey, choosing to be amused by his grumpiness rather than succumbing to frustrated tears as I had done in previous years.

At his grandmother's house, Ethan spoke sarcastically to me in front of various family members. He chose to sit moodily in a corner, texting on his phone, and avoided engaging in conversation. The only time he did speak was to refer to me and his relative as "witches," which was far from an endearing term, though we had grown accustomed to it.

When we returned to our hometown around midday, I asked Ethan to drop my daughter and me off outside the local pub where my own family was gathered. Ethan did not approve of this. As we approached the car park, he deliberately slowed down. However, just as I released my seat belt and prepared to open the door, he suddenly accelerated, causing fear to surge through me as I imagined being kidnapped. Yet, he swiftly turned the car around and dropped off our daughter and me at the end of the road, leaving us to walk to the pub with heavy bags of presents gifted to us by his family that morning. I remember our daughter asking me why Daddy did that, and I struggled to find an answer. How do you explain an adult's childish behaviour to a child who expects them to be a safe and responsible grown-up?

On New Year's Eve, Ethan and I had planned to take our daughter out to feed the ducks in a large, nearby town. However, despite my request, Ethan drove past the town centre and continued towards London. I felt uneasy about his erratic driving and soon began to have a panic attack. After some persuasion, I managed to convince him to turn back and take us home. Throughout the journey, he appeared manic, furious, and swerved dangerously along the country roads.

As we approached a canal bridge, he made a distressing statement, saying that he would drive us into the water and drown us all if we couldn't "be together." He started sobbing, which shocked me because it was extremely rare for him to shed actual tears when crying. He even began banging his head on the steering wheel. In the backseat with our daughter, I discreetly messaged both my sister and his family, informing them of our location in case there was a tragic incident, and we were all killed due to his reckless behaviour. I wanted someone to know the reason behind such a dreadful outcome, and that it wasn't an accident. I know that I was absolutely petrified, but I also know that I remained calm and even sympathetic towards him, to get home safely. I think I stroked his neck, whispering terms of endearment, anything to persuade him all was okay, for my daughter and I to stay alive.

Ethan didn't take anything seriously; it was all just a game to him. I believe he felt that I would ultimately return to him completely. We had agreed to give our relationship another chance, but only after Child Services closed their case, which ironically was when we considered it safe to live together again. However, I had made it abundantly clear to Ethan that I would not go ahead with our reunion unless he changed the way he spoke to me. Every day, I pleaded with him to treat me with kindness, to speak to me differently, and to show me that I could trust him once more, just as I had done once upon a time. Unfortunately, despite being sentenced to a community order for admitting to physically assaulting me, Ethan continued to treat me and speak to me in the exact same manner as he had before I left. Why would he change his behaviour? In the past, I had forgiven him for all his daily mistakes, which I had referred to as "fuckups." So why wouldn't I forgive him this time? The answer was that this time, I had an IDSVA assigned to me, and no matter how much I resisted having Katia in my life, she was persistent and determined not to give up on me. Katia took my situation seriously.

Chapter Seven - Hoovering and Harassment

'A victim of domestic violence is eligible for enhanced services as a victim of the most serious crime, but may also qualify for enhanced services as a vulnerable or intimidated victim.'

Ministry of Justice. (2015). Code of Practice for Victims of Crime

Listen to: Snap Out Of It by Arctic Monkeys

Katia maintained regular contact with me, even though it was evident that I hadn't emotionally severed ties with Ethan. Yes, I had physically left him, but my thoughts were consumed by him and our relationship. Despite believing that he was a 'narcissist', I couldn't untangle my feelings and loyalty towards him for reasons unknown to me at the time. The incident on New Year's Eve made me realise how close he had come to harming our daughter and me over the years, and I genuinely feared that next time, we wouldn't escape the car alive. On New Year's Day, I took a step I had never taken before: I blocked Ethan's number.

I was aware that Ethan would find other ways to contact me, and in a way, I didn't mind. I had grown accustomed to hearing from him. Blocking his phone number gave me a sense of control that I had never experienced before in our relationship, and for a brief period, it felt liberating. However, soon the issue of social media arose. Ethan didn't have genuine social media accounts. Whenever he dabbled with them in the past and posted pictures of himself, he remained secretive, leaving an air of mystery surrounding his living situation, relationships, and activities. It used to sadden me that he didn't share pictures of me or openly express his love for our family when he briefly created an account. He would on Snapchat, but he managed who saw the pictures of me. Clearly, that deliberate choice was meant to diminish my significance to him because after I blocked his number, Ethan started posting pictures of me on his new Instagram page. I won't deny that I enjoyed it. I hadn't received that kind of attention or public display of affection in years.

MUG: An Account of Domestic Abuse

Ethan began contacting me through Instagram Messenger, expressing his love for me. It was something I wasn't accustomed to, and it felt exhilarating that he was making such declarations. He would echo the cliché, "You don't know what you've lost until it's gone." And I fell for it. I thought to myself, "He thinks he's lost me, and it's made him realise that he loves me." As hours went by with his number blocked on my phone, I received increased messages on Instagram, filled with compliments. He didn't just "love" me - he thought I was beautiful, gorgeous! He believed I was a good mother. He acknowledged that he hadn't treated me right, and he was genuinely sorry. He said everything I had yearned to hear for years... and then Katia burst the Love-Bomb bubble.

"My dear, he's lying to you," she sympathetically said over the phone when I explained my dilemma.

He was "hoovering" me; that's what the women on the domestic abuse forums on Facebook said. That's what my friend

Rebecca said. That's what Katia was implying. He was attempting to draw me back into the intimate relationship because, by finally blocking his number, I had regained a small piece of power. How was he trying to hoover me? Through good old-fashioned "Love-Bombing." I contemplated the term "love bombing" in my diary one night. Yes, it felt like the right way to describe it... Love Bombing. Ethan was dropping a bomb of affection onto me, and it was shocking. I hadn't experienced this level of complimentary attention from him in years. However, the fact that he was dropping the bomb after I had blocked his number confirmed to me that he had been withholding affection all that time. He had stored away this bomb, ready to unleash it in case he found himself in a situation where he needed to obliterate my boundaries.

Listen to: Shake It Out by Florence + The Machine

The behaviour of Ethan appeared to align with Lenore E. Walker's "Cycle of Abuse," so much so that I felt I could predict his next move. Taking advice from Katia, Rebecca, and other survivors in support groups, I decided to block his social media accounts. It wasn't an easy decision, but it felt undeniably good once I had done it. Little did I know that this action would open the gates to the next chapter of my journey through abuse. I was starting to act, but my time in The Cycle was far from over.

Towards the end of my relationship with Ethan, I created an Instagram page in the form of a blog, where I documented the local adventures my daughter and I had together. I discussed how this type of "Nature therapy" played a vital role in supporting my mental health. I would also share our environmentally conscious lifestyle and the naturally sourced activities we engaged in. Once Ethan and I were no longer together, I found the page difficult to navigate. Our lives had undergone substantial changes, and I couldn't post the same content anymore. I continued to document our walks and being apart from Ethan made me feel more at ease about speaking openly. I began writing about being a single parent, much to Ethan's displeasure.

I knew that if I wanted to completely block Ethan from seeing my social media posts, I would have to make my Instagram page private. However, that seemed pointless to me. How could I engage in discussions about mental health if my posts weren't visible to others? How could I promote the healing power of nature for a troubled mind if my page was closed off from the world? No, I took pride in the pictures I took, the videos I captured, and the captions I wrote. I wanted my page to be public. But Ethan wasn't going to make that possibility easy for me. He had never approved of me having any social media platform, and during our relationship, I was unable to freely use my phone without Ethan making sneers and jibes about my supposed obsession with a "fake world." Ethan particularly disliked me having the public Instagram account.

No sooner had I blocked one of Ethan's social media accounts from my public page, another one would tediously appear. I found myself constantly blocking him. This was before Meta became Meta and updated its security settings to allow users to block any future accounts created by the same individual or bot. Blocking Ethan from social media became a frequent and daily chore.

As he kept resurfacing under various profile disguises, complete with usernames that held hints to his identity—clues that only I could understand through our private jokes or previous terms of endearment—I started feeling less guilty about blocking him. The final straw came when Ethan began contacting my family members through Facebook Messenger and WhatsApp. It was at that point that I followed Katia's advice and applied for a non-Molestation order.

I don't recall much of the process of applying for the non-mol. I now know that the reason for my lack of memory is because it was intensely painful, and my brain has likely suppressed the recollection of that excruciating time. "That's too painful to remember, best to hide that memory," it seemed to say. What I can tell you is that I was eligible for legal aid, and the process was relatively quick, taking about three weeks from start to finish. In brief, a non-molestation order is a type of injunction that an individual obtains against someone who has subjected them to domestic abuse. Its purpose is to protect the abused person from further harm and establish legal boundaries when the boundaries they have set themselves are not respected by the abuser.

The court date for the non-mol order I applied for was one of the worst days of my life. I had no idea what to expect, and had I known, I might have reconsidered going through with it. While on my way to the magistrate's court via the bus, alone, I wrote the following on my phone:

'On my way to get a non-molestation order against a man I've idolised in some form since I was twenty – almost ten years of my life was spent respecting then worshipping a man I loved to an indescribable extent. I didn't know highs like that existed. And today, I go to get a piece of formal barrier to stop him from coming to see myself or our daughter. To say it's surreal is an understatement, but this is the start of big things for [my daughter] & I. We are such a fantastic team and I vow to show her always that she IS enough. And THAT is why I'm doing this.'

I was informed by multiple services involved that Ethan wouldn't be contesting the non-molestation order and therefore wouldn't be present at court. However, as I stood in line outside the offices, I found out that he would be attending after all. I was devastated. The news hit me like a tidal wave, and I let out a wailing cry, like a tortured wolf. I knew that if I saw him, I wouldn't have the courage to go through with it. Naively, I had chosen to attend court alone, unaware of how harrowing the experience could be. When I learned that Ethan would be there, I did the only thing I could think of at that moment - I called my Mum.

My Mum, a nurse, was working at the time. But on this occasion, she dropped everything and hurried from work to support me. We sat together in a small, plain room at a heavy desk, with a solicitor I hadn't met or spoken to before that moment. I was asked to read a formal report prepared by the solicitor, outlining the reasons for my case. It felt as if I was reading about a completely different person. I remember thinking, "Is this really about me? Did someone do all this to me? Or is it just a nightmare?" And then I heard him. I heard the rumble of his voice, and it felt like a blow to my head. My body started shaking, and my clothes clung to me from the sweat.

Every fibre of my being reacted to his voice in the alien environment. Overwhelmed, I broke down into tearful apologies; I couldn't face him in the courtroom. The solicitor, looking at me with discomfort, went to speak to the judge. My mum sat silently by my side, still in her uniform, badge on, hair tied up, gently stroking my back.

Listen to: Wildest Moments by Jessie Ware

It was so unexpected for Ethan to show up, that the solicitor returned with the announcement that the judge had agreed that I didn't have to enter the courtroom. The hearing proceeded with only Ethan and my solicitor present. It lasted no more than five minutes, and then it was all over: I had a non-molestation order in place. Afterward, feeling weak and far from celebratory, my Mum and I went to McDonald's. I remember her reassuring me that "it was all done now" and that I wouldn't have to go through it again - at least not for some time. It felt like the first day of the rest of my life... for a few hours.

During the period between applying for the non-molestation order and the date it was granted, Ethan was instructed to refrain from contacting me. He did not comply. Ethan not only constantly contacted me through false social media accounts but also made continuous phone calls using 'No Caller ID'. Then he started showing up at places he knew I would be. He would appear outside my parents' house. On one occasion, he showed up at church - my safe space - while I was receiving communion. He grabbed my arm and led me outside, to beg me to take him back. Thankfully, Rebecca had also been there and calmly removed me from the situation. The encounter at the church left me shaken, and I had to report his breach to the police. I knew I had to document every instance of him contacting me.

I had developed a friendly relationship with the vicar and his wife, and they kindly invited me to their house while I waited for the police. While my daughter and I were having lunch in their kitchen, Ethan appeared at the front door of the vicarage. The vicar escorted him away in a kind manner, but also offered him help and support, acknowledging that Ethan belonged to the parish as well. As far as I know, Ethan never took up the offer. I came to understand that Ethan's constant disruptions in my daily life were classified as instances of 'harassment'. I certainly felt harassed. However, alongside that feeling, there was something else I couldn't fully grasp rationally: sympathy. It grew stronger in my mind with each passing day. I found myself feeling sympathetic towards Ethan, especially each time I had to involve the police.

I am naturally an empathetic person - you could even call me an 'empath'. I am attuned to the emotions of others and genuinely feel sadness when things are not going well for them. I always want the best for people. However, I also have a lifelong tendency of prioritising other people's needs over my own. I was aware of these strong personality traits within myself, but I didn't fully realise just how empathetic and compassionate I am until I sought healing for myself and realised it wasn't a straightforward process. How could I begin to heal my own wounds if I was always focused on mending the wounds of others? And if my caring nature led me to feel sympathy for Ethan in the mess he had created, why couldn't I extend the same level of care and sympathy to myself for what I had been through? I often extend grace to others, but rarely show it to myself.

A Narcissistic Abuse expert taught me that narcissists are not born as narcissists; they develop their narcissistic traits because of childhood trauma. For context, let's assume that, at that time, I considered Narcissism to be a personality disorder that originates from trauma. To have the personality traits commonly associated with Narcissism sounded like a solitary, debilitating, and wicked existence for any human being. The more I discovered about Ethan's childhood, the less I saw him as an adult. Instead, I saw a little boy who had suffered severe abuse. I wished I could hold that little boy in my arms, offering him comfort and protection from the harsh and frightening world around him. It hurt me to realise how his own agonising pain had been projected onto me in the way that it had. Ethan had unleashed a nightmare upon me because he had lived and continued to live within a nightmare himself. How could I completely turn my back on that? I didn't believe I could, and I didn't believe I should. In the end, the non-molestation order wasn't a waste of time, but it didn't prevent Ethan and me from staying in contact. He knew that I despised reporting him to the police, and after a few weeks, I stopped reporting him, as if the non-mol didn't exist. It's ironic that, while considering Ethan's childhood trauma, I was neglecting to minimise the impact of it on our daughter.

Listen to: Take Me to Church by Hozier

Ethan, our daughter, and I started spending time together in secret, secluded places, often walking on lesser-known footpaths in the surrounding countryside. Although I didn't feel entirely safe when we ventured off the beaten track, I had been provided with alarms by the police after the non-molestation order was granted. My parents' house had alarms installed at the front and back entrances, and I wore a personal alarm around my neck whenever I left the house. During this period, Ethan behaved relatively well, refraining from saying anything rude or nasty to me. This created a few pleasant weeks of contact, during which I believed I had control because I was the one calling the shots. I unblocked his number and social media accounts, and we would video message each other every night, using our daughter's bedtime as an excuse. While she fell asleep drinking her bottle, I would read her bedtime stories and position my phone by the bed, allowing Ethan to watch via Facetime. Although I had no desire to reunite with him by moving back, a part of me held onto a glimmer of hope that maybe everyone was mistaken - perhaps Ethan was the narcissist who would defy expectations and change? Despite these hopeful thoughts, I stayed firm in my decision to deny him entry into my parents' house and rebuffed his advances when it came to sex. I refused to engage in any form of intimacy with him, as I believed that withholding it gave me back a sense of power.

The Cycle of Abuse had undeniably restarted. On Valentine's Day, I received something I had always wanted - an Emerald ring. It was an exquisite infinity ring, complete with several substantial stones set in a platinum band. It certainly wasn't a cheap gift. My emotions were conflicted. On one hand (excuse the pun), I adored it. It was stunning. On the other hand, it felt like a painful reminder of past disappointments. Valentine's Day had become a sore subject for us in the final years of our relationship. The first one was magical - I was showered with sentimental and expensive presents, accompanied by heartfelt poetry proclaiming that I was the love of Ethan's life and his future wife. However, later celebrations were marked by neglect. Ethan would dismissively claim that he "didn't do Valentine's Day." In truth, I wasn't overly invested in the holiday either, but I yearned for some form of acknowledgment. To then receive not only acknowledgment but also a gift he knew I would adore left me feeling resentful. It highlighted that Ethan had always been capable of celebrating our love, but for years, he had chosen not to. Two weeks later, Ethan and our daughter presented me with a birthday gift for my 30th. It was another emerald ring, this time fashioned into the shape of a flower with four emeralds. Our daughter was thrilled to give it to me. The ring had a white gold band, and the deep green colour of the stones and the delicate elegance of its design showed its significant cost. Ethan knew I would cherish it - and I did. It complemented my infinity band perfectly, resembling an Irish-themed bridal set. I longed to wear them together. However, I couldn't ignore the fact that these rings were tools meant to win me back - and it was tempting to be won over. Unbeknownst to Ethan, there was a complicating factor in the new Cycle of Abuse: I was dating. I had re-entered the Cycle, but I wasn't as easily swayed.

Chapter Eight - Sex and The Perpetrator

'There were 43,774 offences of coercive control recorded by the police in England and Wales (excluding Devon and Cornwall) in the year ending March 2023. This is compared with 41,039 in the year ending March 2022.'

Office for National Statistics, 2023

During the Christmas period after leaving Ethan, I had started casually seeing someone. We had absolutely nothing in common, but our conversations were tolerable because we were always intoxicated when we met. My parents were supportive of my newfound social life, as I hadn't had much of a social life outside of my daughter while with Ethan. This meant they agreed to babysit – a new kind of freedom for me. The Christmas fling extended into the New Year and finally ended on my thirtieth birthday in February. He fit the stereotype commonly referred to as a 'fuck boy' - someone who is only interested in a physical relationship without being upfront about their intentions. I was aware of the nature of our arrangement, but that didn't stop me from daydreaming about what it would be like if we were together. The nights felt less lonely when I had someone to message, and I genuinely didn't want to be alone. My parents had an active social life and were often out in the evenings unless they were babysitting. Having what essentially amounted to a 'Netflix & Chill' companion supplied temporary company because I didn't enjoy my own company. And that was at the heart of my predicament - I didn't enjoy spending time with myself. Instead of finding satisfaction in my own presence, I sought validation from external sources. It was around this time that I realised I relied heavily on validation through sex and what I perceived as romantic attention from others.

Listen to: Coming Down by Halsey

When I reflect on what made Ethan and me so compatible, I can see that it was our shared need for validation. In the first stages of our relationship, like many infatuated couples, sex consumed our thoughts. I wanted him, and he wanted me, and this passionate desire emanated from both of us. I couldn't get enough of his body - his appearance, his movements, and how he looked at me. He would often playfully joke that he was addicted to sex. It's only after leaving the relationship that I realised it wasn't merely a joke; he is genuinely addicted to sex. Sex, for Ethan, is a confirmation of being desired. Sex is his supply. Sex is his means of survival. Ethan survives by eating, drinking, sleeping, and having a lot of sex. He had a lot of sex with me, with himself, and with other women. That's where our shared use of sex diverged - even when my needs weren't fulfilled by Ethan, I remained faithful to him. However, Ethan cannot find validation through sex with just one woman.

Our sex was constant and a combination of frenzied passion, lust, and a deep-seated need. Our exploration was explicitly experimental, encompassing every position, style, and location imaginable. Sometimes, Ethan would shower every inch of my body with kisses, displaying a profound adoration and worship. At other times, he would pour so much champagne on my face while I stood naked in the bath that I would choke and beg him to stop, my senses

MUG: An Account of Domestic Abuse

overwhelmed as I literally drowned. There were instances when he extinguished lit matches on my nipples, causing brief moments of pain. He would occasionally choke me with his hands, his intense gaze fixed upon my eyes, making me feel as if my eyeballs were about to burst from their sockets (for essential information about choking and strangulation during sex, a valuable source is the book 'Block, Delete, Move on' by LaLaLaLetMeExplain).

Ethan would tie me up with dressing gown ropes or wrap me in cellophane, rendering me temporarily immobile. He would insert random objects into me - this was an activity he had a fondness for. Everyday objects were used for this purpose. There was a particular ornament belonging to Ethan that he confessed to having used on 'three different women,' including myself. The thrill of danger always excited me. I relished being considered 'one of his women.' I knew what they looked like, who they were, and I didn't perceive myself to be on the same level as them in terms of beauty or intelligence. I didn't feel worthy of being regarded as one of them. He controlled me during sex, but I showed a willingness for him to do so.

In time, the sexual coercion and control worsened and became exploitive. Ethan would take explicit photos of me during sex and send them via Snapchat to his colleagues or my friends. I hated that, and it became a topic of conversation at the pub for a while. He seemed to take pleasure in humiliating me in front of my loved ones.

Our sexual encounters were often public in nature. We excelled at that. We would engage in intimate moments at quiet spots, bending over bridges, sitting naked in fields, or covering ourselves with my long coat on park benches on village greens. We'd have sex in the sea, under stars or in wildflower meadows. Of course, we also had sex in beds - our own bed, hotel beds, and makeshift beds composed of blankets and sleeping bags that we kept in the car. We would have sex in the sunset with breathtaking views from atop ancient hills, in coastal pillboxes, or beneath the canopy of trees after trespassing into quiet Copses. We could have sex all day, every day - and in the first year, we did. By nightfall, we would still be ravenous and yearning for more. His record was fourteen orgasms in one night. It seemed that nothing could halt our insatiable appetite for sex - not soreness, not familiarity, not boredom, nor anything else... or so I believed.

Listen to: Gimme Shelter by The Rolling Stones

Sex had always been the defining aspect of my relationship with Ethan. In my mind, it was what kept us attuned to one another and added to our exciting blend of fun, wildness and spontaneity. However, within a year of committing to each other, the thrill of our sexual life began to fade. Ethan, who had proclaimed himself a "sex addict," suddenly lost interest in sex. He went from hungrily pursuing me multiple times a day and night to having no desire at all.

Our routine involved early nights, with candles and fairy lights creating a cosy atmosphere. We would watch TV series together, usually from the comfort of our bed. Our bed had been the site of many intimate encounters, until Ethan's sudden disinterest in sex arose. This change in our relationship was as significant as other major milestones couples experience, such as dating, moving in together, or getting engaged. It was marked as the point when Ethan stopped wanting sex with me. If we no longer had sex, what would define us as a couple?

Of course, I believed it was my fault. I started questioning myself. Had I gained weight? Did I have an unpleasant odour? Was it because he noticed a stray hair I had forgotten to pluck? Were my breasts not large enough? I knew he preferred bigger breasts, and mine didn't fit that description. Was it my breath? Did I not clean my teeth well enough? Did I taste bad? Was it my hair colour? He always mentioned that he preferred me as a blonde. Was it because I started removing my makeup with the lights on before bed? Was I no longer attractive? Was I not adventurous enough? Or perhaps too adventurous? Oh God, what had gone wrong? Was it truly me, Beth, who had somehow managed to turn off Ethan, the man with the highest sex drive I had ever met? Had I ruined sex for him? It felt like it had to be my fault.

I decided to step up my game. I realised that my underwear collection hadn't been updated in a while. Perhaps all it would take for Ethan to want me again was to invest in some provocative garments. I spent a fortune in overpriced lingerie stores. For a few weeks, I paraded around my room in corsets, hold-ups, silky bras adorned with ribbons, and the tiniest, most uncomfortable thongs. I propped up my iPhone and posed for hands-free selfies, trying to exude as much desirability and allure as possible. Then, unfiltered and unrestrained, I sent each daring photo to my partner while he was at work. He would message me expressing his eagerness to come home and be with me. As a result, I made sure to shave every part of my body in preparation, applied baby oil to keep my skin soft, and even used scented body wash in places where it shouldn't be used. I was ready to play the role of a porn star.

Ethan would come home and take a bath. He would have the meal I had prepared, waiting for him in the warm oven - usually his favourite dish. He would put on his freshly washed pyjamas that I had carefully folded and treated with fabric conditioner. He would open the energy drink I had gone out to buy for him. Then, he would turn on the TV and watch whatever he wanted. Meanwhile, I would undress and join him in bed, feeling somewhat foolish in my obvious choice of lingerie, which he pointedly ignored. He would snuggle under the duvet and turn away from me, facing the wall instead of me. I would lie down behind him, trying to spoon him and gently caressing his hair and shoulders - something he had once enjoyed. However, he would ask me to stop and move away, claiming it was too hot to cuddle. I would kiss him, but he would tell me to 'get off'. I would make another attempt to arouse him, but he would push me away, saying, 'Get off me, some of us have actually been working hard.' He no longer wanted sex. We had become the kind of dull and routine couple that I used to pity - no sex, no engaging conversations, no excitement after a day of work, and no fun.

After a few weeks, my anger grew. I would snap at Ethan, demanding an explanation for his lack of sexual interest in me. He would dismiss my concerns, calling me 'rude' and citing his exhaustion from work. I would back down and feel ashamed. Perhaps he wasn't the sex addict he had claimed to be all along? Maybe I was the one with the insatiable sexual appetite?

I discovered, through my participation in daily Facebook groups and forums for abuse survivors, that 'sexual abuse' isn't limited violent assaults. I learned that withholding sex could be a form of control. If someone genuinely lacked a sex drive due to fatigue, depression, anxiety, trauma, or simply not feeling up to it, that was different. It is normal and acceptable to say 'no' to a partner when it comes to sex. In a healthy relationship, a partner would understand and respect that, wanting their loved one to have proper rest. In a healthy relationship, insecurities wouldn't arise, nor would suspicions that one's partner was lying or unattracted. In a healthy relationship, appreciation and attraction would be expressed. When an abusive person abruptly stops a particular behaviour, it is a deliberate and premeditated action. They know what they want from their victim and how to manipulate them. In my case, Ethan withheld sex to heighten my insecurities. When I felt insecure, I went beyond to be the "perfect partner," but my efforts were futile as he remained unimpressed. Meanwhile, Ethan enjoyed the benefits of my excessive energy, which he gladly consumed, without considering that I was running on empty once he had drained me. He didn't care about depleting my energy because he could survive on what I had provided. This behaviour is typical of individuals displaying abusive traits; they take your energy without concern for your well-being. Another reason sex is a useful tool for abusers is that it allows them to keep control over their victims. Rape, sexual assault, and abuse can take various forms, including withholding, coercing, exploiting, and trafficking. Lack of physical violence doesn't make the abuse any less severe.

Throughout our relationship, Ethan intermittently used sex withdrawal as a tool of power play to demoralise and control me. During the periods when he withheld sex from me, he sought sexual fulfilment from other sources, essentially replacing me with new partners. By doing so, he could distance himself physically from me while still having his need for validation through sex met by these other women. Additionally, he received pleasure from seeing my insecurities and the excessive affection I showered upon him, all the while satisfying his sexual needs with the women of whom he either paid for or impressed into bed. How often was I cheated on?

MUG: An Account of Domestic Abuse

The entire time.

Chapter Nine -

Affaires

'The abuser's orientation toward sex is likely to be self-involved. Sex to him is primarily about meeting his needs.'

Lundy Bancroft, Why Does He Do That? Inside The Minds of Angry and Controlling Men, (p.174)

Listen to: Gold Dust Woman by Fleetwood Mac

Red Flags I Ignored

The first woman I know of was Hannah, who happened to be a co-worker of Ethan's. She played a significant role in the end of his earlier marriage. Before me, she had claimed to have had an affair with Ethan and even sent a letter to their address while his ex-wife was heavily pregnant. The letter was received and read by Ethan's ex-father-in-law, leading to the eventual end of the marriage less than a year later, before their child's first birthday. Shortly after his wife left him, Ethan started seeing me. Hannah alleged that they were involved in a relationship while he and I were getting together. Frustrated by his choice to be with me, she expressed her jealousy and confusion during a loudspeaker conversation that I overheard. Ethan, of course, denied the entire affair, portraying Hannah as a mentally unstable stalker from work. He explained that a tragic family death had caused her to lose her sanity and become obsessed with him. He denied ever cheating on his ex. I confirmed through social media snooping that Hannah had indeed experienced a terrible bereavement. I sympathised with Hannah for her loss, but I decided to believe my partner. Twenty-four-year-old Beth would have called herself a feminist. Thirty-four-year-old Beth recognises that she had a lot to learn about patriarchal concepts and how women's trauma and grief are used to label them as mentally ill.

In the following years, Hannah appeared to create multiple social media accounts to virtually harass me. While I initially attributed these actions to her, I now question everything and wonder if it was Ethan trying to solidify his lies. However, I did come across her real Twitter profile, where she deliberately posted passive-aggressive tweets, aware that out of curiosity, I might look. One tweet, which said something like "Omg, it lives in my town, drove past it earlier... Dowdy comes to mind," was clearly about me, as I had seen her drive by that day. On another occasion, I encountered her following me down each aisle of a supermarket while I was pregnant, causing me to leave without buying what I had intended. Regardless of the truth, I now understand the dynamics of abusive cycles and suspect that Ethan likely discarded Hannah in a cruel and typical fashion. Hannah was the first likely affair I now know of, but as I disregarded her claims at the time, she wasn't the first instance of cheating I realised.

That was Jenny.

Jenny was a pretty woman and a young mother. It was during the second year of my relationship when she contacted me. At that time, I was working at a pub. I'd just opened, my usual routine at midday, and served the regular old men who visited every day for their lunchtime pint. As a semi-rural pub, it had notoriously poor WiFi connection, and I didn't see Jenny's message straight away. One moment,

MUG: An Account of Domestic Abuse

Jenny was a stranger—the next, I was dissecting her every social media move.

Jenny had somehow come across my Facebook account and seen my happy, smiley profile picture with Ethan. Before opening the message, I could see the first sentence in the notification. It was something like, 'Hey, I'm sorry to do this to you, but Ethan...' My stomach did somersaults, and my whole body felt heavy. With that notification, I just knew that he'd cheated on me. I hesitated to open it, and I decided to browse through the public photos on her Facebook profile, just as I assumed she had done with mine. My overwhelming fear was that she would reveal that her child was Ethan's. I didn't believe I could overcome such a profound betrayal, and panic took hold of me. My body was flooded with adrenaline. Eventually, despite the intermittent WiFi and in-between serving the regulars with a cheerful expression, I gathered the courage to open the message. As the pub shift progressed, whenever I could grab a moment on my phone, I learned from an active exchange with the woman who I felt had just destroyed my life, about Ethan's "casual" affair. Jenny claimed it had been in the evenings, on his way back from work, that he'd stop at hers and they'd have sex. I was able to work out that Ethan's evenings spent with Jenny while her child was in bed had been while I'd worked late shifts on weekdays in a nursing home. Eventually, Jenny had ended the affair because she wanted to be more than just his "side piece."

Initially, Jenny apologised to me and claimed that she had "no idea" Ethan had a girlfriend when she started seeing him. She assured me that as soon as she found out, she ended things between them. I knew she was probably telling the truth, but there was still hope; maybe she was some crazy, jealous woman, making stuff up? I insisted on seeing proof. Jenny sent me the evidence: screenshots of months' worth of messages, Ethan's phone number, and naked photos of himself posing in my parents' bathroom. While most of their communication appeared to be sexual in nature, his written affection for her reminded me of the affection he had shown me at the beginning of our relationship. It seemed clear that he wanted Jenny in a way that he no longer wanted me; it felt painful to see how Ethan would end each message with dozens of 'kisses,' something he had stopped doing with me a while ago.

In their conversations, Ethan eagerly commented on the suggestive photos Jenny sent him, making remarks like, "Can I hold those [breasts] later?" and even the cliché, "I can't stop thinking about you, last night was incredible." When I calculated the timeline of their affair, I discovered that it had taken place over my 25th birthday, which I had described at the time as "one of the happiest birthdays ever." I'd been showered with expensive gifts and vows of commitment. Ethan had even spent the day with my family and friends, enjoying a meal at a pub and drinking with us into the evening. What hurt even more was that his affair with Jenny had occurred during a holiday we had taken together. I had believed our holiday was amazing, but those memories became tainted. There was a picture I had taken on holiday and placed in a photo album of Ethan using his phone. Was he messaging her at that very moment? Could he have been so brazen as to text her right under my nose and in front of my camera lens?

Getting past this seemed impossible. As for Jenny, I struggled to find forgiveness for the woman I labelled a "fucking home-wrecking bitch" in my journal.

Interestingly, what I clung to was one of the screenshots Jenny had sent of their messages. In that exchange, when Jenny had threatened to expose their affair, Ethan responded in a panic, pleading, "Please don't do this to Beth, I love her and want to spend the rest of my life with her." It was a conflicting mix of fury and devastation for me, yet my heart felt a glimmer of hope to see that he had professed such a strong display of what I mistook for love.

Listen to: Behind These Hazel Eyes by Kelly Clarkson

On the day I discovered Ethan's affair, he was working as a manager in a shop. Despite the risk to his job, he dropped everything and rushed to the pub where I was stuck. He refused to leave his stool at the bar as I worked, pouring pint after pint during a busy shift. I did my best to hold back tears, not wanting to ruin someone's drink or smear my eye makeup. Ethan begged me for forgiveness. He promised that the affair had happened during a time when I was tired and stressed from work, and therefore neglected him. I recalled a period of fatigue related to administrative tasks, but I didn't remember taking it out on Ethan by ignoring him. Nonetheless, he had a way of making me question my own actions. My anger was directed more towards Jenny. In her messages, she came across as immature and somewhat blasé about the pain she had inflicted upon me with her revelation.

That night, as I sobbed from shock and heartbreak, yet still climbed into bed with my partner who FINALLY showed me the intimate attention I'd been craving, I messaged Jenny, incensed. I can't recall the exact words I used, but it involved shaming her for being a 'slag' and inviting men she hardly knew into her house for sex while her toddler was in the next room. I will never forget Jenny's final message to me: "It's about time you wiped 'MUG' off your forehead."

The rest of that summer passed by slowly in a melancholic state of disbelief. I felt low and lacking in self-esteem, and this was noticeable to my family. It was unlike me to neglect touching up my roots or be unbothered about wearing minimal makeup. It felt pointless; what was the use in making myself look nice if I'd get cheated on anyway? I even lost weight; eating felt like a chore. The day after discovering Ethan and Jenny's affair, he took time off work and drove me to one of my favourite places, Glastonbury Tor. As we climbed the hill and reached the monument, I could barely find the words to speak to Ethan. He bought me earrings from a hippy shop in town and showed affection at every opportunity. I expressed my uncertainty about how we could move past his betrayal, questioning why he would do such a thing when I believed I was the love of his life. Ethan responded by saying that cheating was the only way he knew how to be with a woman, but I was going to be the woman who would change him for the better. He pleaded with me and made promises that it would never happen again. I'm not sure if I believed him, but I went along with it. The one thing I was certain of was that I desperately didn't want to lose my relationship.

Ethan started to exhibit his best behaviour, and a few weeks later, I decided to dye my hair. I asked him to choose a colour, and he opted for jet black. I also bought some clothes different from my usual style and plucked my eyebrows to be smaller. I'm not sure if I was consciously trying to resemble his ex-partners or Jenny, who were mostly dark-haired, but I know I was deliberately trying to appear attractive to him and not quite like myself.

Despite hoping that our relationship would improve, especially since the frequency of sex had returned, it never quite recaptured that magical "honeymoon" phase. We continued to do things we loved together, embarking on impromptu adventures, discovering new places and people, and capturing our eccentric lifestyle in photos. However, something was missing. Whenever Ethan used his phone, I couldn't help but wonder who he was texting. When he kissed me, I questioned if he had kissed Jenny in the same way. Even when Ethan cuddled me in bed, I couldn't shake the memories of those weeks prior to discovering the affair, when he had avoided physical contact, despite my efforts. I felt perpetually cynical, wondering if he was only spooning me to keep his rent-free accommodation and a convenient sexual partner. The trust was gone. I couldn't confide in my friends because I was too ashamed of his betrayal, so we continued to meet them at pubs and put on a facade of being "loved up."

I observed how skilled Ethan was at displaying public affection towards me in front of my loved ones, but I noticed that his affection dwindled once we were in the car and he was driving me home. This discrepancy further fuelled my distrust. And so, the third person I suspected Ethan of cheating on me with was... his wife.

Listen to: Nothing Compares 2 U by Sinead O'Conor

Discard

In the second autumn of our relationship, Ethan and I attended a fertility clinic. I wanted a baby more than anything, and Ethan was apparently eager to start a family with me. However, we didn't qualify for IVF on the NHS since Ethan already had a child from his marriage. Our only options for getting pregnant were hormone therapy or private IVF treatment.

During the same month, I found a bedsit-sized flat for us to rent in a town over twenty miles away from my home. Although it was difficult to move away from my family, it would bring us much closer to Ethan's daughter, which was his wish. A few months earlier, I had left the job I loved at the nursing home and had been working at the pub in the meantime. The week I secured the flat, I also landed a respectable job as a Senior Care Assistant in a Residential Care Home within walking distance of it. It offered better pay and more responsibilities, and I felt proud of myself. I saw our move as an opportunity to turn the "rocky patch" in our relationship around and begin a new chapter exclusively for us. I was filled with excitement... but there was just one problem.

Ethan appeared to be suffering from severe depression. After work, he began locking himself in my parents' bathroom, which was unusual because I usually joined Ethan in the bathroom. I would wash his hair and sometimes even shave him while he relaxed and shared about his day at work.
"Something isn't right," I confided in my colleague. "He's been so moody with me,

and I can't figure out what's wrong." I was worried that Ethan had changed his mind about trying for a baby and paying for private treatment. I knew that financing IVF was putting a lot of pressure on him. I assumed that my infertility was the problem. We went through a phase of Ethan being the man I fell in love with, for a few days, or even a few hours, and I'd get hopeful that that version of Ethan was going to stay. But then he would slip back into being miserable again, and seemingly unhappy with me, even though I wasn't sure what I was supposed to have done.

Then, for three weeks, Ethan stopped talking to me. He completely shut down. He would silently watch TV in our double room while I sat in bed, engrossed in my journaling. Ethan's messages to me during his working day became less frequent and noticeably lacking in emotion. He stopped expressing his love for me. I started feeling a desperate need to hear the man I adored say that he wanted me. When I asked Ethan if he still loved me, he would turn away and tell me to stop "questioning" him. I could feel him slipping away. There was this sense of impending doom, an intense feeling that he was going to leave me, which felt incomprehensible. Then, on the nineteenth of October that year, he left me. He gave no reason. He offered no excuse. He came home from work, packed his clothes into his bags, and said he was going. I was devastated. I screamed. I fell to my knees, clutching onto his legs, and begged him not to leave me. He went downstairs and apologised to my obviously concerned parents. He told them that he had to end things but thanked them for letting him live there. He said, "I'm sorry it didn't work out." Then he left. As he drove away, my mum held me up as my body collapsed into shuddering sobs. My world shattered.

The next few months of my life were like living in the darkest hole of Hell. After leaving me, Ethan went 'AWOL' for almost a fortnight. Even his work called me, to ask if I knew of his whereabouts. I had already paid the deposit for the flat, so I went ahead with my move to the town where I didn't know anyone. A caretaker at my new workplace used the residents' day trip bus to bring my furniture from my parents' house to my tiny ground-floor bedsit. On the first night there, I sat in an unfamiliar room on a 1970s floral sofa. I drank a bottle of prosecco by myself while watching the film 'Sid & Nancy'. Then, I put on the DVD of a Sex Pistols gig I had attended in the late noughties. In the video, my (previous) ex and I were visibly crowd surfed out. I remembered that moment in all its detail, and something suddenly happened. Not only did I feel a tidal wave of grief for the sudden loss of my relationship with Ethan, but I was also overcome and paralysed with grief over the relationship prior to him, which I had not yet mourned. The only way I can accurately describe that winter of my life is that I crashed - face first - into a pit of agony, despair, and an anguish so raw that the memory of that pain still sends shivers through me. It seemed that if I had to be in hell, then everyone I loved would be dragged down with me.

That December, I did something so diabolical to my best friends, that I lost them. I also drank every day. I smoked when I drank. I self-harmed with nail scissors. I cried. I hated. I hated every single fucking day. I was venomous, frantic, and chaotic. I believed that a demon had taken over my body, I was so ravaged with self-hatred and pain. Not only had a dam of grief given way, but with my self-sabotaging, selfish behaviour, I lost people in the process. Around this time of such self-destruction Ethan emerged from the shadows and began coming over to the bedsit after work for baths, Domino's pizza, and a quickie here and there. I was glad about this and hopeful that he would fall back in love with me. There was no routine, and his timings were irregular, but he would visit, and we would have sex. It was not loving sex; it was not kind sex. It was mostly rough sex and giving him blowjobs. Occasionally, he would spend the night, but he insisted I did not touch him after his routine orgasms. Around this time, I was sure he had left me for someone else, and my suspicion was firmly on his ex, Meg. Isolated from family and friends, I found that I had no one to unload my insecurities on. I worried that I was paranoid or untrusting due to my experience of being cheated on. Without anyone to turn to, Ethan was all I had - and I clung onto him and his sporadic visits whenever I could.

Listen to: Driver's License by Olivia Rodrigo

The Ex

Meg and I don't know each other well, but I've spent years trying to get to know her. Meg is the mother of Ethan's eldest child. It's only recently that I've realised Meg has put up a boundary that I've been ignorant of all these years. For much of my relationship with Ethan, I had no positive opinion of Meg because she was, in Ethan's words, 'The Ex-Who-Wasn't-Who-He-Thought-She-Was-and-Should-Never-Have-Married'.

I had several reasons to suspect that Ethan was either trying to get back together with Meg, or that they were already back together. The first reason was that Ethan's equally deceitful brother had told me so. When Ethan had gone AWOL, I had contacted his brother to obtain any information about his whereabouts. I was worried about Ethan's abrupt change of heart toward our whole lives together. I genuinely believed that Ethan was having a mental health crisis. In a summary of a long, hateful WhatsApp reply, his brother said, "You are a psychopath, and Ethan's getting back together with Meg."

This was the worst news I could hear. Meg had always been the 'third person' in my relationship with Ethan. Not because she is the mother of his eldest child, but because it appeared to be that her rules and actions determined our entire lives (please note the word 'appeared'). For example, I didn't see Ethan on Saturdays because he and Meg would take their daughter out together for the day. It did not bother me that Ethan saw his daughter; I just didn't understand why they had to have 'family days out' of which Ethan was secretive about (he often refused to tell me where they had been if I politely asked). It was not Meg who encouraged me to quit a job I loved, to move from my hometown, and change everything in my life for the sake of living closer to her young daughter. But it stung when Meg continued to not allow me to have any part in her daughter's life, even after I had made those huge changes. I am aware that she had sensible reasons for this, but those reasons were not clear to me at the time. I understand that Meg did not need to justify herself to her ex's girlfriend for the way in which she chose to parent their daughter. But it hurt all the same. I was unable to rationalise any other reasoning for her attitude towards me, other than Meg must still harbour feelings for

Ethan and resented me for being with him. And so, in my head, Meg had stolen back my man. I had no proof that Ethan was cheating on me with Meg, but my gut instinct at the time was that he was trying to resume his relationship with her.

I continued to live a desolate, miserable life in the little, mouldy flat. One day, while obsessively snooping on social media via a brand- new account I had made, I was disturbed to find that after all Ethan's earlier complaints about my personal social media profiles, he had created a Facebook account for himself. Not only had Ethan made a Facebook account where he was friends with all his family and ex, but he had deliberately blocked me on my old account. This behaviour was suspicious. I knew that the only reason for it was that he was either hiding me from his family or hiding 'something' from me. It upset me that I had only met one member of his family (his brother) and that the rest of his siblings did not know me. I, who had been a significant part of Ethan's life for years, and who had cared for and loved him so passionately for a long time. Ethan's brother had called me a psychopath... Was that what they all thought? I wondered. (Answer: Yes, they did). When my relationship with Ethan properly resumed, three months after he had left me, I gradually became friends with his family on Facebook. Consequently, I was confronted with some pictures from the Christmas when Ethan and I were 'apart' (although we were still having sex, so we were hardly estranged). That Christmas, unbeknownst to me, I had been discarded... When I had been severely unwell with depression... When I had chosen to work fifteen-hour shifts throughout the festivities... When I had asked my family not to buy me presents as I couldn't celebrate... When I had avoided discussing the holiday season at all costs... Ethan, Meg, their daughter, and his siblings had all decided that it was the perfect time to have a family meal together. They had never done it before, and they have not done it since. And there, on their Facebook pages, connected by tags, shares, and love heart emojis, was the incriminating proof: happy, smiley, family photos of Ethan, his 'ex,' and their young daughter posing together, sitting together, laughing together in front of a large Christmas dinner cooked by his brother. It might sound like nothing to you as a reader, but it was everything to me. It was not just about the unusual event itself - (It's not for me to write about why they are a complex case of collaborative dysfunction, although there are some positives amidst the negatives). It was the humiliation. It was the secrecy. It was the fact that I had been in a long-term relationship with Ethan, yet he had never formally introduced me to his family. He had shared so much with me, yet he had abruptly ended our relationship without any explanation. He continued to see me for the physical aspect while spending time with relatives he had kept me from and an ex he had previously bad-mouthed and labelled a 'bitch.' I found out about the lovely little occasion months after Ethan and I had officially gotten back together. So, if it had been an innocent occasion, why had I not been informed about it? I checked the date when the pictures were posted. I keep a journal. I document everything. I flipped through my diary, and lo and behold, I had innocently recorded that exact December date:

"Waiting for Ethan to arrive, but his dinner is getting cold. He is having a Christmas do at work. He and his colleagues are at The Wheatsheaf. He says he will be around

later. I hope so, as it's the only time I will see him this Christmas; I am working throughout."

And always, at the back of my mind, was a simple fact: Ethan and Meg were not together... but they weren't divorced either. Meg was his non-estranged wife.

Listen to: I'm Not The Only One by Sam Smith

Eventually, Ethan would claim that he dumped me for those three months because he did not want to "offend or hurt me" by spending time with his daughter at Christmas. I was not able to join him in visiting his daughter because her mother would not let me meet her. He repeatedly said that our relationship prevented him from seeing his daughter because I made it "difficult" for him by "asking questions" and "not understanding." I cried. I said I would never expect him not to spend time with his daughter; I just didn't understand why I couldn't be involved too. Why couldn't he take his daughter out without her mother? Why couldn't we take his daughter out together on a Saturday? Was that so unreasonable to ask? I mentioned that if I ever got angry (which I had), it was because I was frustrated that this woman hated me without knowing me. Meg's apparent low opinion of me made me feel like the evil, absent "stepmother" figure. I felt alone in my feelings.

I later discovered, of course, that it was not all "innocent." I learned that he and his ex-wife had allegedly (note the word "allegedly") joked about having more children at THAT family get-together. I found out that they had given joint presents to his nieces and nephew labelled "Uncle Ethan & Auntie Meg." I have never found out enough to satisfy my questions or confusion. I can honestly say that all of this felt more like a betrayal to me than any of Ethan's affairs did. Yet I will never find any answers in knowing the truth of it all either.

Affaires during Pregnancy

Ethan was largely absent during my pregnancy. Against the odds, I conceived naturally and unexpectedly very shortly after we reunited. He did not have a car that following summer, explaining that it had been confiscated from him when he had driven into a festival with no tax or insurance. We had only had the car for a few weeks, so I was not pleased at the time. By the time I was eight months pregnant, we had moved back to my hometown to live in my parents' spare room, where we had cohabited before. Ethan worked at a distance that was not easily reachable by walking or bus. He'd therefore spend weekdays staying with his boss or colleagues, close to his work. That is what he told me, anyway. I had a niggling feeling that he was seeing someone else, but I didn't know who.

Ethan was not great at FaceTiming me, complaining that his boss's WiFi was always down. That was weird, I thought, for his boss was apparently a millionaire. Surely, he could afford the best in WiFi boosters? When Ethan did make the effort to come and stay with me and the bump, he would leave ridiculously early in the morning to walk to work, which was over sixteen miles away and would take him hours.

I noticed that Ethan had not returned all his belongings when he moved back in with me after our three months' "break-up" - or, as I should refer to it, the three-month discard. I repeatedly asked him where those personal, supposedly "sentimental" objects were, but he insisted he had kept them in the stockroom at his work. However, when he left that job, the objects still did not appear. I suspected that he was probably keeping the possessions at someone else's place. Karen was considerably older than him and had been his landlady once, before Ethan and I were first "official." In the days when he originally lived with Karen, Ethan would sneak me into her house because she "didn't like strangers stopping over." It was while I was drafting this book that I discovered Ethan *had* been lodging with Karen again behind my back while I was pregnant. He had not been staying with his boss. He was renting a room without my knowledge, and he'd rented it from the date he had previously left me. That allowed me to question the dynamic of his relationship with Karen. Formally, it had not made me uncomfortable when Ethan admitted to having once had coke-fuelled sex with Karen in his early twenties, because I knew he was wild, and I knew he had been with a lot of women prior to me. But if he had been discreetly lodging with Karen again during all those nights he was away from me while pregnant... Had he been having a physical relationship with her too? Or had he been seeing other women there while our daughter shifted and kicked and stretched within my belly on my lonely nights in bed? With Ethan's history of lying, it seems likely. I can only assume that Ethan thought he may not stay with me permanently, so it wasn't worth moving all his stuff back into my parent's place.

Listen to: SOS by ABBA

Once A Cheat...

Holly was a beautiful young woman whom as a teenager, Ethan and I had once taken to a football match with her brother and to the pub with her dad. She worked with Ethan, who was her manager. She was quiet and polite, and I had gotten along with her. However, when our daughter was a few months old, on our first Valentines Day as a family, I found Holly's necklace in the back of our car. It indisputably belonged to her because it was a name necklace. With quick and confident amusement, Ethan claimed he had found it in the car park at work and was meant to put it in lost property. Holly gave me the same story a few days later when I confronted her. I didn't like that she messaged Ethan a lot. I would see her name pop up on the lock screen, but he would laugh and say it was because she was part of the work group chat. I tried to brush my suspicions under the carpet.

However, a couple of years later, when I had created my social media platform on Instagram, I noticed that Holly would be the first to watch all the public stories I posted, even though she wasn't following my account. I wondered why she would have such an interest in me when we hadn't spoken since I asked her about her necklace being in the back of our family car. If she liked my social media account so much, wouldn't she just follow it? After several months of observing her watching my stories but not following, I mentioned my suspicions to Ethan. By this time, he was no longer working at the same place as Holly. Yet no sooner had I made my curiosity known, than Holly stopped watching the stories. Somehow, she knew that I had noticed her lurking and found it weird. Had Ethan given her a stern warning? Perhaps Holly had wanted me to notice her? Whatever her reason was, I felt sure that Holly had been one of Ethan's lovers at some point. In more recent years, Holly started watching my social media stories again and routinely following and unfollowing my Instagram account. I don't know if she had an affair with my partner, and I wonder if she had been groomed and abused by him, too, so resonated with my posts around domestic abuse. I'm not sure I want to find out.

Another woman I suspected Ethan of cheating on me with was a mystery person named 'Lindsay'. It was Ethan's reliable relative who informed me about this, as by that time, we had finally been introduced and developed a close friendship. She had heard from Ethan's wife, Meg, that Ethan was seeing a woman called 'Lindsay' whom he slept with in hotels behind my back. Of course, I confronted Ethan about it, but he declared that his sister was lying and merely trying to sabotage our relationship. He also defended Meg, stating that she would never make such an unfounded remark since she didn't care enough about me to spread such preposterous 'lies'. Ethan also added that it was my fault this rumour materialised because I engaged in 'gossip' by talking frequently to 'other women in his life behind his back'. I still don't know who Lindsay is, but knowing wouldn't help me anyway.

Much to my humiliation, and though lacking evidence, I believe Ethan may have had an affair for a brief period with a famous singer and musician. I hesitated about including this in the book, as I often questioned whether I was being paranoid. However, even if my suspicions were unfounded, I don't blame myself for feeling uneasy about what seemed like unprofessional behaviour. In one of his jobs, she was his client, and her daughter shared the same name as ours, which was their starting point for a friendly relationship. There were several weeks during which Ethan would speak about this attractive public figure with admiration, insisting that I watch YouTube videos of her with him in the evenings, despite my annoyance and my previous attendance at one of her live performances. He detailed to me her house, her recording studio, her divorce, and her ex-husband. Perhaps it was merely an infatuation, but he took pleasure in announcing that she had flirted with him in front of his colleagues and expressed her liking for him. Safe to say, I turn her music off or change the channel if I ever hear or see her on TV.

In the fourth autumn of our relationship, I was bathing our daughter when my cousin phoned me.

'Where are you?' She said as soon as I picked up. I knew something was very wrong. 'Are you sitting down?'

Listen to: I Heard It Through The Grapevine by The Slits

It was humiliating. My cousin gently explained that one of her friends had come across Ethan on POF. He was listed as 'single' and looking for no-strings-attached fun. I responded brightly, pretending as if my heart wasn't shattered. I confronted him later that night. This happened around the time when Ethan had persuaded me to agree to trying swinging and registering for an account on the UK's most popular swinging site. He laughed as he told me that his POF account was for our benefit as a couple. I didn't believe him, but I swallowed my pride and told my cousin that it was something we were exploring as a couple. I felt so embarrassed.

Snooping

Later that autumn, a rare opportunity presented itself: Ethan was passed out on the sofa in the three-story townhouse we rented as a family. He usually kept his phone hidden in his pockets, and by this point, he would never have deliberately left his phone unattended. He was not a heavy sleeper, so I knew I was taking a risk by lightly moving his phone from his chest, right where his hand rested on the waves and rhythm of his breathing. I remember how it felt like my heart was vibrating in every part of my body, how I felt hot, sick, and scared. I recall the triumph of retrieving it. I was aware that I didn't have much time to look before he woke up and realised it was missing. I had to be quick and prioritise where I snooped. First, I had to try and guess his passcode, but that was easy. Ethan was so confident that I would never steal his phone and look through it that his passcode was his favourite number, continuously pressed. I marvelled at how well I could know someone and yet, at the same time, not know what they were up to daily. At this point in our relationship, I knew he was cheating on me. I was desperate for evidence, and this was my moment to gather proof. I wondered if I should choose his pictures or the secret social media apps (he had long since 'deleted' his Facebook account). I considered text messages. There was something called 'Kik.' But I opted for WhatsApp. On one hand, I could say I wasn't disappointed with my choice. On the other hand, it literally made me feel ill to discover not just one person he was cheating with (which was what I had suspected), but dozens and dozens, and then some. I managed to skim through his active messages to eleven different women; I didn't have time to read all his chat history. I sat on the edge of my bed, my daughter snuffling and snoring behind me, nestled in the quilt and the lamp light. I had to think quickly. I took snapshots of random sections of the messages to different women and sent them to myself. By the time I had managed to send myself random sections from conversations with eleven of the women he had been contacting, Ethan was running up the stairs, two steps at a time, and I was in trouble. He would have known from the moment he woke up that I had his phone. He knew that I was finally aware of the extent of his infidelity.

One thing I had made sure of was that Ethan didn't know *my* passcode. Although he immediately retrieved both our phones, he couldn't access mine. He had tried the thumbprint method before while I was asleep. I remember waking up with him pressing my thumb onto my phone. Since I didn't have fingerprint recognition, it didn't work. At the time, Ethan pretended he had been moving my phone for me, claiming that I had fallen asleep awkwardly, and as always, I pretended to believe him. I was terrified as he pressed random numbers into my phone, attempting to unlock it—not because I had anything to hide, but because I was prepared for the possibility of physical assault. However, I remained defiant. I remember thinking that he could hurt me as much as he liked (and I was expecting it), but I would never give him my passcode. If he had truly known me, my passcode would have been simple for him to guess. But by then, Ethan no longer knew the finer details about me. He didn't know the woman I was gradually becoming through his frequent emotional discards and devaluation of me. He didn't know the number sequence I used for everything because he had no interest in me beyond my ability to be a homemaker and satisfy his desires. He slept in bed with us that night, a rarity, with his phone tightly clutched in his hand. Ethan changed his passcode.

It was not until the next day, when he had gone to work, that I managed to look through the screenshots, names, and messages I had sent myself. I got up with my daughter, made her breakfast, turned on Cbeebies, and settled down on the sofa. It was sickening. The names of the women were Susie, Lyla, Fay, and Lou. There were six unnamed women, and one addition that reignited my suspicions: his wife, Meg. The "unnamed women" were not so much about him keeping secrets from me, but rather to help him remember where he had "found" each woman. For example, "Hot Blonde Tinder" and "Sexy Woman POF". The women who were of enough interest to him to be known by their first names were described by their location in the world. Susie was "Susie Bodicote", Lyla was "Lyla Marlborough", Fay was "Fay Alton", and Lou was "Lou Swindon". "Swindon?" I thought, "He's driving as far as Swindon for a fuck?" I also realised that there was contact with sex workers from an establishment in a sleepy village on the outskirts of Reading.

Listen to: For Emma by Bon Iver

Reading the messages between Ethan and some of his "bits on the side" made me go numb with shock and denial. I remember feeling overwhelmed by the information overload, with so many names, faces, and intimate conversations to take in. However, the hardest blow came from the confirmation that Ethan was inappropriately messaging Meg. It was the ultimate betrayal for me.

When I say "inappropriate," I'm not referring to any messages suggesting they were having sex. He didn't write to Meg with sexual fantasies or memories like he did with the others. But it was the overly familiar language he used, the persistent pleading, and the regular use of three words that I couldn't unsee: "I love you". Ethan signed off nearly every message with "I love you". Even after several years of being separated from Meg and being in a long-term relationship with me, Ethan still felt the need to tell Meg that he loved her.

Meg was "grey rocking" him – a method of limiting direct contact with an abuser or toxic person. I wasn't aware of "grey rocking" back then. If I had managed to keep the screenshots, perhaps I could have used Meg's cold example of the grey rock method for reference. She seems like a professional at it.

Ethan did not deny cheating on me with the women I had discovered, but he did refuse to explain himself. I asked every day for him to give me the explanation I deserved, but Ethan's response to my questions was to tell me how it 'wasn't important' and I 'shouldn't have been sneaky' and gone through his phone. Ethan would throw accusations at me - that I was probably going home with men after working at the pub, which was ludicrous to suggest since I was earning money, solely responsible for bringing up our daughter, AND knackered every night and day. It was at this point in our relationship when Ethan could not deny his cheating - nor would he show an ounce of remorse. Another woman emerged - a friend of one of his relatives, whom Ethan had been caught Snapchatting. He laughed when I confronted him. (At the time of writing this account, I have discovered yet another woman. Ethan didn't have sex with her, but he evidently tried to).

I don't know how many women there were in total, but it surpassed the 'twenty' mark. I felt worthless, ugly, and miserable. What did they have that I didn't? I gave him everything I had. The women ranged from young to much older women, from redheads to blondes, college students to career-focused women, pole dancers to hikers, hairdressers and beauty salon owners to theatrical actresses and Miss Hampshire. Even when I moved out, but he was begging for me back, declaring his undying love, I was stupidly paying for his phone bill. When I requested his call log, I added the multiple numbers into my WhatsApp and could see each woman's display picture. 'Penny' and 'Kerry' and 'Hetty' and 'Lisa'... Penny even had pictures of him on her public Instagram that I, of course, looked up. Hetty was 'just a work colleague' and Kerry was 'just a friend helping me through a hard time because I love and miss you so much'. More about this discovery later.

During our relationship, our arguments about his cheating escalated, and I sustained some visible injuries that were hard to hide. The more we argued about his inability to be faithful, the more I was put in life-threatening situations. It is truly luck that has kept me alive to be telling this story.

Chapter Ten - Violence

**'Fact: Domestic abuse gets worse during pregnancy.
About 20% of women in Refuge's services are pregnant or have recently given birth.'**

Refuge. (n.d.). The facts.

My first encounters with physical violence by people I loved were not perpetrated by Ethan. Ethan was aware of these incidents, and at the beginning of our relationship, he expressed discontent that I had been hurt by other people who were supposed to love and protect me. During my late teens and early twenties, I was an aggressive person—especially when drunk, which was most days. I often found myself in altercations, and sometimes I was the instigator. When I reflect on my lifestyle and attitudes during that time, I realise that I didn't consider violence as inappropriate or wrong. I saw fighting for your beliefs or defending yourself in the face of adversity as something you naturally did to protect yourself and demonstrate that you were not to be messed with. This often resulted in falling out with friends. Not all fights were my fault, but many of them were.

On one occasion, I was so intoxicated that I forgot I had invited a stranger to a New Year's Eve after-party at my house. When I realised he was there and didn't recognise him, I felt unsettled and initiated a fight, with severe consequences. I am ashamed of that. Similarly, I found myself in situations where others might not have had the courage to intervene. Once, I defended a friend's wife who was racially insulted behind her back. As a result, a large, middle-aged man hit my head against a phone box, leaving me with a black eye. I believed that violence was just a part of life—it happened.

Listen to: He Hit Me by The Crystals

I remember the first time Ethan did something that, at the time, I thought was uncharacteristically aggressive. It was in the weeks after I had discovered his affair with Jenny. He started getting in a bad mood over the littlest things, and I was fed up with treading on eggshells; in my mind, he should still be grovelling for having an affair and making it up to me. We frequently argued about his cheating, and on this occasion, after he had picked me up from work, I was agitated. I felt annoyed when he suggested that I needed to 'get over it' while I was still hurting and unsure how to navigate being cheated on. We had a shouting match in the car. Since I didn't want to go home and potentially face my parents while feeling angry, as I was adamant that no one should know about Ethan's infidelity, we drove about the town and then through a pine forest.

During our intense argument, I noticed that Ethan had locked the car doors and windows in response to my request for fresh air. I asked him to unlock them, but he refused. I then asked him to stop the car, but he refused that as well. Instead, Ethan accelerated. My head throbbed, and I started sweating from quickly overheating. I became nauseous and started to feel dizzy. Eventually, I couldn't breathe. Pure panic took hold, and I screamed. I even tried to grab the steering wheel, begging him to stop and let me out. I remember my heart racing so fast that I thought I might be having a heart attack. At some point, I rationalised that the only way I would get out of that situation alive was if I tried to speak calmly. I sweetly asked him to please stop the car. Finally, Ethan obliged and abruptly pulled into an unnoticed car park. I stumbled out of the vehicle, gasping for air. My instinct was to call my parents, but he snatched my phone away. While I had experienced panic attacks before and knew logically that I wouldn't die from one, it didn't alleviate the terror and panic coursing through my entire body. When I'd had panic attacks before, my fear had been irrational. This time, I had been in actual danger.

Once I managed to calm myself using breathing techniques and the fresh forest air, I reluctantly got back into the car and asked to be taken home. On the way back, as we drove through the pine forest, Ethan punched the windscreen, causing it to rupture into a spiderweb pattern. The sight of the broken glass surprised me into silence. However, he didn't take responsibility for the damage. Instead, Ethan blamed his reaction and the smashed windscreen on my panic attack, saying, 'If you hadn't got hysterical, I wouldn't have broken it.'

The second act of violence I recall occurred when we had "split up," and Ethan was regularly visiting the bedsit for sex. One December evening, as Ethan was preparing to leave, I desperately begged him to stay the night and give our relationship another chance. I don't remember the exact details of how it unfolded, but I do know that he pushed me into the coffee table before angrily storming out. At the time, I believed that he had broken my ribs. I struggled to find a comfortable position, feeling breathless and shocked. Due to the intense pain, I decided to call for an ambulance. The paramedics arrived and assessed my condition, explaining that there wasn't much they could do as my ribs were likely bruised. Instead, they provided treatment for shock rather than a physical injury. I still have the paperwork from that incident. Within a few hours, the police arrived at my door. The paramedics had contacted them. I reluctantly provided a statement to the police, who then referred me to a Domestic Abuse support service. I was hesitant to accept that I had experienced domestic abuse, so I declined the offered help. The Domestic Abuse service suggested that I use "Clare's Law" to find out if Ethan had any previous convictions related to domestic abuse. I chose not to pursue that avenue. Instead, I folded the paramedic's paperwork several times and concealed it in a pair of gloves that I never wore, stashing it at the bottom of my underwear drawer.

Listen to: Your Power by Billie Eilish

The third incident of violence took place when I was a few months pregnant. I don't recall the specific reason for the argument, but it was likely related to his frequent stays at "his boss's house" or another dispute about his unconventional arrangement for visiting his ex and child. I remember being cornered near the front door, with a pen knife pressed against me. Afterward, I went to work at the care home as if nothing had happened.

The next incident of violence that stands out in my memory occurred when I was a new mother. Our daughter was just six weeks old. It was Christmas Eve, and we still lived with my parents at the time. My sister, brother-in-law, and their dogs had left after spending the day with us, and my parents had gone to the pub for the evening. Ethan had a large pile of Christmas presents to wrap for his eldest child. I sat in the living room surrounded by expensive toys, pink princess wrapping paper, scissors, and Sellotape, and carefully wrapped his child's presents as neatly and presentably as I could. I tied ribbons and curled the bows, admiring each gift. I took the opportunity to talk about his eldest child, as it was usually a forbidden topic. Although we had been together for some time, I had yet to meet the little person whose birthday and Christmas presents I helped choose and wrap every year. I believe that was likely how the argument started, as it often did—me asking when I would finally be introduced to his eldest child. The argument escalated, and it ended with me cowering in the corner of the room, screaming, while my partner used a pair of garden scissors to cut chunks off my long, dark red hair, all while I held our new baby in my arms.

Ethan was violent again a few days later. We were in our upstairs room, arguing once more about his weird child visitation arrangement. Downstairs, my Mum and Auntie were enjoying themselves with mince pies and red wine. Ethan silently threatened me with the point of one of his knives, lightly grazing the back of my neck.

I fell silent and went downstairs, putting on a smile and focusing on the company of my relatives. I imagined how horrified my mother would be if she knew what had just occurred moments earlier. I remember thinking to myself, 'They couldn't even guess that this is happening to me, right under their noses.'

The violent incidents became more frequent, and they all blend into one continuous cycle of violence. Towards the end of our relationship, violence occurred regularly—I documented in my journals that I was physically assaulted every other day. The frequency escalated rapidly after we moved into our townhouse, located a mile away from my parents. Our daughter was twenty-one months old, and it was our first family home. I had private concerns about the move, fearing that the violence would intensify. However, I convinced myself that Ethan was simply stressed and that he would improve once we weren't living under the same roof as my parents. Unfortunately, being away from my parents only confirmed my fears of more violence. Within the first few weeks of living there, Ethan escalated his abuse, and I frequently felt terrified of his physical aggression. By our fourth

Autumn together, I was either avoiding Baby & Toddler groups, playdates, and family gatherings or using foundation to conceal the bruises on my face.

Ethan's most usual form of physical assault was strangulation. Even when we lived with my parents, he would regularly place his hands on my neck, leaving red marks, even if my Mum and Dad were in the adjacent room. In the townhouse, Ethan would strangle me to the point where I suffocated. I often had finger-mark bruises on my upper arms as well. As Ethan's violent actions increased, so did the extent of my lies. I became skilled at my craft—an adept and convincing liar. I learned from the best. There were times when Ethan and I lied together, our alibis and falsehoods reinforcing each other. Lying became a survival mechanism for me. If I didn't lie for Ethan, I feared I would be punished later.

There are certain occasions that remain ingrained in my memory more than other instances of assault. One such time, when our daughter was a baby, I was slapped across the face, resulting in a black eye. This was the first slap. I couldn't conceal the black eye with makeup, so I had no choice but to inform my family that I had slipped on a magazine lying on the floor and accidentally hit my eye on our tall chest of drawers, concocting a weird accident. Another excuse I used more than once, was that my energetic baby had head butted me while I was holding her.

On another night, Ethan didn't want to attend my aunt and uncle's 40th Wedding Anniversary party. He assaulted me outside the venue, despite the glass windows making us visible from the party. Though it was dark, the car park was well-lit, and I was sure that my family had witnessed him shoving me and yanking my hair. I cried so heavily that my black eye make-up stained my cheeks, and the carefully curled hair I had styled became dishevelled. Ethan adamantly refused to accompany us. Instead, he drove himself and our daughter back home, with her sitting on his lap for the entire ten-mile journey. Although my family didn't witness the assault, some sensed that something was wrong. Despite this, they acknowledged that he'd taken the baby home and that I was able to have a night enjoying myself, 'child free', as if to commend him for his random act of courtesy towards me. Ethan had the audacity to cause a scene at a family event because he knew I would allow him to get away with it.

Listen to: Love The Way You Lie (Part II) by Rihanna

When we lived in the townhouse, everything escalated after the night I had taken his phone and discovered evidence of his multiple affairs. One day, while I was stirring a boiling saucepan of pasta in the kitchen, with our two-year-old playing nearby, Ethan seized my phone, forcefully shoved it into my mouth, and pinned me against the wall by my neck. I was left with visible marks (which had become normal to me), but I also suffered a cut lip. Although the wound wasn't deep, the sight of blood mingling with my saliva startled me, and my lip swelled. In the following days, I made up a story to explain the injury, claiming that I had accidentally bitten my lip. Soon after this incident, Ethan forcefully covered my mouth with his hands, leaving my face covered in finger shaped bruises. These bruises were not easily hidden with makeup. To account for them, I fabricated yet another lie about having bumped my face somehow. I remember feeling like I was running out of ideas for fibs.

Then there was the argument we had in the car park of the local Leisure Centre during our fourth winter together. It was a rare occasion when I insisted on sitting in the front seat of the car. Ethan didn't approve of it. We had a disagreement about paying for a ticket to the local heritage museum, and as a result, he punched me in the nose. I can still recall the thud of my head crashing against the passenger window, and the slap of flesh upon flesh. My whole head hurt, and at first, I couldn't pinpoint the exact spot of impact. Although I shouted in shock when it occurred, I soon fell into a stunned silence. Ethan appeared panicked upon seeing blood dripping from my face onto my clothes and the car seat. He attributed the bleeding to my piercing, as my nose ring had been dislodged by the impact. Ethan parked the car, got out, and took our shaking daughter out of her seat, refusing to let me hold her. He cradled her against himself. I screamed for help, but despite the presence of over a hundred vehicles in the car park, with members of the public observing and even a shuttle bus passing by, nobody intervened. They simply stared.

No one was helping me, so I surprised myself by feeling compelled to phone Meg. Around that time, I had been wondering if she, too, had experienced any violent outbursts from Ethan. The secrecy of my situation with Ethan was suffocating me. At the same time, I didn't want anyone I loved to get involved, as I felt unable to bear the humiliation, and I knew I'd be told to leave him. Meg was not the person who could offer me help. She sounded annoyed by the phone call and didn't ask if I was okay. Instead, she straightforwardly - but rightly - advised me to call the police. I didn't follow her advice; I was too frightened. Perhaps a part of me hoped she would be the one to call the police instead. Eventually, Ethan placed our terrified daughter back in her car seat, and I resumed my designated spot in the backseat with her, feeling diminished, useless, and dizzy.

There was an incident the following January, when Ethan pushed me by my throat onto the stairs, resulting in a broken stair gate (while he was holding our daughter). The police became involved in that altercation. Ethan was arrested but released a few hours later when I refused to provide a statement. I told the police that I believed the shock of his arrest would change Ethan. Of course, it didn't - it merely reinforced his belief that he could assault me with impunity. Child Services became involved with our case. I convinced them that everything was fine, and they promptly closed the case.

It was the week before a relative's 60th birthday party that spurred a reaction in me, where I decided I couldn't be bothered to act like nothing was wrong. I had been helping my relative to plan a birthday party. I was responsible for the music, and on this day, Ethan didn't appreciate me making a playlist using a streaming app on my laptop. By then, we had moved into our last home together – a large house with a big garden and drive. The conflict resulted in me being slammed against the cold kitchen floor, my face pressed into the tiles, and his entire weight on top of me. He had his hands around my neck, and I knew there and then that with one move, he could snap it. I thought of my two-year-old, sitting in the lounge watching TV, knowing she could hear what was happening as I shrieked, gagged, and choked. I was then thrown onto my back, and his hands were over my mouth and nose. I couldn't use my nostrils to regulate my breathing, and I could see red and orange spots as I entered a state of unconsciousness while he smothered me. I regained my breath as he let go and demanded that I stand up. I dizzily wandered in a daze to the living room, where I picked up my baby and stood with my back turned to him, trembling. Ethan continued ranting, and our baby shook with fear in my arms. I silently prayed for us to be saved. I knew I had nearly died, and I knew our relationship couldn't continue like this. I didn't want to leave him, because I still felt sure he could change. Nevertheless, it was time to get all my ducks in a row just in case I changed my mind. By the end of that week, I had applied for social housing and Universal Credit. All I needed to do was figure out what I could do to make him understand that he couldn't continue hurting me anymore... but first, I was going on holiday for the weekend with my family. I was excited to escape Ethan's moods and hoped to find clarity while we were away.

One of the last assaults was a few days after returning from my long weekend, on a wet, mid-October day. Ethan had returned that morning from yet another night away, clearly off his face on a substance and picking on me for random, nonsensical reasons. In the heat of the moment, I told him that I was leaving him (Note – never tell an abuser that you are leaving them. Just go). Ethan locked me in the house so I couldn't leave and violently assaulted me. This resulted in him later pleading guilty to a charge of 'assault by beating' - the incident that I began Chapter Two with.

Our relationship was incredibly violent, and I haven't detailed even half of the occurrences that demonstrate just how violent it was. However, domestic abuse is a broad term, and although society often associates it with violence, the other forms of abuse are just as deadly and should be documented. This is because physical violence isn't always a factor in an abusive relationship. Coercive control is now recognised as a criminal offense in the UK. Women's Aid describes coercive control as "an act or pattern of acts of assault, threats, humiliation, intimidation, or other abuse that is used to harm, punish, or frighten the victim." Domestic abuse is an umbrella term for a variety of ways in which a person can abuse another, including emotional abuse, psychological abuse, financial and economic abuse, sexual abuse, religious abuse and more. It is important to clarify that ALL forms of abuse are dangerous and traumatic. However, it is not uncommon for victim-survivors to express that enduring mental torment can feel even worse than the fear of physical harm. When the beating is over, we can see and feel it; we know that something bad has happened to us. Mental abuse is confusing; we often don't know if something bad has happened to us or if we have exaggerated it. When we do listen to our gut and understand that we are being abused, it's not easy to prove it. It's harder to evidence an injury inside your head, even to yourself.

Chapter Eleven - Psychological Abuse

'The majority of partner abuse victims in the last year (88%) experienced non-physical abuse,'

Office for National Statistics, 2023

Listen to: Happiness is a Butterfly by Lana Del Rey

Girl Meets Man

There were red flags, left, right, and centre. Let me put it this way: When I entered a relationship with Ethan, my boss took me for an informal, 'off record' meeting to discuss her concerns for my safety. Someone else who knew Ethan warned my mum with some horror stories of his past behaviour; Ethan was known to have stalked, assaulted, and cheated on his ex-girlfriend, who had told me of her trauma firsthand. It's not that I disbelieved her... but I thought that I had changed him; I thought he was different with me. Perhaps that's egotistical of my past self. I'll defend her – my past self, though; By the time all these people had handed me the red flags, I was already deeply emotionally involved – more than they knew. We are not dealing with your regular 'fuckboy'. I am describing someone who is a master of manipulation. Ethan is an intelligent person. Although levels of intelligence are irrelevant to domestic abuse, I do think that Ethan has the advantage of intellect to be extremely calculated in his actions. Ethan has also studied psychology at university (although I never saw proof of a degree). You do not need a degree in psychology to be a fully qualified perpetrator, but it certainly helps you to master your craft. Yes, of course, I could see many of the flags being animatedly waved at me, but the term 'red flag' wasn't even a thing back then. With Ethan, I was willingly colour blind.

When I first met Ethan, I was twenty years young, naive, and hadn't much life experience. He was my supervisor at work and responsible for supporting me in my role. I thought I was happy at the time. It was the end of the noughties, entering a fresh decade, and I had started a new job working with young people with life-limiting, rare conditions. The job demanded my full focus and attention. When I began, I didn't

MUG: An Account of Domestic Abuse

know how I'd ever get the hang of it, but the team I worked with was close-knit and incredible. I felt like I slotted in straight away. However, no one on my team was quite like Ethan. I remember the first time I saw him, and I was shocked at myself. In several years of being in a relationship with my childhood sweetheart, not one person had ever turned my head in terms of attractiveness.

Ethan was older and seemed more mature than my partner or our friends. He was tall, dark, and I liked it when he had stubble. His hands reminded me of Kurt Cobain's, and I found myself always watching them. I loved the way he stood, with his arms crossed, tall, legs wide apart in some sort of regal-like balance. He had an athletic build, with thick dark hair and eyebrows. I loved how he turned his head to look at people while he listened to them speak, twisting his mouth from side to side. That grin... his gleaming teeth, his lips that were full and slightly wonky, and one eye that was the tiniest bit smaller when he smiled. Some people said he looked like a darker-haired version of Jim Carey when he grinned, and when he smouldered, he was often compared to Johnny Depp.

I felt sick at myself for being attracted to him. I genuinely loved my partner and thought he was the best-looking boy on earth. At the time, it was like I lived my entire life with a beautiful boy that I was joined at the hip with because we had grown up together. But when I went to work, it was *my* thing, my thing that *I* did, where I earned ok money and worked with this... this man, who was like no one else I had ever met before. He summoned this kind of magnificent presence, like being around an adored celebrity. Whether he was admired or not is irrelevant; he clearly captivated whoever he was around.

He had a new girlfriend, named Meg. They'd only been together a couple of weeks. I asked my partner if he wanted to go on a double date with them, but he wasn't keen.

A few weeks into my new job, my boyfriend and I had a falling out. We didn't make up before I started work the next day, and I went to work upset. Ethan immediately took me to a private space, and as my supervisor, asked me what was bothering me and shared that I could confide in him. So, I told him. He was supportive, understanding, and reassuring. He validated me. *'He should never have spoken to you like that.'*

Ethan asked me if I wanted a lift home the following week. I had seen him look at me a couple of times, but I was sure it was nothing. Someone like him would never give me a second glance...

He took me home, and we laughed and really got along. He started taking me home more often, dropping me off right outside my front door. He'd always ask me questions and seemed interested in me. He also talked about his own life; how he was close to his grandparents and had lived with them for a long time, and how his mother had died a few years back. He didn't speak to his father, but his grandad brought him up and was a father figure. We found out that we both liked the same bands and going to festivals, and he added me on Facebook. He had Facebook back then. I found myself looking through his Facebook pictures and feeling jealous of Meg. She was pretty and younger than him, although slightly older than me. His ex-girlfriend, who also worked with us, was one of the most beautiful women I had ever seen. Like

Ethan, she commanded a presence when she walked into a room, just by her tall, straight posture, white, clear complexion, dark hair, and big dark eyes. I was curious about how they could have ever broken up – they surely seemed destined together, like a power couple. But I didn't ask at first, and besides... I had a partner.

Listen to: Talk To Me by Stevie Nicks

One day, after work, Ethan didn't take me straight home. He took me to the cemetery, where the old church and yew trees stood, where my grandparents are buried. It was a freezing, icy December day, and the sun was beginning to set behind the silhouettes of newly bare trees. I asked him why we were going there. He said he wanted to take me to see where the badgers lived. He compared me to a badger: beautiful, cute, likes to come out at night, but also wild and vicious. Ethan started calling me 'Badger,' and I began calling him 'Fox'. At work, he would write secret messages to me on the shift planner, even though our colleagues could see, messages like 'Badgers are beautiful' and 'Badger is best.' Everyone just laughed at how weird he was, thinking he was harmless. Then, he began writing

Facebook posts – or statuses, as they were called at the time – 'I love badgers,' right under his girlfriend and our colleague's noses. Still, I didn't tell anyone... In theory, I hadn't done anything wrong. But why did it feel so wrong? If I wasn't doing anything wrong, why did I feel so guilty?

It started happening more often – these local excursions after work. Sometimes I would tell my partner that I'd been for a walk around the Roman walls with my colleague – it seemed innocent enough. My partner never usually wanted to go for walks with me, and I went on walks with other friends or colleagues, too. But I knew he didn't like it. I think he sensed I wasn't myself, that there was an issue – even if he couldn't have guessed what that issue was.

My trips with Ethan after work were usually walks, with scarves, thick coats, and our phones, taking pictures of countryside scenery. He'd upload them to his Facebook, saying, 'went on a walk with a beautiful dream.' Ethan made even the simplest, shortest walks feel exciting by showing me that we could climb that tree, or eat those mushrooms, or shhh... look at that bird. Did

I know it was a jenny wren, the smallest but loudest garden bird?

Ethan was eight and a half years older than me when we first met. After a few months of working together, he repeatedly suggested that he had fallen in love with me. He would express that no one understood him like I did, and no one made him as happy as I did. He claimed that his relationship with Meg was dull and even though he proposed to her, he told me it was entirely her idea, and he didn't know how to back out. He convinced me that he had no intention of getting married, up until the day of their wedding when he texted me that he was only doing it to 'make his granddad proud'. I was bewildered by my supervisor's advances and frightened of the potential consequences if I acknowledged what was happening. I liked my new job. I was in my probation period. Would I have to leave if anyone found out what was going on? And what was going on, anyway? I had no idea I was being groomed, as I thought grooming only happened to school children. I distinctly remember the overwhelming dishonesty in my relationship tearing me apart. I resorted to socialising and drinking alcohol just to be away from home, so that my boyfriend (turned fiancé) wouldn't see the hidden text messages on my phone or detect the guilt and confusion in my demeanour. I would arrive home from work feeling intensely guilty. Sometimes, on the tip of my tongue, would be the truth that I felt I owed my fiancé. But the fear of him not understanding what I couldn't understand myself stopped me. The secrecy created a void where I felt unable to be my true self in my relationship, and my everyday life became entirely consumed by Ethan and the things he said and did and trying to work out my confused state.

Ethan would be in my ear, at the first inkling of a rift between my fiancé and I. He'd tell me I deserved better. He'd make me feel special and valued, because he'd picked up on a lifelong belief of mine - that I wasn't enough. Not pretty enough. Not clever enough. Not woman enough.

But then Meg found his messages to me. And she made him leave our workplace. And I was able to bloom at work and be better at my job. Ethan's absence was noticeable, and I grieved his presence to an extent. His influence had not only negatively affected my relationship with my partner, but also with our friendship group. I pressed a huge self-destruct button and spent most days drinking copious amounts of alcohol, partying hard and getting myself into situations where I let my partner down, and everyone could see that he deserved better than my manic, obnoxious, wild behaviour.

Like many people living with abuse, I already had trauma long before I got into any form of relationship with the abuser. However, this does not mean that the abuse I lived with was my fault - it means that Ethan recognised what he perceived to be a vulnerability in me, which made me a desirable target. As my supervisor, Ethan exploited me. He was in a position of power, and he abused it. Perpetrators often go for the kind people, the caring people, the sensitive, gentle, generous people. We're not 'easy targets' because we're stupid, we're ideal targets because we have the nicest souls, who will give chances, forgive, and see the best in people. We are warm people, friendly people, who will readily accept the perpetrator because it's morally good to be accepting and inclusive. The perpetrator doesn't want a challenge, they want to get their feet under the table of a person who will invite them in.

Listen to: Torn by Natalie Imbruglia

When my previous relationship eventually fell apart, Ethan was lingering in the background, waiting. When his opportunity arose, he swept me off my feet, playing the role of my knight in shining armour, and promising to eradicate all the pain I felt—a pain that he had contributed to causing. I believe that my eventual marriage would have never crumbled if I had never crossed paths with Ethan in the first place because the repercussions of being groomed snowballed into increasingly significant issues, with devastating and detrimental effects.

When a perpetrator of abuse enters your life and decides to prey on you, they will do all they can to possess you. I wasn't just 'love bombed' - I was blasted into another magical world. My journals vividly describe an ecstatic euphoria that I believe I could never experience again unless I were to literally take an illegal opiate substance. I felt drugged, intoxicated - as high as one could possibly be. I wrote incessantly about the colours of the seasons and the sensory wonders of being outdoors. It was as if I had just discovered the world, and it appeared overwhelmingly beautiful; it was as if I had never truly seen the world in colour before, but suddenly, I was perceiving every hue, shade, and contrast. I fell in love with the entire world when I fell in love with Ethan.

When Ethan and I first started dating, he appeared perfect. Nobody could deny that he was perfect for me. That's because he meticulously presented himself as perfect in every way, specifically tailored to captivate me. Once I was ensnared (which happened almost immediately), all he had to do was tighten his grip. He made sure I helped finance his car, he made sure I contributed to his informal child maintenance, he made sure I provided him with a home, he made sure my family paid off his debts, and ultimately, he ensured that leaving him would be too painful and practically complicated for me to consider. Once I was tethered, Ethan's false persona gradually unravelled, revealing his lack of identity. It began with small drips and drops of abuse, around the time we started living together, so inconspicuous amidst all the "good" things about him that it would go unnoticed, until slowly, Ethan's charade crumbled. He went from saying I was 'perfect' to subtly conveying that I wasn't good enough. His soullessness was alien, completely distant from my own personality to which he had once mirrored. At the beginning of our relationship, Ethan and I shared EVERYTHING in common. By the end, nothing that interested me held any interest for him. He had not only deceived me, but he had also fooled everyone in my life who I had enthusiastically introduced to him. Even my colleague (his ex-girlfriend who had lived with his abuse) said, 'I'm glad he has turned his life around for you,' and my once sceptical boss said, 'Clearly, you were what he needed.'

Age Is NOT Just a Number

I believe that age gaps, especially when the younger person is under the age of twenty-five, can be problematic, and the younger a person is, the more problematic it becomes. For example, a twenty-four-year-old will have had at least six years of experience living as a legal adult when entering a relationship with a significantly older person. However, research suggests that, on average, individuals do not complete adolescence until the age of twenty-five. Studies such as that of the The National Institutes of Health (NIH) Adolescent Brain Cognitive Development, shows that our brains continue to undergo growth and development beyond the age of twenty. In 2018, Professor Russell Viner, president-elect of the Royal College of Paediatrics & Child Health, stated in an interview with the BBC that he supported extending the accepted age of adolescence up to twenty-four, and he noted that "many UK services already take this into account."

The idea that the adolescent brain continues to develop until the age of 25 implies that individuals under the age of 25 are susceptible to relationships with older individuals that involve a power imbalance. Although the eight and a half-year age gap between Ethan and me appeared less significant as I grew and matured, I am aware of how different I was at the age of twenty-eight compared to the twenty-year-old I was when I first met him. When I reached twenty-eight, I contemplated how I would feel about pursuing a romance with a twenty-year-old, and I couldn't envision what we would have in common. Despite potentially sharing similar interests and perspectives, we were at entirely different life stages.

Listen to: Somebody That I Used To Know by Gotye

I perceived Ethan as knowledgeable, while I felt unworthy of his level of intellect. He effortlessly educated me and provided me with information I had never had the patience to learn in school. Most of my knowledge about nature, wildlife, animals, science, and even some literature - 'my forte' - was acquired solely from Ethan. Not only did Ethan seem remarkably intelligent, but he was also incredibly handsome. At the time, I felt like I had never encountered anyone so captivatingly beautiful. I was enthralled; in fact, I was obsessed. He became the focal point of my every thought and need. I desired him intensely, day in and day out. For Ethan, being the perpetrator in our relationship, my lust and overt adoration for him were his winning ticket. He could have directed that energy towards other girls, but he chose to demonstrate his commitment to me. I felt special. Do you remember how he was likely involved in a long-term affair with Hannah when he began a relationship with me? She was discarded, and I became the main supply. However, I wasn't just someone he would sleep with and then move on from. Ethan decided he wanted to build a life with me. Despite my recent separation and evident struggle due to the breakup of my marriage, Ethan didn't appear concerned about enticing me into a new life with him. He exuded confidence, even when I displayed signs of wanting to return to my former life. There were moments when my husband pleaded for me to come back, and I considered it because I loved him. As someone whose parents are still married today, I believed in the concept of marriage, and my vows to my husband were important declarations of my lifelong love for him. In the initial stages of our relationship, Ethan used the information I had shared about my marriage breakup to dissuade me from going back. When the parents of both my ex-husband and me attempted to reunite us - and were nearly successful - Ethan would whisper in my ear, *'Remember he did this... Remember he said that....'* I listened to Ethan because I believed he was the wisest person I had ever met. I genuinely believed that Ethan was 'made' for me. He made it clear that he was 'in love' with me from the moment he laid eyes on me. Perpetrators of abuse tend to fall in love rapidly when they perceive potential, especially in a young woman with a history of hurt.

Jealousy

Ethan harboured jealousy towards my ex. Around our first Christmas together, when our relationship was still new, I had an asthma attack after a visit to the pub. At that moment, I believed that Ethan was taken aback and too stunned to use my inhalers correctly. During the asthma attack, I struggled to explain to Ethan how my estranged husband would have handled the situation. I need not go into detail about how this irritated Ethan; a perpetrator of abuse cannot tolerate feeling inferior to another person, especially not a rival for affection. As a result, Ethan seized my phone and sarcastically called my husband for "tips." I cannot recall the specifics of the conversation as I was having an asthma attack, but I remember sounding like a strangled cat in the background, gasping for breath and wondering why Ethan bothered to call my husband instead of fetching my medication. He did it to punish me. This incident constituted not only physical abuse (withholding medication) but also psychological abuse, leaving me (and my ex) confused.

Ethan became fixated on tormenting my husband. I was unaware of it until much later, but he proudly displayed a call log on his old phone where he had copied numbers from my contact list and added them to his. Ethan went through a phase of calling my ex-husband in the middle of the night and abruptly hanging up when he answered. Even before seeing the call log, I knew Ethan was telling the truth. He described my ex-husband's response, precisely the way he would slightly stutter when answering a call. Ethan mimicked, "'H-Hello?'" I was not comfortable with this behaviour, but when I confronted Ethan about it, he questioned why I had an issue with it. I was made to feel as though my concerns were a betrayal to Ethan, as if I still owed loyalty to my ex-husband, who had already moved on by that point.

Listen to: Dancing On My Own by Robyn

My husband had moved on, and I struggled with that reality, finding it difficult to conceal. Ethan was aware that I hadn't allowed myself time to heal from the breakdown of my marriage. During arguments, he would often remind me, "Even your husband didn't want you" or "Your husband didn't love you." Those sentences would linger in my mind for days after the argument. I understood that I was unwanted and that my husband had fallen out of love with me; there was no need to be constantly reminded of these painful truths. By the time my husband divorced me, I was a mother, dealing with a baby and fluctuating hormones, while enduring daily beatings, gaslighting, and manipulation, all while concealing the horrors of my life from those who knew me. The timing of my Decree Absolute couldn't have been worse. On the "bright side," I thought, Ethan had promised to marry me as soon as I was divorced. However, when my divorce papers arrived, Ethan suddenly changed his mind. Instead, he informed me that he would never remarry. So, that's the story I told my family, friends, and even myself—that Ethan and I had mutually decided that marriage wasn't necessary. I changed my surname to Ethan's through deed poll because I desperately wanted to have the same name as our daughter. In my mind, it made us feel like a "real family" and boldly proclaimed, "Look, everyone, I've moved on to better things, too."

Jealousy and Events

Ethan's jealousy would become most prominent around holidays and birthdays. Long before realising I was in an abusive relationship; I noticed the pattern of how his mood changed during birthdays and Christmas. However, in the first year of our relationship, Ethan celebrated my birthday and showered me with attention that I perceived as love. He always bought me expensive presents. While I was still with my ex-husband, before Ethan and I were even together, Ethan – my senior at work - bought me a pet rabbit for my 21st birthday. I was shocked because I didn't have a suitable house or garden for it. To avoid explaining Ethan's unusual behaviour, I fabricated an elaborate lie to everyone, including my ex-husband, claiming that I had rescued the rabbit. It was a secret that weighed heavily on me for a long time, and if I still had contact with my ex-husband, it's something I'd like to admit. I've never shared this before, so it feels freeing to write it down now.

I now understand that Ethan didn't buy me a rabbit because he cared about me; he bought it as a strategic move. He knew I wouldn't be able to refuse it, forcing me to keep it as an awkward reminder of him, impacting my relationship with my husband if he knew the truth. It was a present intended to outdo the gifts from my husband for my 21st birthday (which it didn't; I still have my presents from my ex-husband, but the rabbit is dead), and my parents' gifts. The rabbit was stressful, living unhappily in a cage due to our busy work schedules. It served as a disruption and a message, indicating that Ethan intended to turn my life upside down.

When we officially became a couple after both our marriages ended, my first birthday with Ethan was overwhelming. He spent hundreds on me, bombarding me with expensive jewellery and outfits. We spent an entire weekend celebrating. He showcased me in front of my family and friends, dressing me up and seeming to enjoy having me on his arm as we visited restaurants and bars. I remember everyone feeling sad about my previous marriage ending but being impressed by the effort Ethan had made for my 25th birthday.

Our first Christmas together, following the horrendous incident where he didn't support me during an asthma attack, was turned around by my huge pile of presents. He bought me bags, scarves, dresses, necklaces, bracelets, earrings, rings, makeup... He would personally do up the necklace, zip up my dress, tell me I looked beautiful, then whisk me out to twirl me around in front of onlookers, my family, and friends, saying, 'How amazing does she look today?'

I found that Christmas challenging. It was my first Christmas in many years without my husband, and I had a meltdown on Christmas Eve, where I begged my ex to see me so we could chat. I think Ethan knew I was falling into grief for my broken marriage, so his love bombing intensified. He didn't want me to find time to grieve; he needed to secure his place in my life. By our first Christmas together, my parents were on the cusp of inviting him to live with us, and I was about to pay off some of his debts out of generosity. He needed to up the game at Christmas to seal the fate. 'Forget about your ex-husband; here's £400 worth of jewellery.'

And then came the following birthday and Christmas, and life couldn't have been more different. I had been completely discarded. He'd left me. I didn't receive presents, cards, or even a 'happy birthday' text. It was the worst period of my life, and I attempted suicide. I didn't know how to live; the pain was beyond anything I can explain. When I did see him, he would control the narrative—fuck me, then fuck off.

Listen to: Something In The Way You Move by Ellie Goulding

In the subsequent birthdays, our daughter joined us, and of course, birthdays after having children look very different. But despite this, they were unenjoyable because of how horrible Ethan's mood would be. The first Christmas after our daughter was born, he was extremely violent, and the entire Christmas with my six-week-old was tainted by the fear of having my neck snapped. I lost some of my hair, had a knife pointed at my throat, and got struck on the head with his knuckles more times than I care to remember. He hated the attention being on our baby on her first Christmas. Neither he nor I got much of a look in. I was fine with that.

My 27th birthday and my first as a Mum was much the same. I received some presents, but otherwise, it was a normal day and evening. We went out to a National Trust property, and he somehow made it stressful by refusing to feed or change our daughter. When she was sick in the car on the way back, he shouted at me to sort it out, claiming it was my job. Later, he said, 'You're a mum now,' as if it were a punishment. 'You're supposed to go to bed early; it's not about you anymore.'

My 28th birthday was even worse. Again, we went to a National Trust property, and there was snow on the ground with the first few daffodils bursting through the sprinkling of white. It was such a sunny, wintry day, and I really wanted to enjoy it. However, he was in a horrible mood, snapping and yelling at me. In a huge argument on the grounds of some old Georgian house, with everyone looking, I was provoked into hot, angry tears. He sneered, 'Look at you, you're pathetic. Losing control of yourself in front of all these people and your baby, you're a joke.' We left early, and I remained silent for the whole journey home. Even when our baby was car sick yet again, and he shouted at me to clean her up, I stayed silent. Sitting in the back with my baby, quietly crying, I watched the country lanes fly by, feeling worried about the speed of his careless driving, while wondering how my life had become this place of uncertainty, hostility, and sadness.

It wasn't just my birthday that seemed to trigger anger from him. Our daughter's birthday appeared to annoy him greatly, and he would always pick on me or start an argument to ruin the day. Even if it was one of my family member's birthdays, he would make it impossible to enjoy. He would refuse to drive me to see them or take me but demand we leave early, forcing me to make some embarrassed excuse. He would complain that I wasn't paying enough attention to our daughter or that my family were a bunch of drunks, stating it was a waste of time and expressing false confusion about why I wanted to be there anyway. I was even made to leave my sister's wedding day early due to his discontent at being there.

My 29th birthday was the last one we had together as a couple. I expressed a desire to go out, as I hadn't been 'Out-Out' in years. My parents had never babysat our daughter before so that we could go out late in the evening. By this time, I was isolated from friends, and Ethan was the only person I could go out and celebrate with. We went out to the local town, and he invited two of his young colleagues who seemed to think he was amazing. They had recently embarked on a side hustle of selling drugs together, which I was deeply unhappy about. I explicitly asked for no drugs to be present.

We went to Wetherspoons, and it was disappointing. I asked to go to a bar with music, but he insisted that everywhere else was closed. He convinced me that we should drive to a town in the opposite direction. I doubted there would be any time and that clubs would be closed by the time we got there. I should have known that was never their intention—they just wanted to buy some gear. In the car, before we drove on the motorway, they took some pills and snorted some coke. Then we drove into the next town, with me in the front seat—an unusual occurrence, as by that time, I was not permitted to sit in the front. Ethan shared a risky incident we had once, where

MUG: An Account of Domestic Abuse

I had performed an act on him while he was driving, back in the early days of our relationship. I admitted that it was true but felt extremely embarrassed, wishing he hadn't disclosed this to the two young lads in the back, who I didn't even know. They found it wild, and Ethan boasted about various places and types of sex we had shared. Then, he told me to perform another act on him as he drove. I refused, saying I didn't want to. The boys in the back laughed. He undid his jeans and exposed his erect penis. They laughed even more. I nervously laughed and reiterated my refusal. He put his hand on my head, forcing my face onto his penis. I had no choice but to comply. I couldn't move my head away. I heard the boys laughing in disbelief, saying, 'What the fuck!?' I felt humiliated.

Later, we arrived home, and my parents left after I had lied to them that I had had a brilliant time. Ethan and his two young colleagues continued to snort coke downstairs as I checked on my child, sweetly sleeping in her bed. The boys left. After further checking on my child, I descended the stairs to find a woman in my living room. She was sitting among the children's toys, ball pit, framed photos of my daughter, and all the things we had collected as a family, giving Ethan head. I silently entered the room, and quietly sat on the sofa. Ethan turned her around on all fours, and he fucked her in front of me, as I watched, frozen. She faked an orgasm while staring at me back. I sensed that there was a fear in her eyes, and I feel she could see my own discomfort and dysregulation. It was all over quickly.

Listen to: Vicious Love by New Found Glory Ft. Hayley Williams

Afterward, he handed me some cash and told me to pay her as she cleaned herself up in the downstairs bathroom. I did so awkwardly, and she awkwardly expressed her thanks. I let her out the door, unsure of what to say, so I managed a hesitant, 'Thank you, take care, bye,' as she left my home and got into the black 4x4 parked outside with tinted windows, where she was driven away.

It wasn't my birthday. It was his.

Controlling Behaviour

When you're in a relationship with a controlling person, they chip away at your own perceptions and beliefs, telling you what you should be thinking and attempting to instil doubt in your reality, undermining what you think and feel.

In the first year of our relationship, Ethan would hang out with my friends. We met them weekly at pubs, and since he was mostly a non-drinker, Ethan appointed himself as the designated driver for all of us. While he would buy me alcohol, he disliked seeing me drink. His disapproval was often expressed regarding my preference for beer, insisting that I looked much better with a glass of rosé in my hand. Consequently, at the bar, he would buy me wine instead. I didn't enjoy wine as much because it caused me to become drunk more quickly and gave me terrible hangovers. Despite this, I would still drink the wine. Perhaps Ethan was right? Maybe I did like wine more than beer? Perhaps I'm a wine drinker now, and beer isn't that good anyway?

After a few months together, Ethan started making negative comments about my alcohol consumption. I had already recognised my unhealthy relationship with using alcohol as an emotional crutch for several years, and I didn't need him to confirm that. Ethan would repeatedly call me a "pisshead" or refer to me as a "pisshead like your mum." Then he would laugh and pretend he was joking, telling me to "relax more" and "not take everything to heart." Then he would buy me more alcohol, because despite his vocal hatred of me drinking, he was also the person who supplied me with drink and encouraged me. There was one person he couldn't hide his behaviour from—my close friend, JT.

One night at a pub, JT, Ethan, and I were hanging out when the women's toilets flooded, and women were stopped from using the men's toilets (which, is absurd). I thought, "That's fine, I'll just wee outside like the other women." But Ethan didn't approve of that. He said, "No woman of mine is pissing in a beer garden." JT gave me a look because we had the kind of friendship where we can communicate silently through our expressions. I knew that JT believed this was wrong and that going to the toilet is a basic human right. If I wanted to relieve myself and urinate outside, I should be entitled to do so. We didn't say anything else, but I knew JT saw the red flag. We left the pub early that night because I was desperate to use the loo. I'm certain that was Ethan's intention, but it was masked by the simple fact that I had requested to go home early, for the urgent need to avoid wetting myself. It's strange to look back on this incident with hindsight because absolutely nothing would stop me from using the men's toilet now, yet this was a sign that I was slowly being broken down by dictation.

Ethan despised my tendency to smoke when I was drunk. On one occasion, he took a cigarette that my friend Tav was offering me and snapped it in two, declaring, "No girlfriend of mine is a skanky smoker." I think he tried to turn me against Tav as well. He always had an issue with Tav's cleavage and would often refer to her as a "slut" behind her back. Once at the pub, Ethan claimed that Tav had tried to kiss him in the car park as she was leaving. Tav was a flirtatious person, but I couldn't imagine her loyalty to me waning with a casual kiss to my new boyfriend. According to Ethan, JT's girlfriend apparently had JT "too under the thumb." He believed my friend K8 "loved attention" because of her interest in pole fitness. However, my friend Bari caused him the most discomfort. He hated Barry. Whenever he knew I was going out with her, he would offer to be the driver. He would make comments about my behaviour around her and make faces at Barry when she wasn't looking. He loathed her because her ex-boyfriend was my estranged brother-in-law, which meant we had a shared history and understanding. Nothing Barry did was ever good enough for me in his eyes. Ethan had a way of making me feel like I had terrible friends who didn't appreciate me the way he did. Although I never believed him, I loved Ethan and didn't want to trouble him by hanging around people he didn't like. Slowly, without conscious intention, I started distancing myself from my friends, losing connections with people who had once played big parts in my life, such as being my bridesmaids. This is a common tactic perpetrators use to isolate you from your social circle—they make you feel that you deserve better from your friends. It's as if they're complimenting you when in reality, they're trying to manipulate you into pushing people away. I had friends who didn't like Ethan, although they didn't express it directly to me. They kept their distance because of his presence and probably because they could see I was in a controlling relationship, unable to be persuaded to leave—another way you lose your friends when you're in a relationship with an abuser. By the time our daughter was born, I was almost completely alone. I had gone from having several close friendships to having a couple with infrequent catch-ups.

Listen to: Rockabye by Clean Bandit Ft. Sean Paul, Anne-Marie

There were noticeable changes when our daughter was born. Ethan wasn't the father I had expected him to be. He would become agitated when our daughter threw-up and angry when I couldn't calm her crying. He was not involved in taking care of her. He literally did nothing. I can count on one hand how many times he changed her nappy, and he only did it when my parents or sister were present. I can also count on one hand how many times he fed her a bottle. He would leave for work at six in the morning and return at six in the evening. When he got home, he would hold our daughter for about an hour. During that time, I had to rush upstairs, tidy up the bedroom from the previous night, wash and sterilise all the bottles from the past 24 hours, throw our laundry into the washing machine, take the dried clothes off the rack and toss them on the bedroom floor, change into my pyjamas, hurry downstairs, and take over from him. Then I would take her to the bathroom, where he would sink into a hot bubble bath and tell me about his day at work while I rocked our daughter in my arms. I distinctly remember feeling a deep sense of injustice when, at five weeks old, our daughter broke into her first smile as she gazed at her father, animated as he was while talking to us and squirting Radox. I was utterly exhausted. Weeks, months, and years went by, and he never once allowed me to have a lie-in. The first time I was granted a lie-in after my daughter's birth was the morning after my 30th birthday when she was three years old, and I couldn't physically get out of bed due to my hangover. (Thanks, Mum and Dad, by the way...). Despite knowing that I was the full-time parent to our daughter, I devalued my own feelings of exhaustion and injustice by telling myself that Ethan was hardworking and providing an income for our family, so it made sense for me to bring up the baby while he did his job.

We had a Moses basket and later a cot for our daughter, but Ethan didn't want her in either. He would mention how his ex, Meg, used to co-sleep with their child. I didn't appreciate being compared to Meg, and co-sleeping wasn't part of my original plan. During my pregnancy, I had read that co-sleeping was associated with SIDS, so I hadn't anticipated doing it. However, after a few weeks of breastfeeding while dozing on and off, co-sleeping became our new normal. I became obsessed with checking our daughter's breathing, convinced that she would die if I didn't wake up and check on her every couple of hours. Ethan took this opportunity to sleep separately from me. When we were all sharing a room at my parents' house, he would lay a faux fur throw on the bedroom floor and sleep there. I would ask him to come to bed every night, but he would decline irritably. He had stopped cuddling me in bed long ago, and despite having regular sex, Ethan hadn't shown me any affection. I couldn't remember the last time he kissed me. He would tell me every day that mothers and babies were supposed to sleep together in bed, insisting that was how it should be. This continued when we moved to our three-story townhouse.

Our first home as a family of three was in the centre of the town I grew up in. We were fortunate to privately rent without the interference of an estate agent, as both our credit scores were terrible, and Ethan had massive debt. Our rent was cheap, and the location was perfect for me, a non-driver. The bus stop was right outside our house, as was a parade of cafes, charity shops, takeaways, supermarkets, hairdressers, a post office, and DIY stores. There was also a pub, but there was zero chance I'd be going in there with my non-existent social life. Our house was huge, with three bathrooms, two living areas, a big kitchen, three double bedrooms with inbuilt wardrobes, and an already landscaped garden that caught the sun all day. I knew we had done well for ourselves, and I wanted so badly to be happy. But moving out of my parents' and into the townhouse scared me. I was worried that the behaviour of Ethan's that I was covering up and keeping secret would become worse.

It did.

Our daughter had her own double room, yet she continued to sleep in our king-size bed with me in the main bedroom. Ethan stopped sleeping on the floor beside us, choosing instead to sleep on the downstairs sofa, saying it was because he had to wake up early for work. Each night, my child's father would sit up, cosy under the fur throw, watching TV.

I would bathe our daughter and put her to bed early in the evening, then join her to help her fall asleep, resulting in my own bedtime around 7 pm every night. It was during these moments that I noticed the loneliness. On weekends, I'd hear the rowdiness emanating from the pub I used to frequent when I was younger, contemplating how drastically my life had changed over a decade—never could I have imagined that in my late twenties, I'd be in bed by 7, while my partner chose to do what he wanted downstairs.

The sound of drunken women on their night out would echo outside, reminding me of the times I used to be with my friends, unruly and unrestrained after closing time. I'd catch the sounds of brawls as men stumbled into the kebab shop, throwing punches. Memories flooded back—buying packets of chips there on my way home from the pub with my ex-husband.

Listen to: You Gotta Be by Des'ree

In bed, I would spend hours scrolling through my phone, accompanied by the background noise of football games or documentaries playing downstairs. I would see Ethan online on WhatsApp, but if I sneaked downstairs to check, he would quickly put his phone screen-down on the armchair. As time went on, Ethan started telling me to go to bed with our daughter, sending me off as if it were a command. He would say, "Right, time for you two to go to bed." It was belittling and surreal. By then, I had made friends with other mums from a parenting course. I knew their husbands or partners helped with their children when they returned from work. Some of my friends' partners would bathe their children or put them to bed. Some would even cook dinner. I remember my sister once complained because her husband hadn't given her a lie-in the previous weekend. I felt an unhealthy sense of envy. I realised I was living the life of a single parent, but I couldn't cry or confide in my friends about how tired I was without going into the details of why. My parents didn't offer much help because they saw that I had a partner and assumed I already had support. When our daughter moved into her own bedroom, we got a double bed for her so that I could continue co-sleeping. Ethan still had the TV to himself in the evenings, but the doorway to mine and my daughter's bedroom was visible from the stairs. I couldn't easily scroll through my phone because he would sneak up and spy through the banister, then tut disapprovingly when he saw what I was doing. "Face lit up," he would remark. So, I started reading historical fiction to escape into a different life and century, seeking solace as far away from my own life as possible.

One night, I convinced Ethan to look after our daughter while I walked across the road to the local Indian restaurant to meet the mum friends from the parenting course. He was annoyed about it, stating that going out in the evening meant neglecting my duties and responsibilities as a parent. I promised him I'd be home by 10.

The night turned out to be an embarrassment. Despite being just across the road, my phone constantly rang, prompting me to put it on silent. Message after message notification lit up my phone, demanding to know who I was with, what I was up to, why I was taking so long, and why I needed to be out when I had a child to look after. He said I needed to get back because he had 'work to do' overnight. The rare chance of socialisation was so stressful that I declined most future invitations – it wasn't worth the hassle.

Basic Human Needs

Sleep was a subject Ethan had proudly written his dissertation on during his psychology degree at university. Ironically, he used it as a form of torture, both day and night. He knew I longed for a lie-in, aware of my constant exhaustion from single-handedly taking care of our daughter, managing the household, attending to all his needs, and working part-time. Some nights, even when he slept in a separate room, he would deliberately wake me up to berate me for my loud snoring. Yes, I snored. It was something I was insecure about even before our relationship, but now it's possibly the thing I dislike most about myself. Ethan claimed my snores disturbed both him and our daughter, so he would tap or shake me until I woke up. Additionally, he would intentionally wake me up if I dozed off in the car, which happened frequently given my fatigue. He would swerve the car, causing my head to hit the window or my body to jolt, resulting in a surprised awakening. He even beeped the horn once. And if I fell into a doze during the day, it wouldn't go unnoticed. He would complain about how I "slept all the time" and remark, "It's alright for you two, getting to sleep during the day, but I have to work and get up early." If I had managed to sneak in a nap while our daughter slept, I would try not to let Ethan know. On weekends, if he caught me napping, he would make me feel guilty for "wasting the day." I constantly felt guilty for simply needing to sleep.

My pregnancy was, physically, a wonderful experience, and I consider myself fortunate for having minimal symptoms. However, like many people, I did experience an achy back and requested a massage numerous times. Not once did he offer to massage my back. He would say things like, "You don't massage my back anymore, and I've been working all day." I felt like I wasn't being a good partner if I didn't fulfil his needs or desires, so there were moments when I would massage his back, hoping that in my third trimester, he would reciprocate the gesture. But he never did. He was rarely at home, always "staying at his boss's house," so there weren't many opportunities to even ask for a massage. When he did stay with me, I felt embarrassed because I needed to go to the toilet multiple times during the night. Every time I got out of bed, he would tut, sigh, roll over, or groan... Sometimes, I would try to hold in my wee if possible and rush to the bathroom when he was already awake in the morning. It's no wonder that I ended up getting water infections. He made me feel guilty for needing to urinate.

Listen to: What I Am by Edie Bricknell & New Bohemians

Psychological abuse begins subtly and gradually breaks you down. It's a skill, a craft. Survivors are often asked why they didn't leave sooner, but it's partly because we have been conditioned to accept the cycle of abuse. We become accustomed to that way of life. Although there are moments when we may wish to leave, the thought of walking away can feel unimaginable, especially considering the physical and financial limitations. We find ourselves in survival mode, unable to envision an alternative lifestyle that can satisfy us in the same way as the calm or 'honeymoon' stages of our relationship cycle did. We fondly remember the Love Bombing stage and hold onto the belief that if the perpetrator could be so loving and attentive then, they can return to treating us well. I've heard hundreds of women say that they feel like they're living with a 'Jekyll and Hyde' character, and the 'good' side of him is the man they love—the person they stay for. We hold on to the 'good' we've witnessed, experienced, seen, in the hope that the anger, the selfishness, the sulking, are only temporary. Many women who have lived with abuse have expressed similar feelings to mine, believing that they can tolerate the unreasonable behaviour for the sake of the positive aspects in the relationship. Additionally, some women have agreed with me that they only recognised they were experiencing psychological abuse once they had escaped the situation and received assistance in identifying the abuse for what it truly was. This is because the perpetrator's actions can often be covert and hard to recognise during the relationship.

Being subjected to physical assault poses a life-threatening situation, but the mental abuse inflicted by a perpetrator can be equally perilous. Tactics like gaslighting can make you question your sanity and undermine your sense of reality. There are numerous instances of gaslighting that I could share, and Ethan is an expert in employing this manipulative technique. Like all abusers, he has a way of distorting the truth to make you doubt your own perceptions. For example, if I were to assert that the sky is blue, Ethan would go to great lengths to convince me that it is, in fact, green. One of his frequent tactics involved stealing cash from my purse and then persuading me that the money was never there to begin with, suggesting that I must have spent it myself. Countless times, I arrived at toddler group expecting to find a five-pound note in my purse, only to discover a meagre amount of pennies instead. Upon contacting Ethan and questioning him about it, he would deny any involvement, accusing me of reckless spending and insinuating that I probably squandered the money the previous day.

Coercive Control

A lot of what I have discussed so far pertains to various forms of coercive control. By persuading me that my friends were not beneficial and creating discomfort, Ethan was able to distance me from long-established friendship groups and restrict my social activities. By encouraging me to move closer to his older child, he was removing me from my support network. Isolation is a tactic used to make the abused person feel dependent solely on the perpetrator for support in different areas of their life, including financially, physically, and emotionally. Financial abuse is employed by the perpetrator to exert control over the whereabouts of the abused person and increase their reliance on them. Of course, they also get to steal and use the abused person's money.

In my personal experience, Ethan made it difficult for me to work. The stress of his reaction to me taking shifts in nursing homes or pubs didn't feel worth the harassment. I would be accused of cheating with colleagues or customers, intentionally arriving home late, and being incompetent at my job. He would often say, "Anyone can do that; it's not hard." Towards the end of our relationship, he made it nearly impossible for me to go to work. He controlled my independence by being late from work to take care of our child or not coming home to look after her. Alternatively, after finishing busy shifts caring for terminally ill young people, I'd arrive home around 10 pm to find my toddler eating chocolate with a wet nappy, watching a true crime documentary with her dad, who seemed highly amused. He would argue with me or even assault me before a shift. I remember once showing up to work with a bright red ear and finger marks where he had hurt me, and I can't even recall the reason for his actions. Another time, my scalp was red and sore from him yanking my hair forcefully. I pretended I had a sunburn on my head. Of course, it was always "my fault"; if I hadn't been "provoking" him, he wouldn't have lost his temper. On my way home from work, I use to pray and ask God to keep my daughter and I safe because I knew he'd be angry that I had made him stay at home with the baby.

Emotional manipulation like this is another significant aspect of coercive control. Ethan regularly downplayed my feelings. For instance, he would acknowledge that he cheated, but claimed it was months ago, so I "should move on," "get over it," and "focus on our child, who is the only one who matters." And so what if my day at work was stressful? I was just a carer and a barmaid; those jobs were easy. And who cares if I lost all my friends anyway? They weren't good friends. Emotional abuse made me feel ashamed of myself and guilty or responsible for the abuse. Ethan would gaslight me into believing that I was at fault and undeserving of anything better than him.

Listen to: Have You Ever? By Brandy

Ethan would routinely arrive early to my workplace if he was picking me up and wait outside, or he would call me once or twice an hour to inquire about my whereabouts, what I was doing, why I was online on WhatsApp at a specific time, and whom I was talking to. A perpetrator will survey and monitor your every move, and this behaviour can escalate in severity and frequency, eventually turning into stalking. I will discuss stalking in more detail later.

Ethan would threaten me if I refused to comply, often resorting to violence. The use of strangulation felt like a violent threat of what he was capable of if I didn't conform. If I didn't give Ethan money, he would hit me on the head with his knuckles or put his hand around my neck. I have an audio recording of him being angry at me for not giving him money we needed for bills and assaulting me when he couldn't get his way. In the end, I gave him the money, fearing further violence. The threat of additional abuse through his actions was intimidating, and intimidation is another crucial aspect of coercive control. The perpetrator uses scare tactics to manipulate and control the victim.

Coercive control also includes sexual abuse. For example, when Ethan withheld sex from me, he was purposefully using it as a tool to make me feel unworthy of intimacy and affection. He also used sex as a method of control, pressuring me into engaging in acts I wasn't comfortable with but felt unable to reject. I was also subjected to sexual assaults that I didn't realise were assaults at the time. I recall instances of passing out from alcohol in the passenger seat of his car early in the relationship and being told when I woke up that he had touched me as I slept and that I had enjoyed it. I was drunk and unconscious, so I couldn't give consent—I was violated. However, at the time, I didn't fully grasp the gravity of the situation. There were times when I woke up in bed, and he was on top of me or behind me, penetrating me. I was asleep and unable to give consent, but I'd pretend to be 'into it' because my body was already aroused, so I wanted it, right? I had no control of my own body. Coercive control can lead to rape.

Ultimately, coercive control is a form of psychological, emotional abuse. It is insidious and leaves the victim feeling confused, worthless, and depressed, among other detrimental effects. It strips away a person's autonomy and independence. It is crucial to never underestimate the profound danger posed by psychological abuse; it's just as life threatening as physical violence.

Chapter Twelve -
Do You Remember the First Time?

'Six in Seven rapes against women are carried out by someone they know.'

Rape Crisis. (n.d.). "Statistics: Sexual Violence."

There was a reason Ethan's exploitation on swinging sites didn't feel degrading at the time. Firstly, I felt flattered that I had a partner who wanted to "show me off." Ethan would withhold sex as a form of control; When he promoted me on the swinging site, I felt attractive because he had regained a sexual interest in me, which made me believe I was appealing not just to him, but to other people as well. However, what started happening was that I would be at work while he was supposed to be taking care of our daughter. During my break, I would be bombarded with WhatsApp group messages that he had initiated in my absence, involving random women I had never met. We were on the swinging site for a year, but we never met any women together. Every woman who chatted with us became uncomfortable with Ethan's dominance over the situation. On more than one occasion, a woman privately messaged me to express that other couples didn't initiate casual sex in this way, and that a genuinely interested couple should both equally participate in arrangements. I was asked by two different women if I was being coerced into meeting strangers for sex against my will. I was also contacted several times by women informing me that Ethan had attempted to meet up with them without my being there, and they wanted to know if I was aware of it. Naturally, I wasn't aware, but I wasn't surprised either. Whenever I confronted Ethan about this, he would find it amusing and claim that some "whores" were trying to break us up, hoping to "trick" me into meeting them and having sex with me without him there. He even showed me a screenshot once, which clearly indicated his intentions to cheat. However, despite the undeniable evidence, he looked me in the eyes and denied it. It may be difficult for someone who hasn't been gaslit to understand how an abused person can choose to believe a lie over concrete evidence. That's precisely how gaslighting operates: the abuser convinces the abused to doubt their own experiences, mind, and question what has happened.

Listen to: Unpretty by TLC

Ethan made videos of me without ever asking for my consent. At the time, I accepted it without realising that my consent was required. He would start filming during sex, possibly assuming that I was okay with it because I didn't express any discomfort at the time. To some extent, I was fine with it, trusting that the videos were solely for his personal enjoyment. However, towards the end of our relationship, I discovered that he had been showing explicit videos of me to his colleagues. I felt angry towards the person who told me initially, despite knowing that they meant well in warning me. I revealed that I was aware of the videos and pretended that they were not as 'X-rated' as they had been described. However, the truth is that I was utterly mortified. Learning about the comments made about me added to my distress. There were some disgusting remarks about my body made by Ethan's colleagues that deeply impacted me.

Consent didn't seem to be part of my vocabulary. I felt stripped of my privacy and dignity. I did not know or understand at the time that this was assault, this was rape, this was a crime. I never told him to get off me, I just decided to 'go with it'.

Writing all of this down and knowing that I will be publishing it feels like further exposure of my most intimate privacy, much like when the videos were shared at Ethan's workplace. However, it is my decision to and for the context of this book, I feel compelled to do so. He took away my choice, and now I am reclaiming it. Furthermore, I am going to reveal things about my past that may be triggering or difficult for victim-survivors of sexual assault and rape to read. I have removed a large, detailed chapter of this book that felt uncomfortable and equally cathartic to write. Maybe one day I will release that full chapter into the world.

Rape

The truth is, and it's important to understand the context of my emotional numbness regarding Ethan's abuse, that in my early twenties, I lived through two instances of rape and sexual assault perpetrated by a despicable individual. These attacks happened during the nights when I avoided my first partner because of the guilt stemming from the secret I harboured about my supervisor and his behaviour towards me. The attacker was known to both me and my ex-husband, yet I never disclosed the details of the incidents to anyone because I didn't think I would be believed. Since it happened more than once, I even questioned whether it constituted assault. I wondered if my own foolishness and the fact that I hadn't physically resisted, said no, or removed myself from vulnerable situations meant that it was somehow cheating. I didn't push him away or explicitly refuse because my main priority was survival, which meant enduring the ordeal to escape quickly. At that time, I lacked knowledge about sexual assault and rape, and I didn't feel capable of seeking the desperately needed help. I despised myself for putting myself in a position where, in my misguided perception, I thought he assumed I wanted sex with him. Looking back on this now, I can confidently state that I don't believe the attacker made any assumptions about whether I "wanted" it or not. I don't think he cared about my consent in the slightest. At that time, I didn't even consider myself a "victim."

Shortly after the attacks, was when my Ex and I decided to go on a relationship "break," and I chose to stay at my parents' house for a few weeks. He couldn't understand what had changed between us and I couldn't share with him what had happened. It was after my twenty-first birthday; my bodily fluids reliably informed me that I had a sexually transmitted infection.

Chlamydia

I sat at the local Sexual Health clinic, and to my shame, a mutual friend of mine and my Ex's was sitting in the waiting room. I thought, "Times up." The truth was bound to come out now. But it didn't. Perhaps they were just as ashamed to be in that waiting room as I had been? I knew that he knew I had been 'unfaithful', and from then on, our acquaintance with him felt like a ticking time bomb.

I didn't just leave the clinic with leaflets on gonorrhoea, herpes, and HIV. I left with information about rape—charities I could discreetly call and counselling services I could check in with. It wasn't explained to me why I should call these services. I hadn't even mentioned sexual assault to the nurse.

There is no such thing as "consensual sex" because all sex should be consensual. "Consent" refers to the equal agreement of all parties involved. Any sexual act without consent, lacking equal agreement, constitutes assault and rape. However, I do acknowledge that for Rape survivors, using the word "rape" can be challenging. In some cases, saying "nonconsensual sex" might feel more comfortable. Each person responds differently to the abuse they have lived with, and the language we use, whether it is the accurate terminology or not, can evoke different emotions and reactions.

A few years later, I learned that the perpetrator who attacked me had left our hometown and didn't return to the same social circles because of a rape allegation. He had been accused of raping a teenage girl. The case was dropped for lack of evidence, and the girl received horrific backlash locally. There were other instances as well, of him assaulting women of varied ages.

I didn't have herpes, gonorrhoea or HIV. I did have Chlamydia, though.

Listen to: Do You Remember The First Time? By Pulp

Hyde Park

How do you explain to your loyal boyfriend of many years that you may have given him a sexually transmitted infection? I knew I didn't want to lose him, but I also knew he deserved better. The fear of being without him had overwhelmed me since the moment I realised we were falling in love. The thought of living without my boyfriend was incomprehensible to me. And yet, I found myself pushing him away. I desperately wanted to share intimacy with him, but I couldn't bring myself to do so. Sex had lost its loving and pure essence; it had become dirty and dangerous. I didn't associate him with anything toxic, tainted, or hateful. So, I felt trapped in an internal conflict that I couldn't express, except by pretending to be constantly irritated by him, partly hoping that he wouldn't touch me and partly dismayed that he wasn't touching me.

I could sense that my sudden lack of interest in my partner sexually was eroding his self-esteem. Looking back now, I want to shake myself and scream, "Wake up, Beth! Tell him. He loves you." But I was convinced that he wouldn't be able to get past my "infidelities." In hindsight, even if he couldn't have supported me as a partner, I believe he was decent enough to offer support as a friend, at the very least. But I was terrified of losing him. It's ironic because, by not addressing my trauma, I lost him anyway.

We were enjoying a day out with friends in Hyde Park when I received the news. It was a rare occasion where I could momentarily set aside the atrocities that had occurred that year. I remember sitting on the grass in front of Speaker's Corner, drinking a few cans of lager before heading to a gig where Pulp were headlining.

It was the first time I had developed a skin condition that would plague me throughout my twenties – Folliculitis. The initial occurrence was particularly severe, exacerbated by my recent diagnosis of eczema, which I had never had before. To conceal the raw and bumpy appearance of my legs, I started wearing floaty gypsy-style skirts and maxi-dresses. I now understand that eczema and the resulting Folliculitis can be triggered by stress, and I was certainly under a great deal of stress at that time.

At Hyde Park, we spent the day drinking in overpriced beer gardens after entering the arena. As my friends and I sat in a tight circle, sipping pints from flimsy plastic cups, my Blackberry started ringing. My ringtone was Rihanna's "What's My Name." It was a private number, and I knew it was the sexual health clinic calling. Even before the clinic visit, I had suspected an infection.

"You have Chlamydia," the nurse informed me. "And Bacterial Vaginosis. And thrush. Fortunately, the Doxycycline you've been taking should have treated all the infections. However, it's important that you notify your sexual partners so they can get tested as well."

There, at Hyde Park, I told the boy I loved, of whom had only ever been with me, that I had a STI. The weight of my words settled upon me, bringing forth shame, horror, and self-hatred. But most of all, I felt devastated for him. His eyes, the colour of Maltesers, revealed a deep sadness behind them. His eyebrows furrowed and frowned in response to anything that wasn't funny, further emphasising the downturn of his natural eye slope. I felt like I was in in a dystopian world, where the person I least wanted to hurt in the world was the one who I caused the most pain.

"How?" He asked, and though I wasn't him, I could sense the heaviness in his heart. I am ashamed to say that I proceeded to explain some elaborate lie about how I must have got it years ago, before we were together. What followed was my ex's familiar way of handling difficult situations—he simply shut them out. He turned off his emotions, blocked the pain, and carried on with life. He did this with everything that felt too hard. After agreeing to go to the sexual health clinic himself as soon as possible, we continued with our day out.

Pulp were great that night.

The Truth

The weight of keeping such secrets from my partner caused severe stress. Escaping from home and getting drunk most nights with friends became the norm. The guilt of being around him became an overwhelming burden, and I further pushed him away. We were not only growing apart, but it felt like an insurmountable ocean lay between us, as if we lived in two separate worlds. Even back then, I was aware that I was carelessly pressing a big, red self-destruct button.

Listen to: Born To Cry by Pulp

Not long after, I made the decision to tell the truth. I knew deep down that I was about to lose everything I cared for and loved in my life, but I couldn't bear to continue living the way I had been. I spent hours writing, tearing up, scribbling out, and rewriting letters for my boyfriend while he was at work. When he came home, I handed him a heartfelt yet vague letter, apologising and explaining that I had been sexually assaulted while intoxicated, feeling as if I had betrayed him and struggled to cope with the aftermath. I mentioned that it was likely the reason we both contracted chlamydia. I declared my unwavering love and loyalty, but also acknowledged that I would understand if he chose to leave me. As always, the written word was my best means of conveying what had happened, to some extent. I sat silently in our living room as he read it, completely uncertain about his reaction. I wondered which path he would take—would he be angry... or supportive? Well, what unfolded was all too familiar, it was my ex's way of handling difficult situations—he simply shut them out. He switched off his emotions, blocked out the pain, and continued with his life. He did this with everything, including what had transpired between us. We carried on with our relationship, never once discussing the letter or my revelations ever again. And then we got married.

We separated a couple of years into our marriage and were divorced within six years. The agony was as intense as I had anticipated, perhaps even more so. Probably more.

Chapter Thirteen - Abuse and Misogyny

'Online abuse of women is widespread in the UK with one in five women having suffered online abuse or harassment. Almost half of women said the abuse or harassment they received was sexist or misogynistic, with a worrying 27% saying it threatened sexual or physical assault.'

Amnesty International UK. (n.d.). "Online Abuse of Women Widespread."

Ethan's lack of respect for women is evident. He is obsessed with free porn and introduced me to the world of PornHub. Initially, I watched porn with him out of curiosity, but I also felt pressured to conform to a certain appearance for him. Ethan preferred the stereotypical, exaggerated image of women portrayed in popular porn: vibrant, large-breasted, fake-tanned, heavily made-up, and faking orgasms. These women would have not a hair on their bodies, except for those on their scalps, often enhanced with extensions. Now, if that's how you want to look, that's perfectly fine. However, we cannot ignore the fact that the porn industry promotes a false perception of the "ideal" woman for heterosexual men. Since porn is not reality, the "ideal" depicted in porn becomes a fantasy that many porn addicts expect women to fulfil.

To conform to Ethan's perception of "ideal," I went to great lengths to resemble the porn stars he enjoyed watching. I bleached my hair until it became damaged and broke off. I applied hair removal cream all over my body, leading to allergic reactions and rashes. I posed, pouted, and spent excessive amounts of money on makeup, smothering my skin in expensive foundation, which suffocated it and resulted in breakouts. Yet, when I tried to look like Ethan's version of "sexy," he would criticise my appearance and tell me I looked terrible. All the uncomfortable lingerie I wore for him was labelled as "slutty." If I dared to show any cleavage, I was accused of "dressing like a slut." If I revealed a bit of leg, I was accused of "exposing my body." Even when I applied makeup, he would question why I bothered to wear it. Ethan simply didn't like me wearing makeup. If we were going out and I applied even the tiniest amount of concealer and mascara, he would complain and say that I didn't need to "mess around with makeup."

I didn't consciously decide to revert to a more modest style of clothing. I believe subconsciously, I couldn't be bothered with the hassle and criticism I would face if I wore what I genuinely wanted to wear. It wasn't just my personal appearance that received criticism form Ethan, but slowly, it became everything I did.

Ethan is misogynistic, viewing women as being solely for cooking, cleaning, and having sex with. At the beginning of our relationship, he portrayed himself as a selfless and considerate lover, driven by his toxic desire to outdo anyone who came before him. There had been only one previous partner who had genuinely shown me love, and Ethan felt the need to surpass that. And he did succeed, but only until he had me emotionally invested. Slowly, our sex became solely focused on him, with no consideration for my pleasure or needs. Over the course of a few years, I realised he stopped kissing me before or during sex. Our physical relationship mainly revolved around quickies involving penis in vagina or blowjobs. Our sex life mirrored his general perception of women. According to Ethan, women exist solely for the pleasure of men, and their purpose is to cater to their needs. He saw no reason to provide pleasure to those he believed should serve him.

He once casually mentioned that a man can have sex with his wife half an hour after her death. He joked that if I died, he would have "one last go" with me because, supposedly, it would be legal (This doesn't sound true, and I am reluctant to google it).

Ethan and I conceived our daughter during one of his visits to the bedsit, shortly after his three-month discard of me. Let's just say it was far from meaningful intimacy. He'd do the act hastily and then would promptly dismiss any further connection by either falling asleep or physically leaving.

Before Ethan became romantically involved with me, he was arrested on Oxford Road in Reading. He claimed that he had picked up a sex worker because she appeared upset on the side of the road. Rather than facing other consequences of his actions, he opted to pay a fine and attend a one-day awareness course alongside other men, including professionals like a doctor. However, this didn't deter him from repeating such behaviour, as perpetrators often believe themselves to be above the law. The awareness course seemed to have insignificant effect on him, as he continued to pay for the services of sex workers, becoming even more secretive to avoid detection. This pattern of behaviour wasn't isolated to just one aspect of his life; he paid fines and attended courses for other offenses like speeding, using his phone while driving, and evading taxes, yet continued those actions as well.

I understand that readers may question why I have included an incident that occurred prior to our relationship in this chapter. The reason is that when I discovered Ethan had been charged with solicitation for the purpose of obtaining a sexual service, I consciously chose to look the other way and believe his excuse. I can't believe I fell for it. But I did. Perpetrators of abuse are skilled manipulators, adept at deceiving others. What's more, I felt sympathy for Ethan, thinking he had been trying to help someone in need, only to end up with a tarnished record for future job security checks. Ethan was aware of my tendency to be overly empathetic, and he exploited that sensitive part of my personality for his own advantage. During our discussions about his inability to pursue a career in the public sector due to the requirement of a DBS check, his story of being falsely arrested for picking up a sex worker on the street evoked pity within me.

Listen to: Why Do I Exist by Zevia

You could argue that the sex worker Ethan picked up that night in Reading may have been someone who willingly chose their job and understood the associated risks. However, how can we truly know? We lack information about their age, circumstances, and predicament, if any. Considering Ethan's desperation for his fix, despite being married to someone else at the time, couldn't he have sought services from an agency that prioritise the safety and well-being of sex workers? An agency that empowers women to have control over their earnings, boundaries, and rights? An agency that actively works against coercion and force, and implements safety measures? Because what we do know about Ethan is that he is inherently unsafe, regardless of whether the person who entered his car that night enjoyed their work or not. They were vulnerable simply by being in his presence.

I believe that sex work is a legitimate form of work—hard work—and I support sex workers. My concerns about sex work revolve around the pervasive misogyny and the potential dangers that sex workers face in our patriarchal society. Men like Andrew Tate actively promote content that teaches men how to assert control over women using misguided notions of "masculinity." Drawing from my personal experience of being in a relationship with a predatory individual who often used the services of sex workers, I have seen firsthand how his sense of superiority over women was exemplified through his actions aimed at obtaining power and control. I strongly believe all adult sex work should be legal so that worker's rights – particularly their right to safety - should be considered within a governed framework.

Ethan's lack of respect for women extended beyond viewing them as mere objects of sexual pleasure. He held a disdain for any woman who had a voice or stood up for herself. But wasn't that me? The girl who became feisty after a few drinks in a less-than-pleasant Basingstoke club? What about the girl who confronted the racial abuse directed at her friend's wife behind her back? Or the girl who passionately sang along to Bikini Kill and Babes in Toyland in her bedroom? The girl who named her daughter after Hole lyrics? What about the girl who actively took part in marchs in Westminster, demanded justice at protest gigs, and even faced detention for challenging a teacher's discriminatory values? What about the girl who tirelessly campaigned on social media against the reckless slaughter of badgers? The same girl who was barred from her reception venue on her wedding day for drunkenly and vehemently complaining about months of mismanagement? What about the girl who believed in equal pay for women in the same job roles and with the same qualifications? The girl who advocated for the rights of refugees to live in safety, who championed the rights of trans individuals, supported pulling down statues of slave traders, and opposed the privatisation of the NHS? Where had that passionate girl gone? In the presence of Ethan, she was not allowed to exist, for under the control of a male perpetrator, a woman's voice is silenced. Am I generalising all male perpetrators of abuse with the same Ethan-shaped brush? Yeah, I am. When involved with a male perpetrator of abuse, anyone becomes a victim of disempowerment. Show me a heterosexual male perpetrator of abuse who allows their partners to have a voice. Show me a male perpetrator of abuse who lets their non-toxic mothers, sisters, grandmothers, or daughters have a voice. If anyone can prove me wrong, please do so. However, from both the paid and voluntary work I've done with women who have lived with abuse perpetrated by men, I have yet to hear an account that doesn't involve prejudice against women or non-binary individuals.

Listen to: Lose You To Love Me (Cover) by Bombay Bicycle Club Ft. Rae Morris

Misogyny allows men to be perpetrators. It encourages and perpetuates a culture that normalises and justifies the mistreatment, objectification, and devaluation of women. By perpetuating harmful stereotypes, gender roles, and power imbalances, misogyny creates an environment where men feel entitled to dominate, control, and harm women. It fosters a mindset that disregards consent, dismisses women's voices, and undermines their autonomy. Ultimately, misogyny not only enables men to become perpetrators of violence and discrimination but also sustains a system that perpetuates gender inequality and denies women their basic human rights.

I began reclaiming my voice when I realised, I was in a toxic relationship, but in doing so, I faced further violence. Within the confines of our home, I was unable to fight back. However, driven to assert myself, I sought an alternative avenue—I created my Instagram account. Initially, its focus was on using nature and the outdoors to promote mental health and support children's learning. Ethan harboured a strong dislike for my presence on public social media. Nevertheless, it provided me with a platform to express my creativity, share ideas, and reveal my innermost thoughts—elements Ethan sought to suppress. Through my account, I addressed and advocated for subjects I hold deep convictions about, such as women's rights, socialism, racism, environmental issues, and more. In many ways, my Instagram account became the catalyst for the end of our relationship: regardless of Ethan's violent outbursts, profanities, or tries to silence me, I remained steadfast in keeping my small social media space. I refused to deny myself my voice any longer.

Chapter Fourteen - Sex & Love & Addiction

'We confuse love with neediness, physical and sexual attraction, pity and/or the need to rescue or be rescued.'

(One of the characteristics of Sex and Love Addiction as defined by Sex And Love Addicts Anonymous).

Sex and Love Addicts Anonymous (SLAA). (n.d.). "Characteristics of Sex and Love Addiction."

I once associated a "sex addict" as someone young, male, who snorted coke daily, and was probably a glamorous member of an 80s stadium rock band—I think of "Motley Crue." If you had asked me to describe a sex addict in the 21st century, I would have pointed out Russell Brand in the 2000s. My belief of a sex addict was someone elaborate, outrageously sexual, and open about it. My understanding of sex addiction was limited to modern stereotypes. So, when Ethan casually confessed to being a sex addict, I wasn't surprised, and my ignorance about sex addiction remained unchanged. You see, Ethan was ridiculously handsome, exceptionally charismatic, and extraordinarily unique. He owned the charm and confidence of a Hollywood actor. Once you met him, you couldn't forget him. He didn't dress like anyone else, speak like anyone else, or look like anyone else. He excelled in everything he did and appeared capable of any task given to him. That's what he wanted you to believe, anyway. The truth that an overtly charming perpetrator of abuse cannot bear anyone discovering is that they are none of the things they lead you to believe. Underneath their costume of confidence and charisma lies an insecure individual who seeks validation through love and intimacy. I could devote an entire book to exploring why Ethan is the way he is, but that is his story to tell (and, reluctantly, it would be a fascinating one).

Never in my life had I considered myself an addict, let alone an addict to love and sex. The realisation that I may be an addict is new, and I'm still processing the information I've received through various support systems. When it was suggested to me, I dismissed it. "How can I be a sex addict? I don't even have a dick." But I'm here to tell you that sex addiction doesn't discriminate. It affects men, women, non-binary individuals, queer and trans folk, the elderly, the young, people of all races, heights, educational backgrounds—anyone can be vulnerable to addiction. Addiction arises when you develop a dependency on something. I was craving validation through my abuser, I was unable to control my desire for Ethan, even when I realised that having sex with him was dangerous. Having a sex addiction doesn't mean you go around having sex with everyone and everything you see. It means that you may have a dependency on sex that feels uncontrollable, whether it has a negative impact on your life or not. I have already recounted the beginning of my physical relationship with Ethan and how our connection revolved around a wild "sexual chemistry." Now I understand that it wasn't chemistry at all; it was two addicts feeding each other's highs. I cannot speak for Ethan about our union, but I can describe how it was a euphoric experience for me. And what did I gain from these sex-induced highs? It's that word again—validation. I craved a display of "acceptance." Somewhere along the line as I was growing up, my brain confused "love" with being accepted, and I, in turn, confused sexual intimacy with gaining acceptance. When Ethan began withholding sex from me, my discomfort wasn't only due to the psychological abuse; it also stemmed from the unrecognised withdrawal symptoms of feeling high from acceptance. Remember how far I went to retrieve that validation? I was desperate for my dopamine fix. The irony is that Ethan would accuse me of being a sex addict to gaslight me. But he was right.

Listen to: Rehab by Amy Winehouse

My sex addiction was limited to the intimacy of a single sexual partner to whom I stayed faithful. While it has been damaging, I could envision a complete recovery and a resetting of my perceptions of intimacy – which is where I am finally at now. In comparison, Ethan's addiction is far more destructive.

Ethan's addiction to sex knew no boundaries within our relationship because, for him, there were no boundaries at all.

There was no break in his cheating. I cannot say how often he visited sex workers, but I do know it was a consistent behaviour. As a young woman committed to the relationship, I constantly suffered from the common yet equally embarrassing infection known as Bacterial Vaginosis, or "BV." While BV is not classified as a Sexually Transmitted Infection in the UK, I like to think that this imbalance in a vulva owner's genitalia is "Mother Nature's" way of showing that something is amiss. Why is it that I had rarely experienced BV before having a sexual relationship with Ethan? And why have I not had BV since ending our relationship? Yet, throughout our supposed partnership, I would periodically suffer from BV. I consulted doctors, tirelessly searched online, and did everything I could to prevent the infection. I avoided using soaps, especially perfumed ones, in that area. We rarely used sex toys, and when we did, they were properly cleaned. I refrained from having sex during my period. I even took vitamin supplements in the hope that they would help. However, every few months, BV would resurface with all its characteristic symptoms. While I knew BV was not an STI, I was aware that it could be transmitted through the contact of personal fluids. Once my awareness of Ethan's infidelity was awakened, I couldn't help but wonder if a man could carry the bacteria that causes Bacterial Vaginosis on his penis when having sex with multiple women without properly washing in between (or not washing at all...). I am not a scientist or a medical professional, but as someone with a vulva, I have experienced the unwelcome experimental results of vaginal pH imbalance while being with or without a cheating partner. For me, my flare-ups of BV served as my body's dependable way of saying, "He's been shagging someone else again."

Despite being aware of Ethan's infidelity and the emotional and physical harm he caused me; I still couldn't resist him sexually. Even on the nights when I mustered the courage to say, "fuck you," I would still end up fucking him. This kind of self-sabotage didn't end when I left Ethan; it continued for months afterward. I would go weeks fighting my urges to seek validation through sex with him, and then in a fleeting moment, I would find myself going down on the person who least deserved my attention. These moments were my relapses, and there were many of them.

It wasn't only my sexual addiction to Ethan that I relapsed in; it was my addiction to love. To me, Love was also acceptance. As I mentioned before, I didn't choose to leave Ethan. While I had made up my mind that leaving was the right decision, I didn't want to face it. I was scared, not just because of the potential repercussions of his behaviour, but also because I wasn't prepared to face the loneliness of being single. I had never truly experienced being single before. Instead of confronting that frightening prospect on my own, I chose to remain in the familiar but abusive environment. I wasn't ready to let go of the false notion that sexual connection equalled declarations of love. However, love is not defined by sex. Love isn't about having our needs fulfilled by someone else. There are no healthy substitutes for love because love is love. If others don't show you love, care, or nurturing, it becomes your responsibility to provide those essential emotional needs for yourself. Going through life without being loved is a lonely experience, but you don't have to be lonely or unloved if you can give yourself the love you deserve.

Listen to: Love Fool by The Cardigans

For as long as I can remember, I have indulged in romantic daydreams about the people I have been emotionally involved with. While there have been only a few instances of mutual affection, those individuals have occupied my thoughts completely. They have become my entire world. In my belief, my partners have been a source of sunlight, and I would have willingly followed behind them indefinitely, revering the very ground they walked upon. Ethan would eagerly welcome a relapse from me, and as peculiar as it may sound, my yearning for validation was so overpowering that even after suffering everything he subjected me to, I battled with desperate urges to unblock my abuser—and often succumbed to them.

After physically leaving Ethan, I tried to set up "No Contact" multiple times, but the withdrawal from him was excruciating. It wasn't just a mental discomfort; it manifested physically as well. I experienced headaches, nausea, mood swings, and even had urges to self-harm. I became irritable, grumpy, and sadly, even snapped at my daughter. With the absence of love and sex in my life, I turned to different unhealthy methods as a means of self-medication. Alcohol became a way for me to emotionally connect with my family, with whom I was living. Food became a source of comfort to satisfy my craving for pleasure, which resulted in a dramatic weight gain in the early part of my single life.

I've used alcohol to numb pain, particularly in the aftermath of being raped. During the first UK Lockdown in the Pandemic, I made the decision to embark on a temporary sober lifestyle. I didn't set a specific time limit or have any expectations; I simply wanted to see how long I could go without drinking – which turned out to be a few months and probably could have gone longer if I'd wanted to. While there were challenging moments in the first month when I found it difficult to decline the nightly invitation of an alcoholic beverage, I can confidently say that abstaining from alcohol was a completely different experience compared to abstaining from Ethan. There's no comparison. Overcoming my sex and love addiction, my addiction to the abuser, is unlike anything I've ever known before. I can't compare it to any other experience; it's an excruciating journey.

Many people will call the hardship of going No Contact with an abuser a 'trauma bond'.

Writing it all down may make it sound easy in theory: Recover from your love and sex addiction, your addiction to your abuser, by falling in love with yourself and taking care of yourself. However, in practice, it is not easy at all. I have spent over thirty years of my life not liking myself, and now I am expected to completely rewire my way of thinking about love, sex, relationships, and my relationship with myself? This process requires intensive therapy to undo certain traumas and patterns of thinking. Overcoming addiction and trauma from abuse and assaults is not pain-free; the painful path is the only way to conquer them all. The question is, what is more painful in the long term? Is it the misery of staying in toxic relationships with abusive individuals or the temporary pain and discomfort of the recovery process?

Chapter Fifteen –

Non-Ethical Recovery and Narcissistic Abuse Experts

Fact: Out of the nine criteria that define Narcissistic Personality Disorder by the DSM-5, only five of the criteria need to be met to reach a diagnosis, which can only be made medically by a psychiatrist or psychologist (2023).

Learning About Self-Care

There was a time when I couldn't think of anything more boring than mindfulness. That was because I was caught up in living a fast-paced lifestyle. What enjoyment could one possibly get from meditation? Yoga classes and breathing techniques seemed like boring, hippish, 'la-dee-dah' nonsense. No, I had a pub to go to, gigs to riot at, and lager to spill. There were people to get pissed with, clubs to rave at, and festivals to lose myself in. I was already living in the present, wasn't I? "Living for the moment" and "YOLO" and all that? Well, the short answer is no. I wasn't truly living in the present. Every day, I woke up and lived in my past without even realising it. Mindfulness, though it may have seemed "boring," was exactly what I needed.

Listen to: Put Your Records On by Corinne Bailey Rae

I came to a place where I knew I needed to heal but wasn't sure where to start. My first introduction to self-care came through an online course on mindfulness that I paid for on the wellbeing website DailyOM.com. I dedicated time to learn self-care strategies for myself, after my friend recommended the course to me. Some of them proved to be effective, such as meditation and breathing techniques that I practiced while my daughter was at preschool or before going to work. However, I also developed an obsessive need to "treat myself," using self-care as an excuse for impulsive or expensive purchases that I could have easily done without. For instance, I started doing all the things I couldn't do while in a relationship with Ethan. This included regularly going to the salon for acrylic nails, getting eyelash extensions every three weeks, and getting lip fillers as a thirtieth birthday present. I also satisfied my sexual cravings by having meaningless, casual sex (as documented) and drinking most evenings in front of the TV, just "one or two real ales or glasses of fizz" before bed. None of these things were true acts of self-care; they were reactions to the end of a relationship, distractions from the pain dressed up as 'looking after myself'.

Don't get me wrong – I'm not discouraging pampering yourself, especially after leaving an abusive relationship. It counts as paying attention to yourself and meeting the needs you didn't receive when you were living with the abuse. For me, I had to look at why I was paying attention to myself in the first place to figure out if what I was doing qualified as 'self-care'. I was a skint parent living in a bedroom with my child, and the amount of money I was spending on my appearance was more about temporary fixes for feeling good externally rather than addressing the internal wounds that caused my insecurities. I needed to recognise the deeper needs that required addressing. With some online help, I realised that the pleasure I received from taking care of my appearance and the temporary dopamine boost it provided for less than a few hours was distracting me from the core problems.

Taking care of my appearance was a surface-level way of showing myself love and attention. The dress I would buy for myself on "self-care Saturday" was gorgeous, and I deserved it, but it wasn't the act of self-love I needed to receive from myself. It was an instant, provisional repair, like a bandage on a wound that cut to my bones.

To clarify, I continue to love indulging in gifts to myself and I encourage everyone to do so when they can. However, I had a realisation that self-care is a process that cannot be fully achieved by simply lighting candles during bath time. While such practices can be helpful, true self-care comes when we recognise the inner work we need to do, even when it is uncomfortable and raw. There may be wounds that are momentarily soothed by new outfits, incense sticks, or sharing generic memes on Instagram stories, but they still exist.

For me, self-care truly began when I acknowledged the underlying reasons for needing to care for myself, and this was not an easy or straightforward process. Understanding that healing those wounds would be painfully difficult became a goal of my self-care journey, even though it meant facing interim agony. At times, I found myself wanting to retreat to what I knew and where I felt comfortable. And to some extent, I did return to those patterns. However, I eventually confronted myself with a question: What would be harder? Continuing to suffer and exhaust myself by staying in an abusive relationship and perpetuating my own toxic patterns in relationships, or enduring the non-permanent pain of the recovery process?

I came to the understanding that I had trauma deeper than I ever initially realised. However, I had no clue about the origins of that trauma. How could I tend to a wound when I wasn't sure what had caused it in the first place? Through obsessive research on narcissism and co-dependency, I discovered a popular Narcissistic Abuse Expert who was steadily growing momentum. For a period, she became one of my heroes and my favourite teacher in trauma.

Listen to: Girl On Fire by Alesha Keys

The Expert

Like many Narcissistic Abuse Experts, this person had a free Facebook group. I was in several, and this group was easily the best online support group that I had found. The Expert and her team of moderators were meticulous in checking the group for potential false accounts, ensuring the safety of the many women in the community from abusers, and checking all posts and comments. Additionally, The Expert had a private group that members could pay for, which I felt was worth the money considering the available resources, online group 'therapy', and connections with other survivors who were serious about healing. As the first UK Lockdown began to ease, when I started drafting this book, The Expert facilitated a free online bootcamp. It was during this bootcamp that I decided to sign up for her newly established 'Narcissistic Abuse Healing School'. At the time, I felt like taking the course changed my life.

For twelve weeks, I immersed myself in The Expert's programme, which focused less on the abuse of the 'narcissist', and more on the trauma that allowed me to be in an abusive relationship in the first place. I delved into the understanding of trauma, the human brain, the nervous system, and my own responses to triggering situations. I explored various therapies and theories, and discovered which ones worked best for me. Most importantly, I gained insight into some of the causes of my original traumas.

During this process, I learned that trauma is a complex phenomenon that doesn't always stem from one major event. I discovered that I had inherited generational trauma from multiple ancestral lines, and I also realised that I had experienced trauma as a child without even recognising it at the time. Childhood trauma doesn't always have to be a singular horrific event; it can be a series of seemingly 'smaller' incidents that shape a child's perception of safety. While I won't dive into the specifics of my own childhood traumas in this account, I want to emphasise that overall, I had a happy childhood. However, certain memories where I lacked control became lodged in my nervous system, influencing how I felt and responded as I grew into adulthood, even if I couldn't recall all the actual events.

I want to clarify that this book is an account and not a comprehensive guide to trauma.

If you're interested in learning more about trauma and its impact on us as adults, I will signpost you to some resources I've found helpful at the end of the book. One thing I do NOT recommend, is The Expert. Or most Narcissistic Abuse Experts for that matter. While I think the Healing Programme, online support group and education I received from The Expert was beneficial, it can be easy to be sucked into the beliefs that Narcissistic Abuse Experts financially rely on you believing. I found this out for myself when, upon completing the Healing School, I had a profound realisation that I wanted to work with women in their recovery from domestic abuse. I took the initiative to enrol in Level 2 Counselling Skills at my local college, even though I faced financial constraints as a solo parent relying on Universal Credit. Thankfully, I was able to apply for funding, which I received. The following year, my journey toward becoming a counsellor began.

Things rarely go the way we want them to when we are living with severe trauma. My intentions were good when I decided to enrol at college to learn about counselling skills, but I was not prepared for the eye-opening revelations of the course. I made it through Level 2 narrowly, with my tutor dragging her heels in and pulling me along for a scraped pass. It was clear that before I went on to Level 3, I would need some time out to work on myself. That was okay, I thought – it gave me time to learn some more counselling skills by attending counselling myself and working out the path I was going to go down in qualifying. I decided to take a few months out.

Almost a year after completing the healing school and being a member of the narcissistic abuse expert's paid subscription-based support service, she advertised for a social media manager to join her team. At this point, my Instagram account had progressed from local walks and toddler education to the benefits of nature therapy, mental health awareness and of course, some open discussion around domestic abuse. Multiple people tagged me in the role – everyone who knew me and were familiar with The Expert knew I would be great at the role advertised. I had been running my hometown's community information group for a couple of years and voluntarily led other helpful communities via Facebook, and we were coming out the other side of the global pandemic that had rocked everyone's world. It seemed like a perfect opportunity to build on my career goals. I applied for the job.

Listen to: Lost Heroes by Heavyball

Never Work with Your Heroes

At first, I was turned down by The Expert and her assistant. I was terribly disappointed and therefore, in a bold move, I responded by persuading them to give me a chance because I knew I was right for the role, and they wouldn't regret interviewing me. Impressed with my assertion, The Expert arranged an interview on Zoom. We talked all things social media, and they seemed impressed with my knowledge. By the end of the day, I had been given the job – and it felt too good to be true. Flexible hours? Check. Good money? Check. Understanding of my solo parenting? Check. Work from home? Check. In fact, the job was laptop and phone based - I could work from anywhere. My role would be managing The Expert's several social media groups – the largest with 25,000 women in, maintaining the pages, creating content and initiating and engaging in conversation, promoting the expert's work and signposting women to the podcast episodes, YouTube videos, posts, subscription services and programmes to recover from narcissistic abuse. Overall, I must have been reaching over 30,000 women every day, giving advice and supporting them to understand their trauma and the abuse they had lived with – or were living with. I was provided training to better understand popular social media apps, how to create engaging content and learning about trauma using theory. It ought to have been perfect.

Within the first week of working with The Expert, I was hyped up across her social media groups and pages. She was excited to be working with me – and another newly hired woman from America – and expanding her team to make her groups even better than they already were. She enlisted a small group of volunteers from all over the world to assist me in managing the main group, steadily increasing in numbers. My role became the 'Community Manager', and I felt like I thrived instantly. There were a few things to wrap my head around, but otherwise, I was extremely capable of the role, and my experience in management in the care industry came in handy for my amazing team of volunteers. We were all dedicated to the jobs we had, and we had all completed The Expert's Narcissistic Abuse Healing School. From the start, I was aware that my job would involve constantly promoting and supporting The Expert's work. We had regular meetings, and there were continuous, private group chats where I was encouraged to direct women to The Expert's podcast episodes, YouTube channel, and links to the programmes she offered. However, within weeks of starting the job, I was expected to leave a link to one of her resources with every comment I made and comment on EVERY post made in the Facebook groups. On a busy day, this could amount to 150 – 200 posts a day. Although I was supposed to work only 4 hours a day, I couldn't accomplish everything in that time and ended up working approximately nine hours a day. The role was flexible, so I could choose my days off, but The Expert didn't seem to appreciate me taking time off. If there was little interaction from a volunteer or the Community Manager, The Expert would reprimand us in the staff WhatsApp group. It wasn't just the posts and comments I had to check, but also the members' requests. To make my job even busier, I had to scrutinise each member request (easily over 300 a day due to the advertisement from The Expert's podcast with over a million streams) and ensure that they were from real accounts. If the account was closed and had no profile picture (which is unsurprising since we were working with women who were living with abuse), I would have to direct message them and ask for photo identification of them holding up their name to prove who they were. This process worked fine, but it took hours. In addition to monitoring the groups, empathetically guiding women, educating them, and managing a volunteer team, I was asked to write a weekly newsletter to 800 people in the healing programme subscription service. As a writer, this was a role I relished and knew I was good at. I began experimenting with graphic design, and there were lots of compliments about the inclusivity and care expressed in my work.

Listen to: 9 to 5 by Dolly Parton

Within a fortnight of being hired, my American colleague suddenly disappeared. The Expert explained to me that the role wasn't right for her, but then The Expert wrote a huge post on her public social media page about how someone had criticised her for celebrating her six-bedroom house, stating that it could be seen as insensitive to women who were struggling to live comfortably after abuse. The Expert managed to twist their viewpoint into them being jealous of her success. It was clearly aimed at my former colleague.

Because my colleague had left just before Christmas, I was on my own to handle the holiday season. I was working with over 30,000 women globally across all groups, all of whom were triggered by perpetrators of abuse, with many in dangerous situations, in every time zone. Christmas is a time when domestic abuse tends to escalate, and my Christmas was spent constantly focused on my phone. I had to work for hours because if I didn't, people might not receive the necessary guidance on how to stay safe, be heard, or get the help they needed. I hadn't been in the job for very long, and I wanted The Expert to know that I was worth her investment.

By January, a new colleague had been hired to work alongside me. Changes were being made in the way we ran the groups, and I was tasked with leading these changes. In the subscription service, I had to provide daily self-care posts with mindfulness activities or discussions based on a monthly theme. In the main group, my responsibility was to entice people to join the next free bootcamp. Although my colleague had no social media experience, they knew The Expert personally, and I felt like I carried a heavy load during the first month of our work together. We were also given affiliate links to provide to people in the comment sections, to promote The Expert's healing programmes. The more people purchased the programmes through our links, the greater the chance we had of earning a bonus. The programmes and services ranged from £50 to £350, with private 1:1 therapy costing up to £9,000. Both my colleague and I were expected to sell at least forty £350 healing programmes each.

Privately, I wasn't happy about this. I didn't apply to be a salesperson; I applied to be a social media manager and gain experience working with women who lived with abuse. However, the job came with significant perks, so I decided to continue. There was talk of spa days, retreats, and pay rises. Additionally, I could work during school hours. But it wasn't as flexible as I had imagined; my entire day revolved around work, leaving me unable to relax or switch off. I would spend hours in the evening working instead of doing household chores, watching TV, socialising, or even sleeping. I had less time to spend with my daughter, often relying on Netflix to keep her occupied while I retreated to my room to work. And just when I thought I could sign off for the day, someone would write something that required urgent attention.

The free bootcamp was hectic. I had a new group to manage with 2,000 women, and I also had to respond to comments in the Zoom Lives with a constant stream of feedback. I was instructed to focus on the paid group since they were paying for the service. However, if I took my attention off the larger, free group, I was criticised for not selling enough programmes or addressing enough member requests. The job started to feel impossible, and after four months without a single day off, I began experiencing burnout. I was not the favoured one anymore, despite The Expert initially praising me. My new colleague, who excelled at selling programmes, received all the credit and recognition. I liked my colleague, so I didn't mind, but I started to fear that my job was in jeopardy if I didn't generate enough revenue for The Expert.

Listen to: She Works Hard For The Money by Donna Summer

I held the fort for a week while she went on a business trip to LA. When she returned, she had bigger ideas and told me that if I didn't sell enough programmes, she couldn't afford to keep me in my job. She also started advertising a programme for people to learn how to become a narcissistic abuse expert and work with her.

It all felt very... pyramid scheme-like to me. Suddenly, her kind and friendly persona turned cold, and she began avoiding my messages and dismissing my ideas in meetings. I had feedback based on my own observations and from the members themselves, which I believed would be beneficial for The Expert to hear to improve her brand. Specifically, I mentioned that the groups felt exclusionary, catering only to feminine women and not being inclusive of those who didn't identify as "ladies," or those from queer, non-binary, or gender-fluid communities. However, The Expert completely ignored my feedback - she didn't even respond to it.

After a few months, I realised I was going to lose my job. She sacked one of the social media managers and increased the pressure on us to sell her programmes. She insisted that every comment I left on every post must include my affiliate link. Many members expressed their frustration, feeling like they were being sold a product rather than receiving support, and secretly, I felt the same way. I communicated this to The Expert, but she sent me audios and videos explaining how to sell and gaslit me into believing that it wasn't about profiting from selling a product, but about helping people. She used analogies like comparing it to a hospital, where if you're in desperate need of a doctor, you would pay privately for the best available doctor, not the one with a waiting list who is free. This analogy helped me see how detached from reality she was.

I started to question her actual qualifications and credentials in the field of domestic abuse and therapy. With my completion of Level 2 counselling skills and online courses on domestic abuse, I had some knowledge about ethical frameworks and the importance of governing bodies. I felt that the way The Expert was working with the women didn't prioritise their safety. It seemed like she was exploiting their vulnerability to gain money from their 'victimhood', rather than considering their safety, physical well-being, or financial welfare.

I explained to The Expert that I was concerned. Some of the women I was responding to hadn't even left their abusive partners yet and were in situations where their lives were at risk due to financial and physical abuse. Their immediate priority was to find safety, and they didn't have the means to pay hundreds for a healing programme. However, The Expert maintained that purchasing the programme would be the best option for them. I argued that many women who have just left an abusive situation have limited or no funds and simply need to focus on literal survival before committing to a 12-week programme. She insisted that they would still benefit from the programme, saying, "If they want to heal, they will sign up for it."

It didn't surprise me when my friend realised where she recognised my boss from - a global product that is famously known as a pyramid scheme. My boss had earned a significant amount of money building her business and had given motivational speeches to representatives of the product, one of which my friend had attended. I watched the video of her speech on YouTube and heard all the same phrases, ideas, and terminologies that she'd used to get me to sell. It's one thing to sell a product that enhances someone's appearance and allegedly their wellbeing, but it's another thing to sell products to people whose lives might be at risk because of it.

At this point, I knew I had to get out of this industry because that's exactly what it is - an industry. Part of my job also involved monitoring my boss's equally successful competitors and informing her of what they were posting. For example, if the American clinical psychologist Dr. Ramani had shared something, I would give The Expert the heads up, and within hours, my boss would post her own version of it. I noticed other experts copying my boss as well. They were all competing against each other because, in the end, it was business, and there was money to be made from targeting vulnerable people.

The narcissistic abuse industry thrives on vulnerable individuals believing that they bear partial responsibility for the abuse they live with, as if they attracted the narcissist into their lives. It is true that people with trauma can sometimes attract others with trauma, like Ethan and me who were drawn together by our co-dependency and need for validation. However, while narcissistic abuse experts may claim that "it's not your fault," they simultaneously promote expensive healing processes, suggesting that the victims' wounds are the cause of the perpetrator targeting them. This contradictory approach is, in fact, victim-blaming. The Expert may say, "Narcissistic abuse didn't happen because of you, it happened to you," but then insinuate that the victims' own trauma and vulnerabilities are what attract narcissists and abusers. This implies that narcissistic abuse did occur because of the victim's past trauma.

The narrative promoted by narcissistic abuse experts through healing programmes suggests that victim-survivors of abuse are 'broken souls', falling into predatory traps. It is true that an abuser identifies your vulnerabilities and insecurities and exploits them to manipulate and harm you. But that's not your fault. They choose you as their target because you possess qualities or traits, they desire for themselves. They see the goodness in you and seek to reflect it onto themselves, to their benefit. Anyone can fall victim to this insidious crime. A person whose privacy is violated by having their home broken into and possessions stolen, simply because the thief wanted those things, is not blamed for the burglar's behaviour due to their own childhood trauma. So why are victim-survivors of abuse told that their early trauma has somehow attracted a person who is committing a crime against them?

It's essential to recognise that a healing programme alone cannot magically fix you. The Expert conveys the message that the only path to healing from abuse is through self-healing after accepting the abuse that happened to you, to move forward. However, I don't believe finding acceptance in what happened is necessary. I believe we should allow ourselves to feel as angry as we like for as long as we like, even if that's forever. I can accept an accidental car crash that gave me trauma happened and move forward. Still, I will not accept nearly being murdered and moving forward from that by healing my childhood wounds. We can heal from different traumas in parallel and in different ways.

Listen to: Money Game, Pt. 2 by Ren

Regrettably, this issue is not limited to narcissistic abuse experts alone. It permeates the broader health and well-being sector. Many coaches and self-proclaimed "experts" manipulate individuals by capitalising on their vulnerabilities and blaming them for their past lived experiences. This phenomenon is observable across various domains, including the manosphere, weight loss "health coaches," and even among 'fashion' or 'mummy' blogger-style influencers who have a target to meet. Determining whom to trust becomes a challenging task.

The healing programme and The Expert did not change my life. It was the use of therapy tools and learning about trauma, along with counselling theories, that truly transformed my life. We must take control of our own healing, which includes researching the therapy methods, types of well-being practices, or healing exercises we engage in, as well as the credentials and qualifications of the facilitators, and the ethical guidelines and governing bodies they follow. I became aware of a situation where a qualified educator I know was recommended a 'narcissistic abuse expert' to appear on her podcast. During the pre-episode briefing, it became apparent that this 'expert' claimed to be a "Dr." based on her studies in classical history, rather than psychology or mental health, for instance. She positioned herself as an expert solely due to her personal experience in an abusive relationship, without having chosen to study and specialise in the field. These are the kinds of experts who amass thousands or millions of followers on social media and earn substantial amounts of money.

Abuse can take on various forms, and although it may seem like every abuser is following the same handbook, our individual responses to abuse and the dynamics of our living environments make each case unique. If we choose to engage in a programme, it should be with a counsellor or therapist who can customise the programme specifically for us, rather than following a generic approach. Many of these programmes are unethical, lacking conclusive evidence that they work, and often copied from other questionable 'experts', or regular therapy tools, dressed up as pioneering techniques developed specifically for healing from abuse. Don't buy a 12-step programme from a Narcissistic Abuse Expert - just get a subscription to one of the many therapy resources sites that offer templates of the programmes for less money. Even better – go to 1:1 therapy with a person who can prove they are qualified to support you in a person-centred way.

Chapter Sixteen -
A Plague Upon Both Your Houses

'The London Metropolitan Police Service received a total of 41,158 calls-for-service for domestic incidents between 25 March (following the lockdown restrictions imposed on 23 March) and 10 June 2020. This is a 12% increase compared with 36,727 calls over the same period in the previous year.'

Office for National Statistics (ONS). (2020). "Domestic abuse during the coronavirus (COVID-19) pandemic, England and Wales."

Healing from domestic abuse isn't linear. One moment you're on an upward trajectory and feel like you'll never be fooled by the perpetrator again. The next, you find yourself breaking 'No Contact' and meeting them for a picnic at the park. That's how my healing process started, anyway.

After a few months of being with what felt like half the town's coked-up rugby team, who surely had some kind of bet to see how many of them I would sleep with in my frequently intoxicated state, something unexpected happened. While I was resuming daily contact with Ethan despite the non-molestation order in place, receiving emerald rings, and driving around the countryside after he'd finished work every other evening, that virus in China didn't seem to be disappearing. In fact, around the time of my thirtieth birthday, one or two people in the UK had managed to contract it. But there were always scares like this – I remembered SARS, MERS… even Mumps had had an outbreak. But this one in the news was starting to get scary. Someone died. Then another. And more people were contracting it. Then more. And lots of people said, 'it's an overreaction.' And lots of people said, 'it's a conspiracy.' But one thing was certain – people were getting unwell. Some people were dying.

In March 2020, I had a chest infection, and my asthma was badly impacted. I was advised by my doctor to 'self-isolate' until I recovered. This felt extremely precautionary, but I did as I was told to a certain extent. I continued to go out, but I avoided the shops and pubs. My daughter and I continued to meet her father, and he continued to profess his undying love for me, begging me to move back in with him. And then, there was a big announcement from the Prime Minister. All pubs were to shut for the foreseeable future. What on earth? I was watching Boris Johnson bumbling through a surreal speech, with my mum at the time, and a friend had invited me out. Mum said, 'I'll babysit. You go out... you don't know when you'll get to go again...'. I wasn't feeling well, but that wasn't going to stop me getting a pint.

Listen to: Wait a Minute! By WILLOW

The pubs were packed. Nobody understood what was happening. We all knew we might not see each other for a while, and the landlords needed to sell all their stock. At the local shithole, the beer was cheap, and everyone got as drunk as if it was Christmas or New Year's Eve. Before 10 pm, when the pubs were closing, punters had their arms around each other, swaying and singing 'we'll meet again,' as if we were all heading into World War Three. Police cars were outside, ensuring the pubs were closing at the time the government ordered. It was bizarre.

Within days, the restrictions got tighter. And then, the UK was in complete 'lockdown.' It was eerie, alien, and frightening. Everyone was terrified of catching Coronavirus, or 'Covid-19' as we were learning to call it, and when people we knew got it, we worried for them. The restrictions felt harsh. Schools and preschools were open to children whose parents or carers were 'key workers,' which included me because I worked at a nursing home. My parents, who were also on the frontline as nurses, were working in full-body suits, and my retired aunt returned to nursing to care for Covid patients in segregated wards. It took a while to persuade my boss to allow me to work because I received a letter from my GP saying that, due to the severity of my asthma, I was classified as 'vulnerable' to the virus. I had to sign something to confirm I understood the risks, which I worried about; what if I did die? What would happen to my little girl? After a few weeks, my daughter returned to preschool, where she was spoiled with a ratio of 3 preschool staff to just 4 attending children. This part of my story is not going to be about my overall experience of living through Covid-19;

otherwise, I'd be detailing all the general challenges, government fuck-ups, and world spread vulnerability of the global pandemic. What I want to highlight is how the pandemic affected me as someone living with post-separation abuse.

Post-separation abuse is not talked about enough. Statistically, we know that out of the recorded deaths caused by perpetrators of abuse, a large percentage of the victims are people who have already left the relationship. Leaving the abusive relationship is rarely the end of living with abuse. Ethan, who was furloughed, had all the time in the world on his hands, and he wanted to spend it with me. Fortunately, we were practicing social distancing and were in a 'bubble' with my parents, with whom we lived. The rules stated that co-parenting families were allowed to be in an extended bubble with one another. And while Ethan and I didn't co-parent, we bent this rule for our situation. Government guidelines stated one walk a day, but it was only advice from a government official that a walk should be 'about a mile' or 'about an hour' long. The world was hostile, and anyone walking longer than an hour or for more than a mile faced criticism from angry and hurting people who missed their families, were thrown into unexpected poverty and unemployment, and were losing loved ones. I kept the length of our walks secret for this reason, but for about three months during the first UK Covid-19 lockdown, Ethan, our daughter, and I saw each other nearly every day. We'd walk for miles, with a picnic, down paths no one had ever thought to tread, paddle in streams and trudge over deserted fields and forests. The weather was warm and sunny that spring and early summer, and I remember that I was taking beautiful pictures and uploading them to social media. But no one could possibly know the proximity we were sharing with Ethan or how this time spent with each other was going. He was obsessed with winning me back. He felt that we should all be living together during the lockdown and working on our relationship. He'd changed, he said. He knew what he had lost, and I was the love of his life. He'd only ever loved me like this. Let's get married. Let's have another baby. Please, let's have another baby. And I was tempted to return.

Listen to: All That She Wants by Ace of Base

I wanted another baby. I wanted a family of four. I wanted the three-bedroom house he said he was still living in. I wanted the happy family profile picture on my Facebook. I wanted the annual anniversary post, where I'd write about how lucky I was to be married to my soulmate. I wanted the family and the relationship I had genuinely believed in and thought we would grow old together in. But I knew. I knew that none of this was possible because I knew he couldn't change. To change, he had to show accountability – and he didn't. When it came to it, we'd end up arguing. I'd say, 'Give me space. Stop talking about our relationship and us getting back together. Just show me you're different, that you've grown, that you'll be a better person.' But he would always, always bring up that 'if I hadn't made that police statement,' or 'if I hadn't applied for a non-molestation order,' both of which he considered unnecessary, we wouldn't be in this predicament.

If I knew that Ethan would never change, than why was I unable to stop speaking to him and seeing him? That was a question that I couldn't understand fully, and I felt deeply ashamed and embarrassed at my 'weakness' of being unable to cut contact with someone who had literally pleaded guilty to beating me up. I knew that I could call Women's Aid. I knew that I could phone the national domestic abuse helpline. I knew that I could message my sister, or get in touch with my IDSVA, but all the things I KNEW I could do, felt too difficult. I had lived and breathed for the existence of this man to validate me. I had put trust into this man for the whole of my twenties. He wasn't the only person who had lived off the energy I provided him – I had been living for the intermittent pieces of affection from him.

Due to the non-molestation order in place and Ethan repeatedly turning up at my parents' house at the start of the year while I was obtaining the order, the local authority had classified me as a 'managed move.' This meant I was eligible for emergency housing. The pandemic slowed down this process, but during the first lockdown, I received amazing news: after being a private renter for all my adult life and having dealt with countless exploitative and uncooperative landlords, I was offered social housing. It was a two-bedroom flat in my hometown. I was over the moon. The only problem was that it was ridiculously close to where Ethan was living in our former family home.

By this point, our arguments were increasing, and during a walk in a secluded forest full of fir trees, I genuinely thought Ethan was going to kill us when he took out the knife he always carried and berated me for getting him a criminal record. I imagined, and knew he was capable of him stabbing both my daughter and I, digging a hole in the woods and leaving us to rot in a place no one would ever have thought to look. I decided to contact the police, who arrested him for breaking the non-molestation order. I believe he received a warning, but everyone was short-staffed because of COVID-19, so I never found out the details. I didn't tell them about the knife, but I did admit that we had been meeting up over lockdown. This didn't stop Ethan from contacting me, but it gave me the chance to have some breathing space as I felt smothered by his constant pleas to be a couple again. He'd been warned to stay away.

During August and September that year, I worked hard on decorating my new flat as restrictions around us began to ease. I felt proud of how lovely our flat looked. The main problem was that, since my daughter and I had to literally flee our home, we didn't have any of our furniture, and we still had barely any of my daughter's toys, books, or clothes, nearly a year later. The local community rallied around to help me, and at least three or four charities assisted me in finding furniture. An old friend generously gave me a sofa for free, and my aunt bought me my own fridge. I felt so loved and supported.

Listen to: I will Survive by Gloria Gaynor

During the pandemic, churches had been closed, which had a detrimental impact on my mental health. Towards the end of my relationship with Ethan and at the beginning of the post-separation abuse, the church had been a safe place that didn't judge me but supported me. They prayed for me and surrounded me with positivity, giving me hope and a sense of not being alone. However, services had shifted to Zoom, and it wasn't the same, no matter how much we tried to embrace the changes. I truly believe that if I had been able to physically attend church during this time and not been cut off from the community in a physical sense, I might have had more resolve.

My local council helped me get an oven, and my parents bought me carpets. Honestly, it felt like a wonderful fresh start of independence that I had never experienced before. This was my first place that was truly mine, one that I could decorate without having to share with a partner. I was excited and enthusiastic, and the communal garden had a washing line, stream, and plenty of space for my daughter to run around in. It should have been a home we stayed in for a considerable amount of time, but it only lasted five months. Being so close to our former family home where Ethan lived, and myself initiating contact again because I missed him, Ethan soon found out where we had moved to. I found it hard to resist saying, "come over," and he did. I was strict about him not staying but said he could bring us some much-needed essential shopping that we desperately needed – we were living off food vouchers and Mum's left-over cooking. However, this turned out to be a huge mistake, and proved to be the time that I needed support the most. At this point, I had resigned to the fact that I would always be addicted to Ethan and unable to live without him, despite my new, fluffy grey carpets, navy blue walls, boho tapestries and ability to starfish in my own bed.

I was living without the safety of another adult, although not far from my parents. I was vulnerable, even though I had GPS alarms around my home connected to the local police station, which I could activate with a panic button at any time. I didn't use them. Ethan started coming and going as he pleased, with his usual perceived entitlement to bulldoze my boundaries. His constant putting pressure on me to take him back quickly began to feel smothering and I stopped letting him into my flat. It was clear he was trying to move in with me – after all, the rent was cheap. I asked him for our furniture, toys, and clothes, but initially, he refused. Eventually, he began bringing random bits over and leaving them outside the front door. He did it slowly, probably as an excuse to visit our flat more often.

Around this time, I received a message from the landlords of our old house. They wanted to know what to do with the property Ethan and I had seemingly 'abandoned.' Abandoned? I was confused.

Ethan was still living there, wasn't he? I wasn't naive - I suspected that Ethan might be inviting other women there. In fact, I had done some detective work and created an account on the swinging site he'd signed us up for. I discovered that he had removed me from it and was operating as a single man, where he had 'verified' encounters with women. This is where they described meeting him and going to his home, including details of how kinky their sex had been, and how he was 'safe' to be around. I also saw on the forum that he was asking, 'how do I remove public verifications?' Clearly, he knew I'd do some snooping. But according to the landlords, Ethan hadn't lived there for months, almost a year. He was never there. The home had been left to gather dust, and the Christmas decorations were still up from when I'd gone round and put up the Christmas trees. When I confronted Ethan about this on the phone, he denied having abandoned the property, but I was inclined to believe the pissed off landlords.

Listen to: Buzzkill by MOTHICA

And then, things took a wilder turn. After the landlords complained, Ethan evidently decided to move out of the property permanently, to wherever he had been living, and began transferring all the contents of the large 3-bedroom house to my small two-bedroom flat. Over the course of a week, he continuously dumped EVERYTHING outside my front door. It wasn't just books, toys, clothes, or personal possessions I hadn't seen in nearly a year; it was also broken items, things meant for the dump, spoiled food, a cot our daughter had never used and had long outgrown, opened bags of flour, faulty fans, his DVDs, and even a pair of women's sunglasses that didn't belong to me and I had never seen before. More and more items kept appearing. I lived on the first floor, and the pile of stuff was spilling over to my less-than-pleased neighbour's front door. I'd asked for my jewellery boxes and antique books back, and for our daughter's teddy bears, Barbies and ball pit. I hadn't asked for a truck load of junk.

By this point, I had to block Ethan's number due to the numerous daily calls and messages I received. They ranged from professions of his undying love to furious rants about my decision to leave him. As more and more items continued to appear outside my front door – things I neither needed nor owned – it became evident that he had been picking them up from online marketplaces and freebie sites, presumably with the intent to annoy me. It was unquestionably time to activate the alarms.

The police responded swiftly, issuing a warrant for his arrest due to his violation of the non-molestation order. I was honest, and with shame, explained that I had allowed this contact to happen. Katia, who I had distanced myself from during the earlier part of the pandemic, resumed her support. Child services became involved again. I was told, under no uncertain terms, to vacate my flat until Ethan was arrested, as he was displaying signs of obsessive behaviour and harassment. However, despite all this, the situation continued to escalate. I began to receive a ceaseless stream of deliveries at my front door – pizza, baguettes, fish and chips – all piling up in my tiny kitchen. At one point, while a policeman was taking my statement, his stomach audibly rumbled with hunger. I politely asked if he'd like any of the six different pizzas in my kitchen. They were still edible. Everyone laughed.

The harassment continued. The social media accounts sprung up several times a day. Ethan would use names that I'd recognise as him and send messages begging me to unblock his phone number on WhatsApp so we could talk. I handed my phone over to the police. At one point, he filmed himself outside my home in the dark and added it to his social media stories. The messages became insistent, and I started to want to remove myself from the area altogether. I began looking at homes in Scotland to run away too.

Listen to: Asking For It by Hole

And then I unblocked him. I felt like there was no point in fighting him off. I felt like I was constantly holding up a huge wall to guard myself and he was battering down my defences. And this felt harder than BEING in the relationship. It was far less exhausting putting up with the abuse when living with him. And I allowed him to come over, because he said we could go out somewhere nice, and framed it that he was desperate to see our little girl. And besides, she was missing him awfully, having not seen him for weeks. And so, he came over.

MUG: An Account of Domestic Abuse

And he raped me.

Chapter Seventeen - Rape

'One in Two Rapes against women are carried out by their partner or ex-partner.'

Rape Crisis. (n.d.). "Statistics: Sexual Violence."

My first, personal knowledge of rape was that it was violent. Before that, as a teenager, I had believed that it was always obvious if you've been raped. That you'd sit crying and washing yourself in the shower afterwards, like in films, because you would instantly know what has happened to you. But like many, many other women, I have been raped and assaulted numerous times and can't always pinpoint exactly when. In the relationship with Ethan, I spent a lot of it in a numb, dissociated state and therefore, incidents and occasions of escalated abuse are merged into one big fucked up mess. But because I wasn't living with Ethan at the time, and because I had been actively putting up boundaries, I remember this attack in what feels like a cinematic reel. I remember that from the moment he stepped inside, with bags of food for our daughter, he was pressuring me to have sex with him. Infact, he'd suggested that I just 'stand at the front door, bend over, and he'd fuck me and go'. I kept saying no. I kept saying our daughter was present. He made sure she was watching telly – Cbeebies, to be exact. I went to the bathroom to go to the toilet. He followed me. He shut the door and bent me over. I was facing the mirror. I didn't put up a fight. I knew there was no getting away from it. I knew it would be over quickly. So, he raped me, and while he raped me, our daughter called out for us more than once, and he said in a caring voice to her while he raped me, 'mummy and daddy are just doing something, we'll be there in a moment baby!'.

Afterwards, I pulled up my leggings and the three of us went out for a trip in the car. We went for an autumnal stroll along an abandoned railway line in the middle of a rural village, and I knew that the only way to get through the day was to sweetly smile, laugh and pretend I was having a pleasant time. Appease him. Fawn.

I got home and I don't remember when I called the police – if it was that night, or the next morning. But I did contact two friends from church, who encouraged me to report him.

The next morning, my friend Rebecca took my daughter to her house and the police came and took statements from me. Then an inspector came round to discuss what was going to happen next. They talked to me about crown courts, and prosecutions, and that I'd need to make more statements, and video statements, and how it was decided if something went to court or not. I distinctly remember the inspector telling me that often, it was a victim's word against the perpetrator, and therefore cases would only go ahead to a crown court if there was enough sufficient evidence. That meant that the case would have a high chance of not even going to court. I was also told that if the case *did* go to crown court, that it could take up to two years for that to go ahead. The information I was given from the authorities was a lot to take in, but that was far from the end of the ordeal.

I had to give away the clothes I was wearing in secure bags that I had seen forensic teams use in murder dramas on telly. I gave them my knickers, stained with the traces of substance that had also created something so beautiful – my daughter. I gave them my leggings and even my favourite cardigan. Even worse, I had to give away the toys my daughter had of which he'd left fingerprints on. Light switches, walls and door handles were brushed with swabs, while I provided saliva, and peed in a pot. The bathroom door was closed off with police tape; my own home was a crime scene. It wasn't just my home. Later, my body had to be forensically examined and tested, too. It was one of the most traumatic, awful things I have ever gone through – it felt like being raped all over again. In fact, for me, it felt more intrusive and violating. And this is why I know that people who are charged with rape, are rapists. Because not one person would make up rape for fun, attention, money or revenge, and go through with the investigation. The degradation to your body and dignity during the reporting process makes sure of that.

Listen to: Me and My Gun by Tori Amos

It was only the two friends from church who knew what had happened. Other friends were aware a 'sexual assault' had taken place, with no further details. I knew what had happened was so terrible, I didn't want to burden any loved ones with the knowledge. What's more, I knew that going through with the process would prolong the trauma. With that in mind, I decided not to press charges. This is how I know that people who drop charges of rape are not dropping charges because it didn't happen to them – they're dropping the case because it's utterly horrific to continue with it under the present justice system. I kept the rape secret.

Ethan was still in trouble for breaking the non-molestation order, even though I dropped charges. However, the police couldn't locate him, as he wasn't living at the house we'd once rented together anymore. A warrant was again out for his arrest. I was not allowed to leave my flat. My parents were on holiday, and I needed food shopping. Friends had to help me out with food and my anxiety levels were high. The noise of the GPS alarms was horribly loud, and I dreaded having to press them. I began keeping my curtains closed and my daughter and I lived in the dark for a few days that September.

Eventually, the police arrested Ethan while he was at work. I wasn't to see or speak to him for almost three months – finally, I had 'No Contact', and space to overcome my addiction to this violent, manipulative abuser.

There are things that I wish had happened differently in terms of the support – or lack of support - I received. I was given information on crisis centres to call, but I didn't have the energy to look for counselling. Looking back, it would have been good if someone could have been physically present to hold my hand and phoned a rape crisis helpline with me. I of course had my IDSVA, Katia, but she could only do phone appointments since we were still living in a global pandemic. I was checked for STI's and was free from any infections. And while I felt that I could finally stop being numb and was safe to cry, to scream, to rage (as I did), I was also taken aback by a familiar feeling of longing. A longing for Ethan. This man had nearly killed me on more than one occasion. He had put me in continuous danger every day.

He had lied to me, manipulated me, gaslit me, verbally insulted me, controlled me, raped me. How? HOW did I miss him? I had to be a lost cause. I had to be deranged. There was something wrong with me, surely?

Thank God for Katia, and our social worker, and The Freedom Programme, and for all the women who I interacted with on support forums. Thank God for the church, for the friends trained in counselling and domestic abuse who came my way, and for the ability to be curious and learn. This was around the time that I began seriously researching abuse. I had to understand why this has happened to me, and I had to understand why I felt the way I did; why the rational part of my brain and the emotional part of my brain were at war with each other. I couldn't go on as I was anymore, it wasn't fair on me, and it wasn't fair on my daughter. I was ready, really ready, to heal.

Chapter Eighteen - As We Forgive Those Who Sin Against Us

'The number of non-molestation applications increased by 3.0% in the year ending March 2023 (30,979) from 30,088 in the year ending March 2022; the highest number of applications since our records began in the year ending March 2010.'

Office for National Statistics (ONS). 2023

Going Sober
In December of that year, after weeks of no contact, I went to court again. I successfully obtained a restraining order against my child's father. I felt a myriad of emotions, but mostly, I felt sadness, loss, and grief. I needed to process these feelings – and it was during this time that I had been participating in the online healing programme ran by The Expert. While I strongly oppose the financial exploitation of vulnerable people through the monetisation of the abuse that they have lived with by

unethically practicing 'experts', I do acknowledge that the therapeutic tools introduced to me in the programme played a role in my ability to maintain 'No Contact' and follow through with the court proceedings. This was something the police, Katia, and, most importantly, child services had encouraged me to do. Even though I understood they were right, and that my daughter's and my own safety were at risk, I still missed and loved Ethan. It felt like I was going through withdrawal, both physically and mentally. Physically, I was often getting hot flushes, fidgeting and feeling restless. I was irritable. I had huge mood swings and was generally unpleasant to be around because of my foul temper. I was grappling with the pain and mourning the loss of the life I had desperately wished for but could never seem to achieve. I was also battling profound feelings of guilt and sympathy – not only toward Ethan but also toward our daughter. She deserved to have the 'ideal family' – two parents in a stable relationship, siblings, a secure home, the life that our society encourages us to aspire to. She didn't deserve any of this trauma. But, before I could learn that I didn't deserve it either, I went through a period of reflection about the person responsible for all this abuse. To become the person he is and project his pain onto me and our child, he must have suffered unimaginably at some point in his life. I already knew about his childhood, but I began to slowly uncover more pieces of the puzzle, which made me see Ethan not as a perpetrator of abuse, but as a helpless child. While this perspective can be a useful tool for people living with Complex Post-Traumatic Stress Disorder (C-PTSD) when trying to understand family members who have harmed them, especially during their childhood, it is not always helpful when it comes to understanding the perpetrator of the abuse you have suffered through. This is what The Expert encouraged me to do, and, as someone studying counselling, I later realised that she was not trained in the fundamentals of ethical practise. There were approximately two hundred women participating in the healing programme, and all of us were persuaded to forgive the perpetrator of the abuse we had lived with, by considering them as helpless children.

Listen to: Revenge by Patti Smith

It took a considerable amount of time for me to undo this damage. It required further therapy from qualified professionals to understand that forgiveness isn't a priority in the healing process when you've been nearly murdered repeatedly and raped. It took extensive research, reading, and listening, as I became obsessed with absorbing insights from different trauma experts, ranging from Gabor Mate to Brene Brown, from Van Der Kolk, Judith Herman, and Stephen Borges to Deb Dana. All of this helped me realise that I could acknowledge that the perpetrator of the abuse I have lived with had an unfair and difficult childhood AND that I didn't have to forgive him for continuously violating me.

I'm certain The Expert would respond with, "I'm sorry that you've misinterpreted my lessons," because she excels at gaslighting – yes, the person who taught me exactly what gaslighting is has masterfully gaslit me on multiple occasions. When I began working for her, she attempted to gaslight me into thinking I had agreed to take on a job I hadn't, she gaslit me into believing I was doing the right thing by selling her programme pyramid scheme-style, and she gaslit me into thinking that the abuse was my fault, suggesting that because of 'the hole in my soul,' I had attracted the narcissist into my life.

The Expert, like her competitors, employs excellent tools and methods from various therapeutic theories, but she misuses them due to a lack of training in the fundamental principles of basic counselling skills. At the time of writing, in the UK, anyone can refer to themselves as a therapist as there is no official regulation. While it's recommended to work under the guidance of a professional association such as The British Association for Counselling and Psychotherapy (BACP), it's not legally required. In this way, The Expert falls into the same category as misogynistic influencers and grifters, such as Andrew Tate. These 'businessmen', who rely on social media and capitalism to profit from their influence, also claim to provide a type of programme to men and young boys that revolves around enrolling in pyramid scheme-style plans, grooming consumers into spending substantial sums of money and believing in their harmful narrative, all to keep influenced people subscribed to the agenda that will pay them well. This is how cult leaders have always operated. While it may seem extreme to suggest that narcissistic abuse experts are on par with dangerous misogynists and prolific cult leaders, the availability of internet access and social media has expanded the reach of individuals seeking to amass followings that place them on a pedestal. Their goal is not only to attain external validation but also to achieve financial and economic success. While some aspects of their narrative can be helpful, their primary goal is to have you pay them and keep you engaged. This requires grooming and manipulation and a sense of 'community' to ensure you maintain your belief in and do not unsubscribe to their relentless narrative.

I was drawn into The Expert's agenda and like a clever politician, some parts of it were helpful and true. I couldn't initially see that it was the therapy tools introduced by The Expert, rather than their mismanagement, that helped me gather the strength to obtain a restraining order.

It no longer surprises me to find connections between questionably qualified 'trauma experts,' 'narcissistic abuse experts,' or 'dating coaches,' and misogynists like Tate. Domestic abuse thrives on misogyny, and this holds true not only in heterosexual relationships. Misogyny is deeply ingrained in all of us due to the patriarchal society we are a part of.

The mention of the Patriarchy in this book was inevitable. I firmly believe that in the absence of a patriarchal society, the number of people suffering abuse at the hands of men would be significantly lower. Debating whether domestic abuse is a male-dominated crime is unproductive – I never deny the abuse perpetrated by anyone who isn't male. However, statistics, particularly those concerning the number of deaths caused by abusive men, offer enough evidence that domestic abuse, rape, and other violent assaults predominantly involve male perpetrators. I continue to refer to misogyny and the patriarchy throughout my story, as learning about its prevalence in the world is a large part of my healing journey. This is why I decided to present you with statistics that are relevant to the time of writing this book, as well as resources for further information, found at the back pages. I will also signpost you to books and podcasts that can help you understand the harmful impact online influencers are having on the world, especially on our young people, and how this impact contributes to domestic abuse.

Forgiveness

How do you forgive someone who has committed the most heinous acts against you? And should you even consider it? According to The Expert and her contemporaries, forgiveness is the path to healing from trauma.

But hold on a second.

Dr. Jessica Taylor, a feminist psychologist known for her controversial belief in Anti-pathology, tackles this very issue in her book, 'Sexy but Psycho.' Dr. Taylor dives into the societal pressure on women and girls to forgive their abusers.

I couldn't agree more now. However, during the period when I was financially invested in a monthly subscription service that provided access to a programme aimed at helping me, I genuinely wanted to believe and reap the benefits from everything I was being taught. Consequently, I actively sought to find forgiveness towards Ethan for his lies, cheating, and the mental, physical, and violent violations he subjected me to. This compulsion was further reinforced by another important part of my healing – Christianity. It wasn't solely The Expert convincing me that forgiveness towards the person who had hurt me was necessary.

Listen to: You Got The Love by Candi Straton

Throughout my childhood, my education in Church of England schools, and my subsequent exploration of the Christian faith as an adult, I was consistently taught that forgiveness, the act of letting go, would liberate me from the weight of holding onto grudges.

Finding Faith

During the time I spent living with Ethan, my local church provided me with refuge, away from his rage, his taunts, his silent treatment. I was fortunate to have a welcoming and non-judgmental vicar who offered support. Reverend William and his wife, Mariah, were indispensable to both my daughter and me during the initial years of her life. I want to clarify that this isn't meant to be a narrative that imposes religion on anyone, but it's important to note that Christianity has played a significant role not only in my journey of healing but also in my very survival.

I began attending church when my daughter was a few months old. Much to Ethan's disinterest, I had organised a Christening for her. It was important to me to have her baptised, because falling pregnant with her felt like such a miracle. She had been conceived just days after I had desperately prayed to God, in the side chapel of a cathedral, to give me something to live for. I had just attempted to end my life through the sheer misery of Ethan's emotional discard, while I had been living in the bedsit. I distinctly remember asking, 'if there's anything, any God who can hear me right now, please, please give me something to live for.' Whether you believe in God, Allah, The Universe, Mother Nature, Fate, The Law of Attraction... or just the power of the coincidence - whoever and whatever you believe in, I got pregnant. And if God gave me my baby, my something-to-live-for – I wanted to thank him.

Rev. William came over after a bike ride, not in his traditional dog collar, but his presence and authority was instant. Ethan and I was living at my parents at the time, and our baby was rolling across the floor, the happiest, loveliest baby. It was so nice. We were a family. We talked about how long we had been together. We lied and said we were both divorced (neither of us were yet). Ethan looked at me fondly – the only time he ever looked fondly at me anymore was when he was in front of other people, like he had looked at me back when our relationship was new and exciting and fun. And he said how he loved me. How worried he'd been, thinking our daughter or I might die during what was a traumatic birth. What we meant to him. How we were going to get married eventually, but there was no rush – we were as much as married. How I had changed my surname to match his and our daughter's via deed poll... it was everything I could have wanted. And so, a few weeks later, Ethan and I hosted a christening for our baby girl. It was the first time both our families had come together, and we made a huge fuss. There was a mixture of buffet food – vegan and non-vegan, hot and cold, which lots of people had contributed to. My sister and I had been collecting decorations for months and we made the local memorial hall look amazing – even if I did borrow some of my wedding day decorations... and Ethan's brothers and sisters hadn't been in the same room together for a long time. There we all were—a big, happy, extended family. For a long time afterward, I considered it the best day of my life. I truly believed that Ethan and I would be together forever, and that as we aged, things would only get better.

After the Christening, Rev. William invited me to join the parish emailing circle, keeping me informed about family-focused events in the local community. I gladly agreed, and soon I found myself included in warm, friendly emails that extended invitations to toddler groups, family orientated, informal church services, and provided guidance to support hubs.

The first time I took my child to a service, she was around seven or eight months old, and we attended our first 'Messy Church.' The premise of Messy Church is to create a fun and inclusive environment for all people, with a focus on families, whether they are religious or not. While the church's goal is to bring more people to God and engage younger individuals and children in their congregations, fundamentally, in my opinion, it's a positive thing.

Our local church consistently offers free breakfast in a safe environment, contrary to popular belief, providing non-judgmental support. My aunt once described the church as a hospital for broken people, and I find that to be true. Throughout my time attending our local church, I have never felt judged, coerced, pressured, or had Christianity 'shoved down my throat.' Instead, I have only felt loved and supported.

As a young woman with a baby, navigating abuse yet lacking awareness of what constituted as abuse, receiving love and support was precisely what I craved and needed. At church, I experienced an abundance of it. I also had the opportunity to connect with a group of women, each with young children, who eventually became some of my closest friends. Despite our diverse backgrounds, life battles, and differing worldviews, we met at church—a place of love. Our children had the chance to grow up together, as their mothers weaved through the complexities of life.

MUG: An Account of Domestic Abuse

Listen to: Shackles by Mary Mary

I found myself copying Reverend Williams' sermons into my iPhone notes because they resonated with me profoundly. He dissected Jesus' parables, emphasising kindness, honesty, and vulnerability while rejecting greed, inequality, and judgment. To me, this mirrored the capitalist struggles I faced as a solo mum, being screwed over by the patriarchy, government neglect, and the rich and wealthy.

I had countless questions about God, so I attended prayer meetings and courses to explore them. The answers consistently pointed to His omnipresence and unwavering love. The older members of our church community, both in services and meetings, were inherently good people who hadn't always been so. They openly shared stories of their pasts, revealing moments far from Christian ideals. Witnessing their transformative journeys inspired me as they evolved into inclusive, kind, and generous individuals.

To my surprise, I discovered that some church practices I strongly disagreed with—such as the treatment of the LGBTQ+

community—were not universally accepted among those with faith, including Rev. William. Despite his conservative background, he was a privately staunch socialist. Recognising that there were people within the church who held diverse views was enlightening. I know I am lucky to have this positive experience of church and that the same can't be said for many other people.

While I've never firmly declared myself as religious, I openly attend church, leading some to perceive me as such. I've explored various spiritual paths, including Buddhism, Wicca, Astrology, and even delved into 'The Occult' by Colin Williamson at my father's urging when I was around fourteen. Undeniably spiritual, I consider myself to be explorative of faith and when all is lost – I pray.

With Christianity supporting me through abuse, it seemed natural to find forgiveness for Ethan somehow. If God was to forgive me for my sins, then the Bible teaches that I must also forgive others for theirs. I had indeed been sinful; the divorce from my previous marriage, resulting from a failure to communicate effectively and be honest, still weighed heavily on me as a significant failure. Beyond that, Christianity teaches that all humans are guilty of sin. Reflecting on my life, I acknowledge instances where I have been aggressive, manipulative, toxic, dishonest, thieving, and selfish. Considering these reflections, I questioned whether I was any less flawed than Ethan.

Did I need to apologise to God for all the trauma that had led me to respond with those behaviours? That didn't seem fair. However, accountability is fair, and Jesus teaches us that we can be accountable for our actions and behaviours, not for the trauma inflicted upon us. It felt comforting to realise, in a spiritual sense, that none of this was my fault; it was how I responded that I was responsible for. This perspective aligned with my therapist's and Katia's support – yes, I had done bad things, and I am accountable for those actions, but I am not responsible for the abuse that happened to me. It was time to try and transfer the sympathy I felt for the younger version of Ethan and apply it to myself – to feel sorry for ME. It's challenging, as a lifelong lesson I've had engrained into me is that feeling sorry for yourself is unhelpful and self-serving. But where do we begin in our healing if we cannot find empathy for our own traumas and hardships? For ourselves?

Despite the restraining order in place, I experienced a second January of Ethan violating my boundaries after our separation. He resorted to creating multiple daily social media accounts again, bombarding me with desperate declarations of his 'deepest love'. Faced with his relentless behaviour and feeling emotionally drained, I was left with the decision of whether to reconcile with him so he'd stop, or involve the police once again. However, going back to him was not an option anymore, especially with Child Services and the police assessing my daughter and me as 'high risk'. Monthly meetings with various professionals, including child services, my daughter's preschool, Ethan's probation team, and others, focused on our safety and well-being. With numerous court proceedings, professional input, and support, our priority remained our daughter's safety – both physically and emotionally.

I opted for calling the police.

Chapter Nineteen - Stalking and Harassment

'Stalking is characterised by fixation and obsession from one person to another. Stalkers often use a combination of online and offline behaviours to gain contact such as calls, texts, contacting family, friends and work, sending gifts, researching online and using fake profiles.'

Aurora New Dawn. (n.d.). Help for the Stalker.

Listen to: Why Do You Love Me? By Garbage

Cyberstalking

Message received from Ethan via a random Instagram account:

'So I am at the stage where I can't change any of the past or my past but I can create a future

Hope I can show my girls a wonderful future full of adventure and love and health and happiness

I will do all I can'

Nothing had changed. Although we hadn't physically seen each other for months, Ethan continued to create social media accounts and cyberstalk me. He would engage with me on my public page under the guise of someone interested in the topics I discussed. Once I joined the conversation, he would reveal his identity. He'd follow me with usernames connected to my life or our relationship. His distinct way of typing also gave him away. Making his account public, he would 'like' all my posts, flooding me with notifications. Despite knowing I shouldn't watch his stories, I did, feeling compelled to know what he was saying. I would screenshot most of the stories, keeping the evidence in a secure file. Every day, I felt stressed as more accounts popped up for me to block. In retrospect, I can see that I was living in a dissociated state, exhausted and numb.

While attempting to go to work at the nursing home, Ethan would call my work number and speak to my colleagues. One of my managers had to intervene, asking staff not to pass on messages to me but directly to her for police notification. I felt constantly targeted—both at work and online. The numerous contacts with different professionals were draining and repetitive, as I had to reiterate the same information. For a long period, I was in contact with the police, victim support, child services, health visitor, preschool, Katia (my assigned IDSVA), a link relationship officer communicating with Ethan's probation officer, a solicitor assigned via a domestic abuse charity, my GP, a crisis counsellor, regional manager at work, housing officer, and countless others.

Solo parenting while living in a bedroom with my parents (staying in our flat felt too risky), enduring a year of a global pandemic and its strange restrictions, added to the difficulty. Katia and my link officer Shona, who was a huge support, encouraged me to call the police. However, the prospect of more interviews, statements, and reports felt utterly exhausting, contributing to the trauma. I was torn between not wanting to be harassed and lacking the energy to report him. I was completely broken down.

Then came The Netflix Breach. I had a notification from Netflix that evidenced Ethan was using my email address and password from the property he was residing in.

The audacity. This man wasn't paying me child maintenance, hadn't paid the 'victim damages' as the court had mandated, however pathetic that sum was. All I had asked for was ONE THING – Be a better person. Show me you're a better person. But he couldn't. He wouldn't. And now he was using my username and password to watch Netflix. I was paying for him to watch Netflix. To have comfort and enjoyment wherever he was, while treating me with such constant disrespect for my boundaries. And for some reason, that one thing really, really pissed me off. So, in a phone call with Shona, who routinely checked in, I expressed just how pissed off I was. She alerted the police. When the police came to my parents' house to speak to me, I cooperated.

'This is more than breaching the restraining order,' one of the two male police officers said, clutching his bleeding arm after I had warned him not to stroke my feral cat, 'This is stalking and harassment.'

A warrant went out for his arrest.

Stockholm Syndrome

That's when the harassment abruptly ended, after making statements with the police and a follow-up phone call confirming a warrant was out for his arrest—possibly another call saying he had been arrested—I can't remember the finer details due to how dissociated I was back then. The sudden silence on social media was validating — I wasn't going insane. It really was him creating this steady stream of fake social media accounts. But I also felt... bereft? Ghosted? From being constantly assured multiple times a day that I was desperately 'loved,' wanted, beautiful, perfect... the silence felt deafening.

Before becoming a victim of stalking, I would never have imagined the complex feelings that came with it. Stress, frustration, anger, and exasperation lingered in every waking minute of my day.

Paranoia about where I would see him, who was calling me, or that my friends, family, colleagues, and church community were messaging me to alert me that he had contacted them brought shame and embarrassment. But there was also a weird kind of 'kick' from being told I was wonderful every day; It was all I had ever wanted him to feel for me and communicate to me. Once it was gone, like a switch turning off from the moment he must have been arrested... I was faced with something I wasn't used to; safety. Peacefulness. Time. Time to process. Time to grieve. Time to discover what adult life was like without Ethan in it. Without being abused. Time to observe the damage.

Listen to: Would If I Could by Melissa Auf Der Maur

I didn't realise he would go to prison. I knew if he carried on the way he was, it was a possibility. But his breach of the restraining order meant he remained in custody until his court hearing, where he pleaded guilty and was sentenced to a few weeks locked up. I can't remember when or how I found out. I think it was his sister who phoned me to say that Ethan had done the unthinkable and contacted his equally abusive father after two decades of estrangement, asking to be bailed. He wasn't bailed, but a colleague seemed to be present for Ethan's hearing and relayed the information to his sister, who informed me. I was shocked. No one had told me the time, day, or what would happen—what the outcome would be. You might have expected me to be happy that there was some form of justice, but I wasn't.

I felt chronically severe guilt.

I knew he had committed many wrongs, not just towards me, but also towards my daughter and others. Those are their stories to tell. I acknowledged his responsibility for that behaviour. Yet, like our daughter, he had been a little boy once too—a little boy who craved love, safety, and care. Having seen numerous pictures of him as a child, our daughter bore a noticeable resemblance to him, sharing the same expressions, the same smile, and the same look in their eyes.

Initially, Ethan had painted his childhood as happy when we first met. He frequently reminisced about the joyful, fun things he did in his early years, but it took a considerable amount of learning about him, listening to his family, and piecing information together for me to realise that his childhood wasn't as always enjoyable as he portrayed it to be. While the stories he shared were indeed happy, they might have represented the few moments of joy amid the constraints of his cheating, controlling father and reactive mother. I now understand that much of the initial part of our relationship involved a childlike escapism and a pursuit of adrenaline, attempting to recreate our happiest childhood memories—being outdoors, exploring, and having adventures.

Our shared desire to find a fun fix of dopamine was where we met in the middle. It's also the reason why I struggled so much to let go, even attempting to revive our adventures after our separation during lockdown walks and restricted drives due to COVID-19. However, by then, escapism was no longer possible—not when I knew the truth about who he really is, and he knew that I couldn't unsee the reality. There was no mask for him to hide behind anymore, no exciting adventure that could erase the knowledge that he was inherently an abusive, violent, and dangerous person.

The risky behaviour that I once loved so much lost its appeal. I was rightly frightened, and we couldn't bring back what once was. None of us can escape the truth forever.

I knew the truth, but I had also seen the boy. I knew him. And now, visually, as I had brought into the world a person who was 50% biologically that boy, I could see him even more clearly. The fear I witnessed in our own daughter's eyes when Ethan's behaviour escalated—when she trembled in my arms on that icy cold December night—I could see it in the little boy confined in a prison cell. He was cold, confused, desperate to break free. He didn't want to be locked in; he needed an escape. He longed for fun, adventure, something to make him happy—anything but being locked in with his fears, his harsh reality, every day, all day. With no one to love him. No one to nurture him.

He yearned for the trees in the copse by the street in the village where he had grown up. He craved the treehouse he had proudly claimed to build and regularly slept in throughout his life. He wanted to ride his bike by the canal, skate to the park, spy on the badger Sett. He needed to be free from the restraints that held him captive and miserable.

I cried every day. Often, I would call his sister and tearfully speak to her over the phone, expressing my regret for involving the police. I wished he had just listened, heard me, and done as I asked—left me alone to think, breathe, and work on himself. An overwhelming sadness consumed me as I thought of his child self. I felt desperate to hold, mother, look after, and provide for that little boy, yet he seemed out of my reach. I felt incapable of giving the care and love 'the child' needed and deserved.

If he had had his needs met as a little boy, he could have been a better person, a great person. There was so much potential for him when he was little. He was intelligent and knowledgeable. His passion for the outdoors had taught me more about nature, animals, and excitement than anyone else on earth. He had possessed the potential to have lived a wildly different life. What could that little boy have been...?

Listen to: Realeyes by Babes In Toyland

I imagined him crying. How were the prison officers talking to him? Did they provide him with vegetarian food? How would he cope without his energy drinks? He'd get headaches. Would he have access to free dental care? I worried about his toothache. How much time did he get outside? Was there grass? Were the people nice? What about using the toilet? He didn't like being around other people... did he share a room? Did they hurt him? I found out he had COVID. He was isolating. He was alone. What could he do? What could he read? Write? Did he just sit with his thoughts?

This wasn't his fault. It was his upbringing. It was his dad. It was the teachers who didn't understand him. It was the love he never received. He was a victim, too. I had seen goodness in him before—perhaps that goodness would grow while he was in prison? Maybe all the bad, the abusiveness, would melt away? What if this is what needed to happen? What if he changed? What if prison really did change him? What if he had to receive counselling? Could the little boy inside him finally be saved?

NO. NO. NO. NO. NO. I was experiencing what is commonly referred to as 'Stockholm Syndrome.' I found myself empathising with the person who had held me captive, violated me in every possible way, and put my life at risk for their own gain. Once I was free from his constant presence on my social media, once the harassment stopped, my nervous system began to move out of a state of dissociation, and my brain felt safer using different coping mechanisms while processing the enormity of everything that had happened to me. This was a part of recovery—I was healing, even if it didn't feel that way. I was transitioning away from the instinct to survive at all costs, starting to realise the very real danger my daughter and I had been in. I had to move through this coping mechanism first to get to the next stage:

Liberation and freedom from the captor.

Chapter Twenty -

Freedom

'There were 700,236 stalking and harassment offences recorded by the police in the year ending June 2023.'

Office for National Statistics. (2023). Crime in England and Wales: Year ending June 2023.

'Stalking can cause victims to feel extremely hyper-vigilant. Try not to dismiss their feelings as many victims know what the person stalking them is capable of.'

Black Country Women's Aid. (2023). 5 things everyone should know about stalking during Stalking Awareness Week 2023.

Ethan's Instagram Story on a random account:

'Miss Everything,

About that girl,

Miss all she was inside my world,

Miss the way she treated me,

Miss Badger, that's she,

I promise My World,

I'll show you things,

I promise my baby'

Anger Is an Energy.

I was inexplicably paying for his phone. I couldn't rationalise it; my financial management skills were considerably lacking (an understatement), and I struggled to keep track of bills. I didn't always forget, but my brain seemed to want to ignore it. However, during his time in prison, after days and weeks of intense guilt, I began to feel less disoriented. According to polyvagal theory (I'm really into that), I was moving up my ladder (regulating my nervous system) and a sense of anger started to surface. What the hell was I doing, funding his phone bill with my low wage?

Then, I had an idea. It was devious, but I felt like some clarification was the least I deserved. Earlier in this book, I mentioned that I had gone through Ethan's call log. Ethan's call log was linked to my online account with the provider, something I hadn't realised until then. Did he actually love me as much as he professed every day on Instagram before he went to prison? I saw a way to verify his lies.

Listen to: Blood One by Bikini Kill

I examined his call log, discovering weeks' worth of numbers he frequently called at various hours of the day (and night). I knew it might hurt, being reminiscent of the last time I had gone through his phone, but curiosity got the better of me. I added the numbers to my WhatsApp and looked at their profile pictures. It was no surprise that they were nearly all women—each woman distinctly different from the others. Some profiles seemed vague, so I phoned them. I had nothing to lose. It turned out these numbers belonged to sex workers or were connected to sex work establishments.

I observed that there were certain women he spoke to slightly more frequently than the others – Kerry and Hetty in particular. Notably, he had even been calling Kerry in the middle of the night. On seeing Kerry's profile picture, I was driven by a sudden rise of fury that had been dormant in me; I messaged her. She never replied. It dawned on me that he probably had girlfriends – plural – while stalking and harassing me. Suddenly, I didn't picture a little boy in a prison cell anymore...

I was angry, sickened. A large part of those emotions stemmed from the stark reminder of when we first got together. I spent some time reading through my old diaries and reflected some more on Hannah; it was at that point that I realised he had likely started seeing me around the same time as Hannah, all the while attempting to reconcile with his ex-wife, Meg. I felt foolish, worthless, livid. The words of Jenny, the first person I caught him sleeping with—
'Time to wipe mug off your forehead'—
echoed in my mind. I hadn't taken that advice all those years ago, but it was time to now.

I cancelled his phone bill and threw away clothes he had bought for me. If he crossed my mind, it triggered rage. Initially, there was a strong urge for vengeance to make him pay for the torment and humiliation he had inflicted on me. But he was in prison, facing his version of hell, alone with himself, with no way to track what I was up to.

The new ability to use social media or my phone without the constant stress of Ethan's harassment felt surreal. I recognised that I had been limiting myself in what I could write or post due to fear of his reactions. Slowly, I began testing the waters on Instagram, discussing domestic abuse in a more personal manner. It was simultaneously terrifying and liberating. There was no longer anyone to fear— I was no longer constrained; the captor couldn't reach or touch me.

Listen to: Hand Grenade by Be Your Own Pet

As I spoke more openly about my experiences with abuse, I found a growing sense of courage. Strangers reached out to share their own stories of suffering abuse, creating real and powerful connections. Life began to show glimmers that had been absent for years—freedoms I had gradually lost during the abuse. I could listen to music in the kitchen while preparing food, watch telly, and stay up past six o'clock in the evening. Opening a beer, talking on the phone, making a cup of tea—these simple acts were no longer sources of guilt. I could excuse myself to use the toilet and sit in the front seat of the car without fear of consequence and punishment. Everyday activities, often taken for granted, had been absent from my life for years. Embracing my freedom took a long time, as I felt incredibly overwhelmed and alien to the prospect of living life without feeling frightened of what would happen to me if I stepped out of line and put the kettle on or dared to scroll through Facebook in the presence of someone else.

I was catching glimpses of a life I had never experienced before. I had never been single, officially lived on my own, learned to drive a car, attended a gig, or holidayed alone. As pandemic restrictions eased, opportunities for dating without social distancing opened to me.

I enrolled in college, got a provisional license, and bought my own furniture. I decorated exactly as I wanted, without compromise. I talked to men, flirted with whoever I wanted to, and wore whatever I dared. With the further easing of lockdown restrictions and when I could get childcare, I socialised with whoever I wanted, wherever

I wanted. My sadness and fear diminished, and the world began to regain its vibrant and exciting colours. I discovered that I could still have adventures without the need for an escape. I was creating the life of my dreams alongside the daughter of my dreams, determined never to let another person hold me back. Life was about to become bigger and brighter, and it no longer mattered if I remained single forever—I was starting to feel like I didn't NEED a relationship while I learned to healthily maintain the one with myself.

I attended online CODA (Codependents Anonymous) meetings and SLAA (Sex and Love Addicts Anonymous). Instead of seeking advice on domestic abuse support groups, I found myself in a position to give advice — good advice! Drawing on the skills I had learned from completing my Level Two counselling course, I even established my own online support group. This group was specifically designed for women who had lived with trauma, with a particular focus on offering support to women who, like me, had been cheated on or abused. It was, after all, my speciality.

I sought counselling for myself, exploring various counselling approaches to determine what worked best for me. This process largely aided part of my personal growth in self-awareness, helping me understand areas where I needed to be accountable for my past actions. I recognised how awful I was in establishing boundaries to safeguard myself (physically and emotionally) and respecting the boundaries of others. Many aspects of my life, that I once viewed as dark and unchangeable, became clearer, shedding some of the shame associated with them. Shame... it was something I felt strongly about so many different things; my failed marriage, being a divorcee, my vulnerabilities, staying with someone who serial cheated on me, having to be rescued over and over by family, friends, tutors, vicars, the police... God? I had been drowning in shame for most of my life and it's taking a lengthy time to cleanse myself of it, but I was finally in a place where I had the tools to heal and want to use them.

Listen to: Drain the Blood by The Distillers

MUG: An Account of Domestic Abuse

In reflecting on my life with a violent man, I became interested in learning more about male perpetrated violence. I have identified as a feminist since my early days in secondary school, recognising the importance of women, particularly woman artists. However, it wasn't until I fled an abusive relationship that I explored what feminism truly meant to me and how I personally defined it. During my teenage years and early twenties, my perception of feminism was cantered around my obsession for woman musicians, especially the women in music who screamed, snarled and rioted. I spent much of that era of my life trying to look like an indie version of Courtney Love.

Now, feminism holds a much deeper significance for me. It is about asserting my identity as a person without seeking acceptance from anyone, particularly not from men. To me, feminism is recognising that women are not safe. It's recognising that women deserve safety and advocating for that safety. It involves acknowledging that men are currently the main perpetrators of violence against all people. Feminism, for me, means understanding that I can provide for myself without relying on a man — be it income, housing, meals, love, sex, or a baby in my belly.

Feminism is about the belief that I, a woman, deserve fair judgment, the equal right to be believed when using my voice, the way a man is automatically believed when he speaks out about domestic abuse or parental rights. It is about advocating for the rights of those like me – and not like me. Feminism is advocating for those who are less privileged but equally deserving of opportunities and respect. Feminism rejects the idea that I should be doubted in my capabilities simply because I am a woman. Feminism is a fight for independence and the knowledge that the oppressed WILL be heard. It is how we eradicate the toxic influence of capitalism, misogyny, and privilege that poisons the world. Feminism is the only way to combat the global crisis of domestic abuse, to reform the justice system, and to keep children safe with their mothers. It is the way we will prevent women and girls from dying at the hands of men and dismantling the patriarchy.

I am a feminist. It is my lifelong mission to witness the decline of violence against women and girls and be part of that decline.

Domestic abuse didn't become my life's purpose, but it revealed the woman I am. I AM a woman. And in the words of Courtney Love— a nod from my fourteen-year-old self— 'I am a force of nature'.

No one, especially no man, will ever attempt to bury me again because I soar above them, rising higher than those who have hurt us can ever ascend.

And borrowing from the words of Maya Angelou—

I rise.

Chapter Twenty-One - Freedom Fleeting

'..the summary-only offences of stalking (section 2A) and harassment (section 2), which carry the maximum general sentence a magistrates' court can impose. As summary offences, an information must be laid within 6 months of the commission of the offence. The 6 months' limitation runs from the date of the last incident comprising the course of conduct.'

"Stalking or Harassment" - Crown Prosecution Service, Director of Public Prosecutions v Baker [2004]

Message received from Ethan on a new number:

'Would be so nice to just talk like we have been I will leave it to you as I love you both and would love to be part of something nice with our baby x night'

I would have loved to end this book on the previous chapter. What an amazing ending that would have been! But this is the nature of post-separation abuse and the behaviours of a stalker. Ethan was released from prison, and by spring, he was in contact with me again, despite my having blocked him. Even with an epic restraining order in place, virtually banning him from being within a 20-mile radius of me, he persisted. He began to message me via social media, creating multiple email addresses, using different phone numbers, and creating endless new accounts. I kept this contact secret because sometimes... I replied.

For someone who hasn't lived with abuse, it might be easy to ask, 'Why did you reply? Why didn't you call the police straight away?' But the truth is, despite acknowledging how much I enjoyed my freedom, I had a problem – my daughter. At that point, she was four years old and unable to sleep in her own bed or spend a night away from me. While she was happy at preschool, it had taken a lot of time and effort to support her in being there without me. She would cry if I went into a different room in our small flat, following me everywhere, and interrupting every phone call.

Listen to: Song For Our Daughter by Laura Marling

I remember a day when I needed to speak to the GP during a phone appointment. My daughter screamed and cried until I was forced to end the appointment and comfort her. She incessantly talked about her father—asking where he was, why she couldn't see him, when she would see him again, and why other children had their daddies with them every day, but she didn't.

It broke my heart to witness my child longing and mourning for her father. She was too young, too innocent to know the awful truth, but she wasn't oblivious. She realised that our family wasn't 'normal.' She saw other Dads at preschool nativities or waiting to pick up their children at home time. She knew our 'mother and daughter' routine was different from what she saw on her favourite TV shows – Peppa had two parents, so did Bluey, and even Bing Bunny had a father figure (whatever Flop was to Bing!). I loved Bing Bunny. Flop, his 'caregiver,' seemed to be a 'solo' adult household figure who nurtured Bing as part of a... unique... knitted community. Voiced by my favourite actor, Mark Rylance, Flop had a gentle, calm manner when addressing Bing, even when Bing was being difficult. I wished to be more like Flop, but the more I tried to 'gentle' parent as a single mother, the more I seemed to 'fail'.

After four years of parenting on my own — neglected, rejected, raped, strangled, punched, pulled, betrayed, lied to, gaslit, disrespected...after over four years of sleepless nights, surviving on pennies scraped from the bottom of my purse, constant moving, rental deposits, police statements, courtrooms, social worker visits, and a truckload of trauma... I was exhausted. I wasn't the gentle parent I wanted to be. Often, I was grumpy, snappy, and sometimes even a shouty parent. I hated being a shouty parent.

It dawned on me that I had always been the sole parent, whether in a relationship or not. I was parenting alone in the present and had done so even when I was with Ethan. I wasn't a single parent, as my relationship status didn't reflect my parental role; I was a solo parent, and I was tired.

Ethan wanted to see our daughter, and she wanted to see him too. So, I didn't call the police. I gave up. I felt utterly defeated. Despite him having been to prison, it hadn't stopped him. Could I manage what other mothers in the abused women's social media groups did? Many of them practiced something called 'parallel parenting', minimising interaction with their ex, while maintaining communication for their children to have a relationship with both parents. Parallel parenting involved accepting that the toxic parent wouldn't be fair or cooperate with the safe parent. Instead, the safe parent focused their energy on ensuring their children felt consistently safe with them.

I was researching family courts, hoping to avoid them entirely. I hadn't encountered a mother with a positive experience in family court, either in the UK or elsewhere. I'd heard dreadful stories where women fought for their children, incurring tremendous debt, yet a judge often granted custody to abusive men, posing a danger to their children's lives. I was fiercely protective, unwilling to let my daughter be alone with a man capable of nearly killing us in violent outbursts. Over my dead body would he have any court ordered custody.

Perhaps, allowing communication would allow me to negotiate a limited format where he had some involvement in her life, but I could closely monitor every action and counteract any harmful words he said to her. I craved some form of control.

By early summer, I allowed our daughter to FaceTime her father, which seemed to improve her mood and reduced her questions. However, it also placed incredible pressure on me from him to allow in-person visits. I gave him an inch; he expected a mile. At this point, he didn't know our new address after the last stalking incident, and I had no intention of revealing it. The local authority had, by this time, moved me three times to hide my location from him. But one day, as I grew complacent during my four-year-old's FaceTime call, doing the washing-up while she chatted to him, he asked her about the new outside views from our windows. Before I could intervene, she had showed him the landscape. Within hours, he was parked outside our new home.

'He's outside! Mummy! Mummy! He's outside!'

GPS alarms were installed in my flat—at a considerable cost to the public sector—connected to the nearest police station. Panic buttons were placed in discreet areas of my home. An alarm was constantly worn around my neck. Even my phone number was flagged with the local police station. All the precautions I could have taken. All the precautions I should have taken.

But I opened the door. I let him in.

'Surprise!' I exclaimed to my daughter.

Listen to: Praying by Kesha

He didn't leave until we both put her to bed, and she fell asleep tucked in between us. I knew it was a mistake. Every part of my body was on high alert—my heart racing, head pounding, feeling nauseous. But when I opened that door, I reacted with a sense of appeasement. I slipped into the 'fawn' response. I descended my regulatory ladder straight into basic survival mode—open the door, appease him. Be polite, appease him. Say yes, appease him. And then, as our daughter drifted into what seemed a contented sleep... he resumed it all once more.

'See? This is how we can be. We can be good. We can be a family. You don't know how much I've changed. We can move away. We can go somewhere else. People would start to understand once they see how much I've changed. This is our family. I love you. I have never loved anyone more than you. I fucked up, I know I fucked up. Let me show you how much I've changed...'

It was the same spiel from his 100,000 Instagram accounts he'd bombard me with every day. It was the same pleading he'd done throughout the COVID pandemic, during lockdown when we were going for walks in our family 'bubble'. And it was meaningless now. It meant nothing to me. It was empty.

'Go,' I said. But he wouldn't leave. I began to shift from my 'Fawn' mode into 'Fight'. 'GO. Now.'

'Don't be like that, you know I love you. You KNOW I do. It's us. We're us. Let us be us again. Let us adventure like we used to.'

'I wanted us to do all that again when we were together... but you cheated. You were horrible to me. You hated me. No. No. NO. GO, Ethan. GO.'

'No.'

'Go now,' I trembled, 'or I'll press a panic button. The police will be here straight away.'

'You wouldn't. Don't do that. There's no need to do that. You're being stupid.'

Stupid. I'm being stupid, I thought. And all the words he had ever said started ringing in my ears. Stupid. Thick. Useless. Pathetic. Retard. Stupid. Thick. Useless. Pathetic. Retard. Stupid. Thick. Useless. Pathetic. Retard. Bitch. Dog. Cunt. Bitch Dog Cunt. BitchDogCunt. BitchDogCuntStupidThick. Useless. Pathetic. Dog. Dog. Dog. Dog.

'Get out. Get out. GET OUT NOW.'

I remember him cursing me as he pounded down the stairs, but I don't recall the specific words he used, as all the previous hurtful words he had called me were chiming in my ears.

Gone. He was gone. I locked the door, put the chain over the lock, and slid down against the door as he began knocking again.

'I'm sorry! Let me back in so we can talk. I'm sorry...'

Stupid. Pathetic. Thick. Cunt.

Victim Vs. The Police

'Hi. Are you safe?'

It wasn't uncommon for my child's preschool to phone me. We were in more contact than other families. They had been involved in all the risk assessments, kept informed about child services and the police. They knew that legally they couldn't prevent my daughter from going home with her dad, but they could alert the police immediately if that happened. Since her father had never once taken her to preschool—and if I hadn't forced him to attend sports day once, he probably wouldn't have known where she went to preschool—my first thought was that he had turned up to collect her. Shit. We hadn't spoken since we'd argued a couple of days beforehand.

'I'm safe, why?'

'No need to worry, she's fine,' they reassured me, 'but I'm afraid we've had to contact the police. We received an anonymous call saying that Ethan is hanging around the area.'

I was panicked. Obviously, he was waiting for me to pick her up. And who would contact the preschool? Who knew me well enough to recognise Ethan and not directly contact me, but instead alert my child's preschool? It didn't make any sense. It still doesn't. I've never found out who alerted her preschool. They never disclosed it themselves. Of course, I asked around. Everyone else seemed as confused as I was—and said they would have informed me if they'd seen Ethan hanging around.

Listen to: Fidelity by Regina Spektor

I don't believe Ethan was lingering around the preschool. I think my daughter told her preschool teachers that she had seen him, that he had been around her flat. I think they lied to me and pretended that someone had anonymously tipped them off.

And I think that's why Child Services came down so hard on me.

Later that night, after my daughter was safely tucked up in bed and I was ready to join her, there was a terrifying banging on the front door. By this point, I was already frightened of knocks or rings on the door, in case it was Ethan turning up again. I froze. They banged again. My daughter woke up, startled.

'It's the police, open the door!'

Frightening thoughts raced through my mind; was it my parents? Had they been in an accident? Was it about the unpaid council tax? It couldn't be about Ethan and what the preschool had said? Not at this time of night? My daughter was crying, she was scared.

As I went downstairs to the front door, the blue lights flashing into my hallway, I felt absolutely petrified. I opened the door. I didn't have time to process what was happening—four police officers barged past me and headed up the stairs. Another stood by the front door, waiting. I followed.

'You're upsetting my daughter!' I screamed at them.

'Ethan?' They called out, searching through the bedrooms, even the one where my daughter sat up in bed crying, pushing back curtains, checking the utility cupboard, and inspecting the bathroom... 'Ethan, come out!'

'He's not here!' I kept screaming. They didn't listen.

After less than two minutes of checking my tiny flat, one of the police officers said to another, 'Go and inform PC {name} that he's not here, we'll take it from here.'

I was pissed off. I had a scared child to tend to in the bedroom, and two police officers in my messy living room, saying they needed to question me. I felt protective over my personal space. I informed them that I would not be answering any questions until I had settled my child back to sleep. Unfortunately, there was no settling down. Eventually, I ended up giving her the iPad and told her Mummy would be back to cuddle her as soon as I could.

'Sorry about the mess,' I said as I re-entered the living room. I said this every time the police came; it was like a routine.

The two male police officers informed me that they had been told I was back in a relationship with Ethan and that he was currently staying at my flat. I stated that it was nonsense and demanded to know who had told them. They mentioned that the preschool had tipped them off from an anonymous call. Yeah right. There was absolutely no one in my life who would suspect that, let alone tip off the preschool without asking me first. Our flat was so small with paper-thin walls, I knew my daughter could hear us all talk.

I explained that I was NOT in a relationship with Ethan, that I did not want to be with him, and that I was rather annoyed about the way they had entered my property. They made no apology. I was informed that Ethan's probation meant that any reoffence would send him back to prison—yet more information I was never given before. I reiterated again that Ethan and I were not in a relationship. But then they asked if he had been to the flat. If he had entered it. Even then, even after everything that had happened to me, there was still a part of me that wanted to lie for him, to protect him, to not see him get into any trouble. But I couldn't lie. I knew that child services would be on my case. I knew that this wasn't the normal way the police had approached me about Ethan—this time I was being treated like I was the criminal causing the offense, hiding the perpetrator, and lying to them. I had to tell them the truth.

'He was here two nights ago.'

And so, I made my statement.

Victim Vs. Child Services

I knew Ethan had been arrested while at work the next day, but I had no further information. There were no follow-up phone calls from the police. I assumed the silence meant there was nothing to report. As for Ethan, he hadn't created any social media accounts or messaged me; he was probably laying low. The silence was somewhat comforting. Yet, that wasn't the end of it.

During the Men's Football Euro's that year, England were performing well. One weeknight, I said to my daughter, 'If mummy buys you a McDonald's for dinner, can you go to bed early so that mummy can watch the football?' We struck an easy deal.

We had a McDonald's delivered, and then I began preparing my little girl for an early bedtime. Suddenly, there was someone at the front door. I froze. The doorbell or knocks on the door were having a severe effect on my mental health.

As soon as I opened the door, I recognised her as a representative from Child Services. She held a folder in her hand and wore an ID badge around her neck. She arrived alone, yet she was a senior Social Worker. This was an unexpected visit, and although I had been anticipating Child Services to get in touch, I hadn't quite expected this. Previous social workers had been full of kindness and advice, supporting me as I navigated life after an abusive relationship and learned how to parent a child dealing with trauma from domestic abuse.
However, this time, it was *my* parenting that was being questioned.

Listen to: Former Lover by Saint Etienne

Why had I let him in? Why had I engaged in conversation? Are we together?

Then came the questions my daughter was asked.

'What do you like the most about Daddy living here?' It was a horrible question, because she was extremely aware that Daddy didn't live with us and that we hardly saw him.

'Daddy doesn't live with me.' She said.

'What do you like about Daddy coming to see you?'

'Daddy doesn't see me very much.'

'What do you like the most about living with Mummy?'

Her face lit up.

'She always gives me McDonalds to eat then puts me to bed early so she can watch football.'

Thanks, daughter. I laughed nervously and said it was just tonight that was happening.

There were more questions, designed to trip us up, but there was nothing to trip us up over. Eventually satisfied yet warning me that if I were to get back into a relationship with Ethan, my daughter would potentially end up living elsewhere with a trusted friend or relative, the senior social worker left. I didn't feel much like watching the football anymore.

We haven't seen a social worker since. Additionally, my daughter was signed off from the health visitor team, and the following week, she left preschool. It felt like a new chapter of our lives was beginning. We had our new home, we had each other, and my daughter was about to start school. I'd had a few days of not being harassed, and child services were happy with my parenting. There was something else, too... someone else.

Chapter Twenty-Two - Dating With Trauma

'PTSD is experienced by 51% to 75% of women who are victims of Intermate Partner Violence (compared to an average of 10.4% of women in the general population).'

"Post-Traumatic Stress Disorder (PTSD) and intimate partner violence" by B. Golding et al

<u>Message from Logan, after several dates:</u>

'I am glad we're on the same page. I like that you are beautiful. Like I go to find a stupid meme to send my friend and I see a photo of you and it makes me go 😍 . And aside from the fact I find you very attractive. I love that you are so strong as a person. I don't think of things you have dealt with as "baggage".'

I had been dating Rick for a long time. He was someone from my past, and we had matched on a dating app. When the first lockdown restrictions eased, we went on socially distanced dates. It was a huge development for me. Despite having obvious differences in our lifestyles, we got along well, and I cared about him a lot. Rick was an archaeologist, having previously served as a sniper in the army. I believe part of what brought us together was the severe pain left over from my marriage before Ethan, as my former husband had joined the army when he left me. Conversations with Rick confirmed for me that people change in the army, and I wouldn't have enjoyed the lifestyle restrictions, such as living far away when I couldn't drive or having to up and leave when I was feeling settled. Rick had been injured in the Iraq war and subsequently discharged from service. After studying to become an archaeologist, he found a new path in life. Unfortunately, he was severely affected by his time at war and suffered from PTSD. It was highly eye-opening to learn about the lack of support for veterans. Rick was staunchly Labour and detested capitalism, blaming it for war, where men were made to feel important but were 'merely numbers.' Still, I observed him changing his profile picture on Facebook regularly to images from his time on tours, days gone by when he was just a child, carrying a government-issued gun and encouraged to participate in acts of violence no child should have to know.

Our first date was lovely. It was socially distanced, so we didn't kiss. I was glad about that, because I had explained to Rick that I needed to take things slowly and didn't feel ready for intimacy. However, we did go for a long walk where he took me to a location, he suspected was the site of an Anglo-Viking battle—a hellishly boring date for some, but geek heaven for me. Unfortunately, I hadn't realised the walk would be so long, and I had dressed inappropriately in a short, cleavage dress and white converse. My thighs chafed in the heat, and my heels literally bled all over my white shoes. We also forgot to bring a drink with us and became extremely thirsty. But it was very romantic when a huge herd of deer ran past us amid the pink poppy fields, almost like a Disney scene. I enjoyed his company, but he knew this would be a slow burner, and it would take a lot for me to trust anyone again when it came to dating and relationships.

Listen to: Archie, Marry Me by Alvvays

Like with other men I've been interested in, I began daydreaming that Rick and I would up and leave, taking my child to Scotland, where we'd live off-grid. It felt exciting when he said he wanted us to move to the Highlands, live in a country that serves its people better, and hunt deer that he'd gut and cook himself in the evenings. I am a big *Outlander* fan, so this obviously sounded appealing... as a fantasy.

I didn't know about limerence back then. I only learned about it through @lalalaletmeexplain a few years later, on her podcast *'It's Not You, It's Them... But It Might Be You'*. In a nutshell, limerence is when you develop a fixation or obsessive liking for someone before you know them properly. I could not stop fantasising about the potential future I might have with Rick and would constantly think about whether he really felt the same way. Limerence isn't falling in love but rather agonising over the object of affection and whether they will reciprocate the excitement and caring feelings you have for them. We didn't have much in common, but I would focus on the small amount we did share, as if this was a perfect match.

However, it's not like love bombing a new or potential partner as a perpetrator of abuse will do because the infatuation is not about asserting power and control but the excitement of finding the potential of love. Ultimately, in limerence, you're a victim of yourself. You form this amazing idea in your head about what your life will be like with this person in it, attaching yourself early on. Then, as you get to know the person more, the bubble often bursts. Suddenly, that cute, endearing thing you liked about them gives you the ick. You realise that you're not actually that compatible. You realise it's not going to work. In fact, you think to yourself, what was I thinking?

I never thought, 'What was I thinking?' with Rick. It was more like, 'Why aren't I thinking?' This man seemed completely head over heels for me, and as our dating progressed, I grew less interested because I could see our lives were heading in different directions. His dreams didn't align with mine, especially as I had a young child. I turned cold towards him, something I deeply regret. When he continued to be as nice and loving as usual, despite distancing myself, I finally expressed that I didn't think we were going to work out and asked if we could just be friends. It felt horrible to let him down, after I had shown so much interest and suggested we would turn into the real thing. The guilt I felt for speaking honestly about my feelings didn't sit well with me. I hate hurting people, letting them down, or making them feel sad. Unfortunately, our friendship couldn't continue due to his feelings for me. I care a lot about Rick. He was the first man after I'd lived with domestic abuse to show me that not every man was going to harm or hurt me.

But I was talking to someone else. I mean, I talked to loads of people. I could spend a lot of time writing about how frustratingly shit dating apps are, but there are already great authors and creators producing work that details that – see the back of my book for recommendations. Yes, it is a giant sleaze fest of misogynistic arseholes who just want to have sex and may or may not be single. But among the 4,000+ men who liked my profile – yes, I subscribed to see who liked me, yes, I am aware of how many likes that is, and yes, I feel embarrassed, even though I shouldn't, as clearly my profile was amazing – I found a gem. What's more, I'd swiped for this one... it was a match because I was interested in him without seeing if he was interested in me. We started talking. I think it was me who initiated it.

His profile said, '2 truths and a lie... 1) I'm in a band, 2) I'm a professional wrestler, 3) I've been on TV.' Well, his pictures were of him wearing flamboyant velvet jackets and patterned shirts, and his hair was long with dark ringlets, like how I'd imagine Marc Bolan's to be if he lived through the eighties. He was definitely in a band, and maybe that band had been on telly.

Listen to: Baby It's You by London Grammar

Wrong. He was a professional wrestler. I knew nothing about wrestling, except that it was this weird fake thing people stayed up all night to watch. Interesting. I kept talking to him.

Logan says I was cold at first, and hard to talk to. I didn't give much away, and he even broke his rule of double messaging after I hadn't replied in several hours. But after a few weeks of talking, the conversation began to flow easily, and I realised I really liked the sound of this person. So, we agreed to meet for a date, the very same week that Ethan had been arrested.

It was meant to be a lunchtime date, where we met at 12ish, and then by 2, I'd leave to pick my daughter up from preschool. But the moment we met, we hit it off. Logan was very funny and charismatic, but not in the charming way. More like he had funny stories and wasn't afraid to sound silly. It was a sunny day, and we sat in the garden of the local pub, the sun beating down on us, and the cider flowing. I did something I'd not done before, and asked my dad if he could pick my daughter up from preschool because my date was going well.

Very well.

We left the pub at last orders and ordered wine from Deliveroo to my front door. We watched Pulp re-runs at Glastonbury Festival on the telly on BBC iPlayer, laughed, talked, and then we kissed. I knew he was going to be my new boyfriend.

We dated for five weeks before I introduced him to my daughter - something that surprised me. I had always imagined that I would wait a long time, but because it was the summer holidays, the only dates we could have were around my flat while my daughter was asleep in bed. I was worried she'd wake up and find a strange man in the flat, so I decided to introduce him as my friend. She seemed unsure at first.

My relationship with Logan was slow. We were intimate, but he respected that I needed time to trust and that there were things about relationships that I'd forgotten were normal. The first time he made me a cup of tea, I was honestly in shock. He was taken aback by how amazed and grateful I was and how I kept pointing out his kindness. This would be a repeated cycle over many things that happened in the first year of our relationship. When he gave me a kiss on the top of the head, just because, I'd be stunned at the affection, given freely without my request. Logan was thoughtful, caring. He listened to all my stories, and I told him the bad, hurtful or toxic things I had done in my life. We started our relationship by revealing the skeletons in our closest, as so the frankly disturbing saying goes. As our relationship progressed, I felt comfortable and therefore more able to tell him things about Ethan and of what he had done to my daughter and me. Logan was the first person that I felt I could tell, in detail, in my own time, what had happened to us.

Another reason why all of this felt easy, was because Ethan couldn't reach me or take away this happiness from me. I was safe...

...Ethan was back in prison

Freedom, Fight or Flight

It took a fortnight for me to find out that Ethan was in prison. His relative informed me that Ethan had handed himself in after two days of a warrant being out for his arrest. After weeks of silence from the police, I decided to investigate myself. When a police officer eventually confirmed over the phone that Ethan had been in prison for two weeks and would remain there for another six months, I was utterly shocked. I had anticipated the possibility, awaiting news of a court hearing, but I never expected him to be sent straight back inside.

Discovering the prison he was in, I talked to his family, who were equally astounded. Yet, this time, I didn't feel guilt. I didn't want him to be released. My life had never felt so empowering; I finally felt free again.

That summer was incredible. Falling in love with someone I was getting to know, spending time with friends, taking my daughter for walks along the river and to the park without my phone notifications constantly buzzing, or fearing my Ex was following us—it all felt liberating. So did my ability to write.

By then, I had gained a couple of thousand followers on Instagram and was connecting with many women who lived with abuse. With Ethan in prison, I felt safe to share more of my story, to be open about the abuse, stalking, and harassment I had lived with. As I spoke more about these experiences, I found more people who resonated, building a loyal following of individuals who appreciated connecting with me.

Listen to: Out of My Head by First Aid Kit

I consider this time in my life as positively happy—as if my life was on an upward trajectory. My daughter was grieving for her father, and I chose to be open and honest with her. I explained that her dad wasn't seeing her because he was in prison, not because of anything she had done. To cheer her up and support her through her grief, I got her a kitten, and they soon became inseparable.

Life was really looking up. I was a student, had a lovely home, a healthy daughter, a wonderful little cat, and I had landed myself a boyfriend. Moreover, everyone kept noticing how well and healthy I looked; fewer bags around my eyes, a fuller figure, shining hair, a natural smile replacing my former worried, serious expression—overall, a more relaxed demeanour. But the calm lasted barely five minutes.

My nervous system heaved a sigh of relief, finally feeling that we might actually be safe.

...until the doorbell rang. Or the phone rang. Or the microwave went ping. Or someone shouted. Or my daughter touched my neck. Or I stood at the bus stop. Or a white van driven by men went past and beeped at me. Or I heard a particular song. Or I walked past certain areas. Or I heard the word 'stupid'. Or thick. Or useless. Or bitch. Or dog. Dog. Dog. Dog.

Or I heard a police siren. Dog.

Or I went to sleep and dreamt...

Dog.

Or I saw Meg's Facebook profile picture pop up on my phone.

Mug.

Or my boyfriend had to apply the brakes on the car slightly harder than usual. Mug.

Or I dreamt some more and -

Witch.

My daughter was shouting at me. Screaming. Crying. Tired from her new school routine.

Witch.

'I want a cuddle!'

Witch.

'Mummy, I WANT it, that's not fair!'

Dog..

'I don't want to go to bed!'

MUG: An Account of Domestic Abuse

Mug.

'I want this one!'

Mug.

'I'm hungry!'

Mug.

'I...'

Mug.

Mug.

Mug.

It's time to wipe *'MUG'* from your forehead.

Mug. Useless Mother. Stupid Bitch. Fat Cunt.

Cunt.

Bitch.

Dog.

PTSD.

Chapter Twenty-Three - Post Traumatic Stress

'Estimated risk for developing PTSD for those who have experienced the following traumatic events: Rape (49 percent), Severe beating or physical assault (31.9 percent), Other sexual assault (23.7 percent).'

https://www.ptsduk.org/ptsd-stats/.

<u>Message received from Logan, after four months of dating:</u>

'Obviously I wasn't around when you were going through these bad times but from what you have told me it sounded horrible. You never deserved any of that and I'm glad you can see that now. It makes me feel really sad to know that someone could do that to you. I just think you're an amazing person and i love you, so the thought of anyone being cruel to you is sad.'

It was evident that my mental health was suffering. However, it took a couple of years to receive a diagnosis of Complex Post-Traumatic Stress Disorder. Over that two-year period, my C-PTSD worsened. There are signs that are obvious to me now, indicating that I had been living with C-PTSD while in a relationship with Ethan, and that my nervous system was doing everything it could to protect me. I spent most of my relationship with Ethan in a state of fawn, appeasing him to stay safe from harm.

While Ethan was in prison, I was given the opportunity to live in complete safety. Although I was happy, my nervous system couldn't shut off completely. As my daughter started school, I found the rush of the school run every morning incredibly difficult. The pressure of catching a bus on time and not being listened to by my four-year-old triggered a response reminiscent of when I was deliberately ignored by her father and when he scolded me for not being fast enough. I often heard him in my head as I ran around the flat searching for her school bag, my keys, my purse, her coat... 'Come on, for fucks's sake. You're fucking useless.' The school run became more than stressful for me; it was distressing.

My poor child would enter school either feeling dysregulated in her own nervous system because of the chaotic mornings with me or arrive late and miss register and class. She used to ask me why we were always late. I ended up with a letter from child services at the end of the first term, stating that my daughter's school had reported her lateness. Fortunately, as we were already known to child services, they listened to me when I expressed how overwhelmed the school run had me feeling.

Listen to: Shitlist by L7

It wasn't just the getting ready and leaving for school that triggered my trauma. Standing at the bus stop also affected me. I had never liked standing at the bus stop for others to drive past and see me due to a lifelong history of insecurity about my appearance. However, when Ethan left prison months earlier than initially intended, my PTSD kicked into full swing.

I was informed by the professionals involved with both of us that Ethan was being released due to good behaviour. He was to move to a new address, where he would be under day and night monitoring due to an enforced curfew. Additionally, he would be required to wear an electronic tag. I knew he would hate this. He had already attended a programme called 'Building Better Relationships,' which Katia had told me she didn't agree with.

'These manipulative, controlling men attend this course only to learn how to be better at coercion and control.'

I had heard similar sentiments from other women in support groups. Ethan had also been doing community service since the first conviction of him assaulting me, which had been prolonged in duration due to COVID and the succession of convictions afterwards. I knew he had more added on with his current prison sentence – and rolled my eyes when I discovered what his 'punishment' was. Ethan was a landscape gardener, doing gardening for community service. He had a strong work ethic and worked hard, so for him, it was additional work with no financial gain. However, it sounded like he was gaining the validation he always required, by being praised for his work and dedication by probation officers.

Before his prison sentence, Ethan had wasted no time in telling me that the community order was enjoyable and that the staff were impressed with him. He mentioned he was getting to maintain old cemeteries, find bones from graves, tend to trees, and be around old churches and beautiful views – all things that he and I were morbidly interested in. (I studied church architecture at university, okay?). I imagined he was continuing more of the same, and it felt like a pathetic punishment. He'd been convicted twice for not adhering to a restraining order due to stalking and harassment—what was the point of reduced prison terms? What would it teach a person like him, other than fostering resentment and anger toward the victim? Because when he contacted our very small mutual circle, that was what he conveyed. There was no 'I love her,' no 'I've changed.' There was only a strong sense of hatred. He referred to me as a lying witch, a psychopathic whore, a fat, ugly dog. Ah, there he was... the man who had supposedly 'turned his life around' and vowed never to disrespect or mistreat me again. I was terrified of his anger toward me.

I was paranoid about standing at any bus stop, especially on mornings when I had to take my daughter to school. Despite the initial restraining order prohibiting him, I was convinced Ethan would ignore it, just as he had disregarded others, and drive past us anyway. After reading news articles about acid attacks on former partners by perpetrators or their angry relatives, I convinced myself that Ethan had made friends in prison who would have no problem throwing acid on me as I left my house or waited for the bus. I was constantly on edge, waiting for my skin to suddenly burn each time I opened the front door.

Listen to: The Thin Line by Blondie

I worried that Ethan would drive by, slow down, and either stare at me, shout, or try to force our daughter and me into his car. I lived in a constant state of dread. I had never given myself enough time to completely cut contact with him, so his prison sentence had gifted me emotional space. Even if I hadn't responded to him for months, he would still find and contact me through social media. But now, even out of prison, I heard nothing. There was no contact. And this silence was new and alien to me.

I was able to think about the disgusting ways he had treated me without feeling any empathy or compassion for his own hardships that might have led him to behave that way in the first place. Now, with Logan in my life, I was aware of how I should have always been treated and understood that it wasn't that Ethan was incapable of showing me respect, but that he hadn't wanted to. If he hadn't respected me when we were together, or even when he was pleading for me back while disrespecting my boundaries, what was he capable of since I had made the statements that ensured he went to prison for his actions, not once but twice?

My experience with PTSD manifested in ways that a typical Hollywood War film might predict; loud noises would often startle me. When my daughter unexpectedly jumped out and said, 'boo!', it felt like my heart would race a thousand times faster. Even simple noises like my

Mum clanging the cutlery drawers or putting plates back into cupboards would leave me feeling shaky. Sudden entrances, loud exhausts, or fireworks would also trigger a startle response in me. Once, I was in a pub watching football with my parents. When one team scored and the pub erupted with the roar of middle-aged men, I could vividly hear Ethan clapping and shouting 'yes!' as if he were right next to me. It felt like I was completely losing my mind.

I would hear Ethan's voice regularly, have nightmares, and certain tastes, smells, or sounds would trigger dysregulation. If possible, I tried to avoid places that might trigger these reactions. When I couldn't, I would dissociate; it was as if I was absent or vacant half the time. My short-term memory suffered. I experienced typical brain fog, walking into a room and forgetting why I was there or the task I needed to do next. However, there were also strange gaps in my memory—I couldn't recall what I'd done the day before, forget responding to messages, and even forget whole conversations with people. Sometimes, I'd unintentionally repeat myself. I'd forget my work or college schedule and even the day of the week. Worryingly, I would frequently forget to take my medication. There were instances where I'd forget to eat or drink until I felt weak or had a headache. This memory loss also posed dangers for my daughter and me; I'd forget about a burning candle, an oven left on, or accidentally boil an empty kettle. The fire alarm's noise triggered me too, and I'd worry it was Ethan or his relatives setting fire to my home. I was scared that I had early onset dementia.

Listen to: Survivor by Destiny's Child

Even my safety alarm, which I always wore, would startle me if it went off. That high-pitched noise led to an incident when my daughter accidentally set it off in a public space, causing the building to be evacuated due to the noise. We laughed about it afterwards, but it was terribly embarrassing. The panic I felt when my phone rang, especially if it was an unknown number, prevented me from answering important calls. I missed many crucial communications because my brain was convinced it was him calling. The doorbell sound sent me into a complete panic; I would hide and pretend I wasn't home for as long as I felt necessary. Life became a series of frightening events, and I constantly felt unsafe.

After my diagnosis, I was deemed permanently 'unfit to work,' relying on benefits and recognised by the government as having a disability—though proving an 'unseen' disability in forms like PIP was extremely challenging. At one point, I had to quit college while studying my Level 3 in Counselling and restart several months later. Activities I once enjoyed became too stressful to pursue—simple things like going for walks or writing journals that had previously benefitted my mental health became overwhelming. The PTSD I was living with was utterly debilitating.

I believe two contrasting reasons contributed to the severity of my PTSD. On one hand, I met someone who provided a safe space for me to unravel—Logan's support has been nothing short of amazing. He's made me feel incredibly secure. However, on the other hand, my PTSD worsened as Ethan's restrictions eased.

Around the third Christmas after our separation, I was informed that attending court for Ethan's restraining order renewal wasn't necessary. The restraining order was granted without me being present. Yet, the fourth Christmas after our separation, I was told I had to attend. I went with Logan for support, and I was permitted to enter via a private back entrance. In the lead-up to the court date, I had asked for a video call appearance, but it wasn't allowed. Insisting on a dividing screen, I was initially told it would be permitted. However, upon finally going to court on the day, the staff seemed confused. They mentioned that due to the offenses committed, they hadn't expected my attendance and said a video call was recommended instead. Struggling to regulate my nervous system after weeks of anxiety, I could barely speak, and this time, I didn't have legal representation. All I had were Katia's instructions: requesting Ethan's restriction from my entire hometown, a step less than his prior restrictions but enough to ensure safety on public transport. Katia anticipated it would be granted. Logan stepped up and unofficially represented me as negotiations took place in a small waiting room. I was extremely emotional and concentrating on breathing techniques and focusing on staying in the present. I remember thinking that I hadn't even wanted any of this, how was I here? I wanted to get up and run out of the door, but how would that look to child services? Being at court felt more difficult than the abuse itself, because of the trauma I was being brutally confronted with, and unable to hide from.

Unlike me, I knew Ethan had a lawyer, and it worked in his favour. The previous restrictions of Ethan's restraining order were waived. Consequently, I, or rather Logan, considering my emotional state, requested Ethan's prohibition from my street, the adjacent one we walked daily, and the main road where my daughter and I caught the bus to school. However, the judge declined this request. Ethan was only barred from entering my street and the next one, while he retained access to the main road where we waited at the bus stops. This main road, however, he no longer used, as he had apparently relocated, and his work didn't require its use. I knew that not being required to use the road wouldn't stop Ethan from driving it and turning up at the bus stops we used at school drop off hours. Despite the considerable support I received previously from the justice system throughout my court proceedings, this time, I felt thoroughly dismayed – not so much for my daughter and I, but for other victims. How could these kind of rulings ensure the safety of people who have lived with stalking and abuse? When it comes to addressing stalking and harassment, the British justice system still has a long way to go in improvements.

Life became more challenging when I realised Ethan would be following me wherever I went. I understood that prison hadn't reformed him, and he would likely become more adept at stalking me. While I lacked evidence for this and might have appeared paranoid, I knew Ethan well enough to understand that he never stopped pursuing someone he'd been involved with. This awareness stemmed partly from my connections with some of his past partners. Ethan had a history of stalking his exes, something I knew when beginning my relationship with him.

Knowing about Ethan's stalking behaviour wasn't entirely new to me. Among the many red flags I'd encountered, warnings about his stalking behaviour were also given. Yet, I was so infatuated, so enamoured, and so deeply in love with him that I consciously disregarded these alerts. I ignored warnings about his controlling nature, finding it attractive that he wanted his women all to himself. I romanticised his history of stalking his exes, by viewing it as an indication of his unwavering love. As for his past infidelities, I rationalised them by thinking that if he cheated on me, then he would eventually return to me – being his woman meant more to me than anything else. My self-worth was so diminished that I failed to recognise these behaviours in his previous relationships as red flags—back then, we didn't label them as such. If you had asked me in my early twenties what a 'red flag' in a relationship was, I wouldn't have a clue what you were asking me. So, besides loving him, why didn't I leave when I began witnessing the dangerous behaviour that I had been warned about in my relationship with him?

Listen to: Shame by PJ Harvey

I was twenty when I met Ethan, and throughout each transition of our relationship —from mere colleagues to intimate lovers, from a passionate couple to a cohabiting family, it felt like we were living in a world of our own, detached from reality. Our life was a movie, full of dramas, crises, and dangers as otherworldly as our intense connection, our impromptu adventures, and our seemingly explosive 'love' for each other. We existed in our own wild world...

...until we weren't. For a long time, I harboured self-hatred for my naivety, my blind sidedness, my mistakes. But now, I understand that I was a victim of grooming—a part of domestic abuse that isn't often discussed in detail. Grooming is such a huge part of my story, as well as many others', that I mentioned in an earlier chapter. I've encountered numerous comments on social media, overheard conversations in real life, and even experienced it myself—that blame is often shifted onto the victim for being put in a position to be abused, assaulted, or raped. *'What did they expect dressed like that?' 'They shouldn't have drunk so much alcohol.' 'They should have listened to the warnings.' 'They shouldn't have gone there...'*

Being subjected to victim-blaming is a likely part of living with domestic abuse. Whether directly confronted or stumbling upon a stranger's thoughtless comment on your

Twitter feed, encountering victim-blaming is inevitable, and it can feel deeply personal.

However, I discovered that, for many years, I engaged in self-blame. Thoughts like *'If I had stayed in my marriage and made more effort to make it work...'* or *'If I had just told my boss about his inappropriate behaviour...'* or *'If I hadn't gone out that night...'* regularly crossed my mind once I understood what I had lived with. It's remarkably easy to blame the victim, especially when the perpetrator is so skilled at manipulation.

Ethan excels at grooming people. While his choice of partners may vary in appearance, clothing, music preferences, or location, a consistent pattern emerges—they always possess a personality trait that Ethan perceives as a vulnerability. Contrary to the assertions of so-called narcissistic abuse or trauma experts, the perpetrator accessing that perceived vulnerability is not the victim-survivor's fault. Ethan is a classic example of how a perpetrator preys on a part of a person that he regards as a weakness, and masterfully uses that part of who they are to manipulate them. However, what a perpetrator perceives as vulnerability or 'weakness' is often a survivor's superpower. Qualities like empathy, faith, trust, a caring, kind nature... these are our strengths and how we can live a life after the perpetrator. Of course, in many cases, victims of abuse will have very real vulnerabilities they cannot help having, such as age, disability, financial situation, environment, dependency... these factors will also be exploited by an abuser, particularly in the grooming process.

Listen to: Zombie by The Cranberries

My personality traits that Ethan apprehended as parts of me to exploit were the things about me that make me an inherently good person: my desire to help people, my generosity, my kindness. The vulnerabilities that he saw in me that were real were my lack of self-worth and my lack of life experience. I was twenty; he was twenty-eight. We were in different life stages. Legally, I had lived 90% of my life as a child. Two years living as an adult by law didn't mean I had the brain of an adult. I was still growing, evolving, learning who I wanted to be... and then I gained a supervisor at work whose job was to guide me, teach me, support me...

I was flattered. I was riddled with guilt for feeling flattered due to being in a relationship with someone I deeply loved. I felt confused. I felt angry at myself. I self-harmed by drinking excessively, pushing my future husband away, staying away from home so he couldn't read the guilt on my face. In hindsight, it's easy to wonder what would have happened if I had told my higher-up that my supervisor was flirting with me in supervision, commenting on my breasts while I leaned over at work, and months later, saying he didn't want to get married because he'd fallen in love with me. What if I had had the ear of someone older, more experienced, whom I felt I could confide in without getting into trouble and losing the job that I loved... would they have told me this was harassment at work? Would they have disciplined him? Would I have felt like I could tell my partner what was happening? Would we have ever divorced?

When I went on to get married to the man who truly loved me, with such big secrets, it could never last. I understand that. In a different place, in a different time, in a different life, maybe. It felt so unfair to me that two people so compatible, so in sync, who bounced off each other with ease and adored one another in the way my ex-husband and I did, could be driven apart by our lack of communication and understanding of one another's situations. We split up because he joined the army, and I felt hurt that he was leaving me for extended periods of time, that I couldn't go around the world with him when I had been given a promotion in the job I loved, that I had to cancel our fertility treatment together.

But after a few weeks and then months, I knew that all of that didn't matter to me anymore: I would travel the world with him, forgo fertility treatment, find another job because I loved him, and being apart from my husband was worse than our marriage problems. But very quickly after we had separated, when it was all fresh, and I didn't believe the separation could last, Ethan was there. He took me to Brighton on a nighttime adventure, where he bought me a bottle of champagne to drink on the way to the beach. He had picked me up after a late shift at work. We were still in occasional, weird contact because he had a Twitter account that would tweet me random things from time to time, and I watched it curiously. He would only ever tweet about me, and no one followed him. He didn't have a profile picture of himself, but I knew it was him because of the cryptic nature of the tweets. And when he found out my marriage was on hiatus at the very least, he swooped in. He was freshly separated from his marriage, he said. He'd always felt something strong for me, he said. Let's be friends, he said.

It wasn't really a friendship, though. On the way back from Brighton, after I had passed out from champagne, he joyfully informed me upon waking me up and dropping me off at home that he had 'fingered' me as he drove, and I had enjoyed it in my sleep. I didn't view that as sexual assault; I saw it as me being disloyal to my estranged husband and a nail in the coffin of our relationship.

A huge part of the Post Traumatic Stress that I live with revolves around trust. Dating didn't come easily to me; I've been told by the men I dated that I came across as cold and distant. That's because I was. In the span of a few years, I went from being a trusting young person to becoming disillusioned and severely suspicious. It amazes me that there were at least three men who managed to break through the solidness of the frozen walls I had barricaded myself behind. I rarely make new friends. I have reconnected with the long-term friends I lost during my relationship with Ethan, kept the friends from church, and have no capacity for any more deep connections. I cannot let you into my circle and give you my energy. I am traumatised. I am distressed. I am tired.

Grooming is a topic I feel passionately about. I wanted to discuss grooming in more detail in this chapter because I think it's easy to view the Post Traumatic Stress that people live with as mental suffering after extreme acts of violence, assault, and invasion of privacy. But through grooming, victims of abuse are coerced into dangerous relationships that, in some cases, can end their lives. The process of being groomed is as harmful as an act of physical violence against us. It *is* violence.

And yet, despite the mental and physical damage that has occurred to us, we are still not believed or considered seriously. Is it any wonder why most people who have lived with abuse deal with some form of mental health issue, such as Post Traumatic Stress? And how do we heal from Post Traumatic Stress when the trauma continues long after the main events? Traumatic experiences, such as going through courts and reliving what happened to us, are exacerbated by the language and agenda made public by the judge or jury, the media, social media users, far-right ideologists, misogynists on podcasts and TikTok, and actors and musicians receiving standing ovations as a display of sympathy even after literal evidence has been provided of them assaulting intimate partners. My trauma was literally reported in the media three times. How do I heal while I am bleeding from wounds that keep being slashed open?

This is why I say that I am not a survivor – I am surviving.

Chapter Twenty-four - Speaking out and Post-Separation Abuse

Email received from a follower:

'Hi Beth. I just want to say thank you for posting about your solo parenting on top of recovering from domestic abuse. It's so nice to read everything you put up and feeling like I wasn't so alone, that there are other women that go through what I did. I'm just not as brave as you to write about it. I can't even think of mine without going into floods of tears. I went to a support group the other day and said do you ever heal from it? Because I feel like it's consumed my life.'

DM received from a follower:

'You inspired me to leave. I felt brave enough to go alone and be a single mum.'

Listen to: I Don't Care Anymore by Kelis

I have always been an open person, much to my detriment. In fact, I am an oversharer, which, in recent years, I realised was a trauma response. On too many occasions to count, I have sensed that someone is uncomfortable or surprised at my level of openness. In recent years, my trust has waned, and I am not as forthcoming in my immediate, casual reveal of my life situations or things I've lived with.

I started speaking out about the domestic abuse, stalking, harassment, and cheating I had lived with when Ethan was in prison. It felt liberating to speak openly. I did this via the social media account that had once been a place to document escapism with my daughter on our woodland walks. I lost plenty of followers who only liked our pretty nature walks with jangly songs, but I gained plenty through talking about abuse. Interestingly, I had women approach me in my DMs to say that they couldn't follow me because of the abuser in their life checking their socials, but that they appreciated my posts.

I created a Patreon so that when Ethan was out of prison and without a restraining order, I could write about what was happening to me or what had happened in a controlled environment, where I could manage who was reading. But in the last twelve months, I've been unable to write openly on my social media account about things that have happened or are happening to me because Ethan has regained access to our child. I will do everything I can to keep her safe, which includes not publicly posting her face on social media anymore and not 'poking the bear' with my posts about the abuse he has subjected my daughter and me too.

Since our daughter began to see Ethan (supervised) again, the abuse has continued. It was suggested by professionals that Ethan see our daughter in a visitation centre – but that having 'turned his life around,' this contact would become unsupervised in time, and he would be able to have our daughter for extended periods of time, including the potential for overnight visits. I have never bad-mouthed him to our daughter, but after not seeing her father for over two years because of his stints in prison and disrespect for my boundaries, she was adamant she did not want to have alone time with him in that way. I sought advice from solicitors, who said the easiest thing to do was to mediate outside of the courts.

Knowing that Ethan would not actually want to parent our daughter and therefore would not care to have her overnight in whichever abodes he resides in or be responsible for her basic care needs, I broke 'No Contact,' and as if nothing had ever happened, we were in phone communication again. We decided on a routine of every other weekend, for a few hours, where he could have supervised access. To begin with, this access was with a trusted person. But in time, I realised that the only person I trusted with my child's safety around the person who caused us so much harm was the person who had protected her fiercely throughout her life and cushioned her trauma as much as they possibly could. Someone who would lay down their life for her. Someone who knew how to survive Ethan better than anyone else on earth: me.

It came with much objection from family and friends. The only person who really saw my point of view – even though he didn't like it – was Logan. Out came the alarm. Out came the Hollie Guard app (more information on this at the end of the book), out came the Grey Rock method, and out came my fierce survival mode. Ethan only decided to ask for access to his daughter once he discovered I had a boyfriend. He had not phoned or asked for any information once during his time in and out of prison and with a restraining order preventing him from contacting me. But the professionals involved with us were always aware that I wanted him to know he could request contact with our child, be that through a visitation centre, phone calls, and so on. At one Christmas, our daughter did Facetime with him with the support of our social worker. But otherwise, once the justice system had deemed him as an ex-offender who had 'learned his lesson' from his slap on the wrist, I was on my own.

We continue to meet in public places. I tell people where we are. I hate it.

Ethan quickly returned to his usual self, the self before he begged for us to get back together and harassed me while declaring his undying love. He became grumpy, moody, and would mutter under his breath. Initially, he would not look me in the eye or speak to me directly but conveyed messages via our daughter. He hinted to her that my family was drunken, fat, lazy, and rude. He would say that 'mummy was silly.' Every visit, he made sarcastic comments about Logan. The Post-Separation Abuse is not over yet. However, as the months have gone by, like what happened with his older daughter from his marriage with Meg, the visits have shortened in length and became more spaced out. He shows a lack of interest in being more present in our daughter's life and did not contribute to child maintenance until I went through the CSA. I know it sounds sad for our daughter, but I've never said a bad word against him. I want her to see and experience for herself the kind of person her dad is and come to her own conclusions, as long as she has my unconditional nurturing and love.

Listen to: Brave by Sara Bareilles

Despite him gradually disappearing from our daughter's life again, I still feel I cannot be as open as I want to be on social media. It is not worth the risk to our lives if I speak candidly, despite the amazing connections I have built with followers on social media, who come to me with their own stories and advice after resonating with mine. It is too dangerous to speak out so publicly, which is why I am writing under a pseudonym.

When a Victim-survivor speaks out about abuse, or even when they don't, they are often met with what we call the 'smear campaign'. This is when the perpetrator of abuse will spin the narrative to victimise themselves and make it appear that the abused is actually the abuser. A typical smear campaign from a perpetrator sounds like this:

'She's lying. She's crazy. She's a psychopath. She's mentally unwell.'

or

'She's making it all up to cover up what she's done.'

And often, from a convicted perpetrator, we hear:

'She set me up. I had to plead guilty, or I'd get into trouble because they believed her over me.'

With convictions of perpetrators of rape, domestic abuse, stalking and harassment as low as they are, and victims often choosing not to report escalations of violence and coercion in the first place, having someone wrongly convicted on the basis of evidence is extremely unlikely. But by the time a perpetrator is wrapped up in a smear campaign, in which I wonder if they actually gaslight themselves into believing, they have usually moved on to a new victim that they are love bombing or have their feet firmly under the table with, swirling them around in the dizzy cycle of abuse. People believe the smear campaign because perpetrators of abuse can be so manipulative, so conniving, so charming, that lying is second nature to them.

It's not just the new people in their lives that they've groomed into unseeing the red flags. It's the family and friends around the perpetrator who will commonly believe that the perpetrator has been wronged by the victim. I've spoken to many women who have disclosed to me how frustrating it can feel when former in-laws can't see their loved one for who they are. Interestingly, it seems siblings of perpetrators will often show support more than any other family member, from my own personal experience of supporting thousands of women who have lived with abuse.

In my personal experience, Ethan is mostly

estranged from his family because he chooses to be; therefore, I haven't faced any huge backlash. In fact, a handful of family members have offered me support. However, in Ethan's family, there are some prominent members who have abused and cheated on all their partners.

Ethan's brother and father have a similar history to Ethan in terms of lying, living double (or triple...) lives, and being abusive towards partners. I am in contact with some of Ethan's ex-partners who can relate in some way to the abuse I lived with, and I am friendly with some of his brother's ex-partners, who were also abused. Ethan's brother has directly called me a psychopath and relays this to the partners that he is with at the time. It is Ethan's dad who caused me distress, however.

Despite Ethan not being in contact with his father for decades, his father found my social media page. On a post where I was most open about my abuse, I rather hesitantly posted a picture of an injury I had photographed while in a relationship with him. Ethan's father commented accusatory remarks, calling me a liar, making up claims of abuse, and portraying me as insane.

These comments were jumped on by far-right trolls, who were potentially friends of his and commented with abuse. One troll wasn't connected to Ethan's father but took the cue when seeing the abusive comments. Regarding the injuries in the picture, he said,

'If that's all you've got to show for it, you're a poor man's Amber Heard.'

Cutting a long story short, it turns out that particular troll was a proud misogynist who was charged with inappropriate behaviour towards children in a playground. I never followed up on the case after I reported him to the police and blocked him. I had to block his email address as I was receiving endless emails from him too.

Trolls nearly always seem to be far-right, women-hating men. I created a TikTok account that slightly diverged from the content I made on Instagram, with a more direct message about domestic abuse and violence towards women and girls. One video went semi-viral, but even on the videos that haven't gained much attention, I have been met with more trolls and trolling comments than I can count, even on my small platform. I've been called chubby, ugly, delusional, mentally unstable, on drugs, worthless, pathetic, a narcissist, a misandrist, judgmental, a liar, and more. A small proportion of these trolls have appeared to be women, but it's important to point out that it is common for men's rights activists to pose as women and 'radical feminists' to provoke attacks from fellow men's rights activists to push an agenda that all feminists are discriminatory towards men. Sadly, *'not all'* men's right's activists are men.

Speaking out about abuse feels risky because there's a chance you will lose friends. As Ethan doesn't have friends, that wasn't an issue for me. However, I know through working with women who have been abused that losing friendships has been a difficult part of ending the intimate relationship with the perpetrator. Some perpetrators are covertly abusive and able to maintain a reputation for being a 'good person,' hiding under the guise of a charitable, helpful, seemingly caring individual, often with community values. They may also promote their spiritual or religious beliefs and work in positions of trust where one would not expect a perpetrator to be hiding in plain sight. Perpetrators like this will keep hold of friendship groups, and the abused person will lose the support and respect of the people holding the perpetrator in high regard. In these situations, it doesn't feel worth it to be open and tell people what you have suffered if you cannot trust they will believe your story or if they have a mindset of 'there are two sides to the story' or 'giving the benefit of the doubt.'

Listen to: Hey Queen by Beautiful Chorus

Having now worked with thousands of women, all with their own unique circumstances, cultures, backgrounds, upbringings, yet seemingly telling a story that makes me feel like perpetrators read the same 'how to be an abuser' guide, I do not blame anyone who feels they cannot be open and honest about the suffering they have lived with. There is deep pain in not having your suffering truly heard when you've taken a vulnerable step in speaking about it.

Victim-blaming is like a disease, swirling around all parts of the world, even catching and infecting those whom you believed wouldn't succumb to such poisonous accusations, such as, 'If it was so bad, why didn't she leave?' or 'Yeah, but she did behave in this way...' and worst of all, is when someone says, 'He's never done anything wrong to me.' And so, they continue to be friends with that person, holding space for them and not holding them accountable for their dangerous and insidious behaviours. You will lose people when you speak out about abuse.

I have personally experienced losing closeness to friends or family members who didn't have the capacity to support me in my process of leaving Ethan and then embarking on a rollercoaster of a recovery journey. At times during my healing process, I've felt sad, bitter, and sometimes resentful of this. But I have enough compassion now to know that it's really hard to hold space for someone who needs much more than you can give them. And sometimes, there will be loved ones who just don't know what to say or what to do, so they'll avoid you. That feels hard, too. Again, they don't have the energy to hold space, and so the victim-survivor must find acceptance in order to move forwards. And then there's the survivor's own life changes once leaving abuse;

The world becomes a remarkably different place when our life moves further and further away from the abuser. And we can outgrow the people that were in our lives previously. They may not have a place in our new, healthier lives. That's also a difficult truth to face, but a truth nonetheless. In order to grow, we sometimes have to let go.

For me, writing this and speaking out on social media and in endless DMs has been a cathartic part of my recovery and growth journey. I don't regret speaking out, although sometimes I wince when reading things I've written. I don't delete them. At the time, I needed to document what I was thinking and feeling, and where I am now is testament to where I was then.

Chapter Twenty-five - The Future

<u>Message received from Becky, 'Blue', a few weeks before she passed away:</u>

'You are a lioness.'

I used to look at the future and see nothing else, but The Dream sold to me: marrying a dark, handsome man who was masculine and fathered my two or three kids. We'd all be happy, growing old in the village I was born in, and enjoying everything life had to offer, such as the money I was undoubtedly going to earn, the home I was undoubtedly going to buy, and the kids I would so easily have.

As we know, life doesn't pan out the way The Dream tells us it will. I never expected to be divorced by twenty-seven and holding a baby at the time that wasn't my ex-husband's, but a man who was cutting chunks of my hair off because he didn't like me asking questions and sticking his penis in anything that moved. But there I was, smiling in my winged eyeliner and never seen without a pretty dress on, pretending that was all exactly how I wanted it, thank you very much.

I know now that the future is something to consider lightly; I don't know what will happen tomorrow, therefore I'm very much living for today. I know I want to earn money, own a little cottage, rescue loads of old cats, have a writing room, a bedroom always ready and prepared for my daughter wherever her life takes her, and a yearly holiday to Cornwall, Glastonbury Festival, and, if I were rich, an escape to the sun during my January blues. That's the dream now. It's far more realistic and achievable, but I don't think about it too much. I tend to see the future as the stretch of months in front of me -

As I write this, I am excited about having Glastonbury tickets for the first time ever. My daughter and I are going with Logan, and I'm apprehensive about rain but so excited to experience it together. I am looking forward to going to Cornwall, to Manchester, to the Forest of Dean, maybe it's even time to reclaim Brighton. I am excited to pass my driving test. I am excited

MUG: An Account of Domestic Abuse

to pass my course. I am still training to be a counsellor. After working with thousands of women with The Expert, I did a Level 2 in Understanding Domestic Abuse, and I will be taking that further, maybe to train in psychology and specialise in supporting women and children through domestic abuse, stalking, harassment, and rape. I look forward to publishing this book that I've been writing on and off for four years. I'm looking forward to the other book I've got in the pipeline. I'm looking forward to creating more content and engaging with more followers who have lived with abuse, too. You may not know who I am, but I will be making a lot more noise for women and girls. And Logan and I have discussed potentially moving in together – we'll see.

Who knows if my daughter and Ethan will be able to continue their relationship, and what our daughter will make of him as she grows older. I don't like to think of it too much. What will be, will be.

Right now, I'm enjoying the little things; recently, Logan's been helping me during a severe period of overwhelm and anxiety. Having someone help me wash up, fold my laundry, sit with my child while I have a driving lesson... even make me a cup of tea just how I like it. It's amazing. He cooks for me, he takes me on holiday. I know that when I am qualified and I've sold millions of this book (ha, my goal is to sell 50, and even that is a massive stretch, I'm sure!), I will treat him to lots of nice things because I want to. I like sharing life with him.

I'm not going to finish this heavy, dark book with a sparkling, shiny, smiley, happy ending where I say that everything is better, because it's not. Ethan is still asserting control over me in terms of visitation and money arrangements, but life has improved so much more and become much safer in the last few years. I didn't think I could get through another moment at one point. But here I am, finishing the last chapter of my book. And I'm happy. I'm still living with Post Traumatic Stress, but I'm happy.

And if you have read this and you resonate or relate in any way, and you're not in a positive place right now...

...you can reach here. I am aware that, in a weird way, I am fortunate to have had the perpetrator of abuse convicted of his crimes and that I was mostly supported by the police and child services, where I am able to live every day with my daughter. I have found solo parenting incredibly hard, but I am also grateful to be able to solo parent. I am devastated for the mothers who have their children ripped away from them by the family courts, in the UK, in the USA, and around the world, when they have spoken out about abuse. I thought about writing more about this horrific, common occurrence across the world, but I want to save space for the voices of women such as Brody Dalle, Tina Swithin, and the women I have spoken to who have their voices silenced and without public platforms, who have reported abusers and had the courts rule in favour of the abuser due to apparent 'parental alienation.' Finding light after abuse takes faith in yourself and the journey. It isn't linear, it isn't kind, it is ugly and sore and emotional. It is scary and sad and frustrating. It is revealing, reminiscent, and wretched. But it's also revitalising. Liberating. Freeing. It is power. It is courage. It is being kind to yourself. It is everything you deserve and more;

You deserve to be happy, to be loved by yourself, to be respected by yourself, to be free of the restraints that kept you imprisoned – you are worthy.

MUG: An Account of Domestic Abuse

We are worthy.

Useful Resources:

Helpful organisations, charities and services (UK):

CALL 999 IN AN EMERGENCY.

Use the Domestic Violence Disclosure Scheme (DVDS) to find out if your partner or a loved one's partner has a history of *reported* abuse or violence. You can request 'Clare's Law' by making an application at your local police station.

Install the Hollie Guard App to your phone. By pressing the alarm in the app, your camera and microphone will pick up evidence of what is happening, and your chosen emergency contact will be notified with a web link to your location and the evidence your phone is sharing.

https://hollieguard.com

National Domestic Abuse Helpline:

0808 2000 247

Refuge:

www.nationaldahelpline.org.uk/

Women's Aid:

womensaid.org.uk/

Scottish Women's Aid:

womensaid.scot/

The Men's Advice Line / Respect:

0808 801 0327

https://mensadviceline.org.uk/

National LGBTQ+ Domestic Abuse Helpline / Galop:

0800 999 5428

Galop.org.uk

Rights of Women (support in legal matters):

rightsofwomen.org.uk

Samaritans (help with depression and suicidal thoughts):

116 123

Southall Black Sisters (specialising in supporting minority groups):

020 8571 0800

Southallblacksisters.org.uk

Aurora New Dawn (domestic abuse and stalking):

02394 216 816

aurorand.org.uk

Paladin (National Stalking Advocacy Service)

020 3866 4107

Paladinservice.co.uk

Suzy Lamplugh Trust (National Stalking Helpline)

0808 802 0300

suzylamplugh.org

Victim Support

0808 16 89 111

victimsupport.org.uk

Relate (counselling around relationships)

0300 003 2972

Rape Crisis England and Wales:

0808 500 2222

rapecrisis.org.uk

Rape Crisis Scotland:

08088 01 03 02

rapecrisisscotland.org.uk

Rape Crisis Northern Ireland:

0800 0246 991

rapecrisisni.org.uk

National Male Survivor Helpline and Online Support Service:

01926 402 498

safeline.org.uk

Shout (text helpline):

Text CONTACT to 85258

PTSD support:

ptsduk.org

Campaign Against Living Miserably (CALM):

0800 58 58 58

The Survivor's Trust (Rape and Sexual Abuse Services)

0808 801 0818

thesurvivorstrust.org

The Freedom Programme

01942 262 270

Help@freedomprogramme.co.uk

https://www.freedomprogramme.co.uk/

Must Read Books

A selection of books that helped and inspired me while I wrote this account:

Men Who Hate Women by Laura Bates

Dangerous Relationships And How They End in Murder by Jane Monckton-Smith

Codependent No More by Melodie Beattie

What Happened To You? by Bruce D Perry and Oprah Winfrey

Fix The System, Not The Women by Laura Bates

Sexy Buy Psycho by Dr. Jessica Taylor

All About Love by Bell Hooks

Block, Delete, Move on – by LaLaLaLetMeExplain

Tinder Translator: An A-Z Guide of Modern Misogyny by Aileen Barratt

Hood Feminism: Notes From the Women White Feminists Forgot by Mikki Kendall

Everyday Sexism by Laura Bates

Untamed by Glennon Doyle

The Archetypes and the Collective Unconscious by C.G Yung

I Am Not Your Baby Mother by Candice Brathwaite

No Bad Parts by Richard C. Schwartz

The Women In Me by Britney Spears

Why Did You Stay? A Memoir about Self-Worth by Rebecca Humphries

Fight Like A Girl by Clementine Ford

Polyvagal Theory in Therapy by Deb Dana

From Swansea to Hornsey by Jack Jones

The Body Keeps The Score by Bessel Van Der Kolk

She Must Be Mad by Charley Cox

Wedded Wife, A Feminist History of Marriage by Rachael Lennon

Femina: A New History of the Middle Ages Through the Eyes of Women Written Out of It by Janina Ramirez

I Don't by Clementine Ford

Client-Centred Therapy by Carl Rogers

MUG: An Account of Domestic Abuse

(I know there's more than this and I will be kicking myself by the time this is published).

Relevant podcasts I listened to while writing this book:

It's Not You, It's Them... But It Might Be You with LaLaLaLetMeExplain

Manosphere Debunked with Aileen Barratt and @The_Nice_ish_Psychologist

Untethered with Clementine Ford

Crime Analyst with Laura Richards

iWeigh with Jameela Jamil

Behind Closed Doors: The Domestic Abuse Podcast. with Jessica Clare of North Devon Against Domestic Abuse

Thankyou:

To ALL the loyal followers across social media, particularly those who trusted me enough to pledge to my Patreon page, including:

Jimmi – *In the past, you have given me friendship, consideration, knowledge and advice. You have listened to me. You have provided me with a huge catalogue of music to check out, as well as your dating disasters. You deserve to be very happy. Thank you for your support.*

Tania – *Your commitment to my writing is greatly appreciated. Thank you so much for believing in me.*

Rachel 'Poppet' – *You have always believed that I will become an author and write books. You remain someone I admire greatly for your strength, resilience and faith in people. I consider it an honour to be your friend!*

A special note to 'The Church Girls':

Kristina H – *Strong, brave, beautiful, and consistent; you have inspired me from Day One. Your endless endeavour to nurture* *your children in the way that little K was not gives me hope for their generation and the next. Your honest dedication to living a fulfilling life by opening your heart to God, Sobriety, Self-Partnering, Solo Parenting, and growing in your career lights up the world around you. We were not brought together by coincidence – it was always the plan.*

Michelle – *The world is a better place because of the lessons you have learned and the experiences you have had because your growth is an example to us all.*

Kayla – *You loved and nurtured us since the moment you came into our lives. You have slowly revealed to me the hardships of your own life story, and it empowers me to see you brave and tall, raising your arms to your love of Jesus and the trust you have placed in Him. Your wisdom and experience have given me the courage to continue with tough decisions and trust the process. Thank you.*

Nikki – *For your strength, faith, trust in me to share deep feelings, and for your company.*

Rachel A – *For your creativity, vulnerability, overflow of artistic ideas, and the warmth of your heart. You were surrounded by women who have lived with domestic abuse. This is so you can provide nurturing, support, and hope to our lives. You asked for signs, and I think your connection with us was a significant one! You are capable of so much love, and it is powerful.*

And to my Sister – *For calling the police and getting me out.*

Brish, Girl, K8, Barry, Tav, Joss:

The length of time between us meeting never changes our love and respect for one another, nor the abundance of experiences we have shared together. Without your love and forgiveness, I would not be here, writing this right now. Each of you means so very much to me, and you will always be my friends forever.

RS – *You taught me one of the most valuable lessons I have ever received: You taught me that not every man is going to* *harm me. Your life has been tremendously hard, and your determination to live a life of your choice is inspirational. Thank you for treating me with so much unforgettable kindness and respect.*

T – *I have so many words to say, but they don't all belong here. I hope one day we can sit and laugh and forget all the pain that was had between us. I forgave that pain long ago. I always knew you would be whoever you wanted to be, do whatever you want to do, and be the best father. You're the one who left the small town and got away and I am proud of you. My heart is filled with happiness to know that yours is. It is all I could have hoped for and more. Thank you for making me the person I am today.*

My Boyfriend – *I didn't think I could fully trust a man in a relationship again. You've shown me that I can. You've shown me that a relationship does not have to be codependent, toxic, or full of drama. You've shown me that I can love with ease. You've shown me that dating can be simple and fun, not nerve-wracking. You've shown me that relationships can have room for* *different interests and views. You've shown me that asking for help is okay. You've given me so much fun and support in equal measure. I look forward to everything else we are going to learn together, because you make loving easy and joyful. The value you bring to my life is immense. The support you endlessly provide me is an honour. I feel grateful, lucky and blessed to have you by my side. You are loved, appreciated and admired beyond measure.*

Witch Sister – *I knew the moment we first met that we had something instant and special. It seems rare to meet someone who just knows... but you do just know. I do not know whether that is good or healthy, but we are bound together in a relationship that no one else can begin to understand! Thank you for always believing in me and encouraging me not to make reckless decisions! I know this book will be hard for you to read. I know that I will tell you not to read it, but that you will anyway.*

Your lifelong bravery has helped me write this book. I watched you stick two fingers up to life's shit with the courage of a lioness. You are spectacular and supply a significant role model for how to keep going when it feels like the world wants to knock you down, time and time again.

An added shout out to the following inspirational people who I have the pleasure of knowing:

Jenny C for your validation and support.

Angie S Because your future is bright

Amy A For trusting me

ChloeM L For trying to break trauma chains

TJ One of the bravest men I know.

JB For THAT hug.

Bex For your courage and strong will

Sandy For your prayers and belief in me

...And to all the people (mostly women) who have left or are living with abuse that I connect with on Instagram.

To my parents: *Hopefully you will never read this 'thank you', as I have put in a boundary that I'd rather you not read this* *book. But thank you for your support, as always, and that of my family members such as my aunts who have provided me with help and support over the years.*

Finally, to the children. *I'm sorry this is so hard. I hope you don't read this, but I know that you might one day. To my own Daughter, please never forget that I love you and that you are safe, you are loved, you are enough.*

Sources, Citations & References:

AN IMPORTANT NOTE:

At the time of publishing this book, it was revealed by the UK Domestic Abuse Commissioner, Nicola Jacobs, that in June 2023, the Home Office instructed the police to stop counting crimes of threatening or abusive messages when a victim reports abuse. It was suggested that the ONS overview for Domestic Abuse in England and Wales in 2023 has nearly 18,000 domestic abuse crimes missing from statistics. Therefore, while I have provided references to the overview released in November 2023, I want to make it clear that the number of reports is inaccurate. Additionally, it's important to acknowledge that most incidents of domestic abuse go unreported.

Office for National Statistics (ONS), released 24 November 2023, ONS website, statistical bulletin, Domestic abuse in

England and Wales overview: November 2023

Women's Aid. (2023) The Domestic Abuse Report 2023: The Annual Audit, Bristol: Women's Aid.

Women's Aid. (2022). Come Together to End Domestic Abuse: A Survey of UK Attitudes to Domestic Abuse 2022.

Refuge. (n.d.). The Facts. Retrieved from https://refuge.org.uk/what-is-domestic-abuse/the-facts/

HMICFRS. (2019). Increasingly Everyone's Business: A Progress Report on the Police Response to Domestic Abuse. Retrieved from https://assets-hmicfrs.justiceinspectorates.gov.uk/uploads/increasingly-everyones-business-domestic-abuse-progress-report.pdf

Women's Aid. (n.d.). The Survivor's Handbook. Retrieved from https://www.womensaid.org.uk/information-support/the-survivors-handbook/

Ministry of Justice. (2015). Code of Practice for Victims of Crime. Retrieved from https://www.gov.uk/government/publications/the-code-of-practice-for-victims-of-crime

Bancroft, L. (2002). Why Does He Do That?: Inside the Minds of Angry and Controlling Men. Berkley Books.

Rape Crisis England & Wales. (n.d.). Statistics: Sexual Violence. Retrieved from https://rapecrisis.org.uk/get-informed/statistics-sexual-violence/

Amnesty International UK. (n.d.). Online abuse of women widespread. Retrieved from https://www.amnesty.org.uk/online-abuse-women-widespread#:~:text=Contrast&text=Online%20abuse%20of%20women%20is,threatened%20sexual%20or%20physical%20assault

Sex and Love Addicts Anonymous (SLAA). (n.d.). "Characteristics of Sex and Love Addiction." Retrieved from https://slaafws.org/download/core-files/Characteristics-of-Sex-Love-Addiction.pdf

American Psychiatric Association. (2013). Narcissistic personality disorder. In Diagnostic and statistical manual of mental disorders (5th ed.). https://doi.org/10.1176/appi.books.9780890425596.dsm09

Office for National Statistics (ONS). (November 2020). "Domestic abuse during the coronavirus (COVID-19) pandemic, England and Wales."

Aurora New Dawn. (n.d.). Help for the Stalker. Retrieved from https://www.aurorand.org.uk/services/help-stalker

"Stalking or Harassment" - Crown Prosecution Service, Director of Public Prosecutions v Baker [2004] EWHC 2782 (Admin)

(https://www.ptsduk.org/what-is-ptsd/causes-of-ptsd/domestic-abuse, Post-Traumatic Stress Disorder (PTSD) and intimate partner violence" by B. Golding et al)

https://www.ptsduk.org/ptsd-stats/

https://www.drlenoreewalker.com/research/

https://www.polyvagalinstitute.org/about-deb

Black Country Women's Aid. (2023). 5 things everyone should know about stalking during Stalking Awareness Week 2023. Retrieved from https://blackcountrywomensaid.co.uk/5-things-everyone-should-know-about-stalking-during-stalking-awareness-week-2023/

Mayo Clinic Staff. Narcissistic personality disorder. Mayo Clinic. (Oct 2019). Retrieved from https://www.mayoclinic.org/diseases-conditions/narcissistic-personality-disorder/symptoms-causes/syc-20366662

Domestic Abuse Commissioner. (25th April 2024). Nearly eighteen thousand domestic abuse crimes missing from statistics. Retrieved from https://domesticabusecommissioner.uk/nearly-eighteen-thousand-domestic-abuse-crimes-missing-from-statistics/

Office for National Statistics (ONS), released 8 February 2024, ONS website, article, Homicide in England and Wales: year ending March 2023

Women's Aid info on coercive control – https://www.womensaid.org.uk/information-support/what-is-domestic-abuse/coercive-control/

'Adolescence now lasts from 10 to 24', 2018, Katie Silver, retrieved online:

https://www.bbc.co.uk/news/health-42732442

Printed in Great Britain
by Amazon